JOE NAMATH
and the
OTHER GUYS

JOE NAMATH
and the
OTHER GUYS
by RICK TELANDER

Holt, Rinehart and Winston
New York

Library of Congress Cataloging in Publication Data

Telander, Rick.
Joe Namath and the other guys.
1. New York Jets (Football team) I. Title.
GV956.N42T44   796.33′264′097471   76-4731
ISBN 0-03-017396-5

FIRST EDITION

Printed in the United States of America
10 9 8 7 6 5 4 3 2 1

ONE

You must stir it and stump it,
And blow your own trumpet,
Or trust me, you haven't a chance.
—W. S. GILBERT

What value can there be in
fantasizing about such false idols as
professional athletes?
—ROBERT LIPSYTE

In January of 1969 the upstart New York Jets of the upstart American Football League prepared to play the venerable Baltimore Colts of the NFL for the championship of pro football. In the two previous Super Bowls the AFL representatives had been trounced. This time was going to be no different. You could get odds to prove it: ridiculous pregame spreads giving as much as 17 points to those pretenders from Manhattan.

But the Jets were making strange noises. They thought they could win. Joe Namath, their bonus-baby quarterback and the biggest wise guy of them all, *guaranteed* a Jet win. He smiled and posed with girls and wore sunglasses and told anyone in need of a good laugh that the Colts would be lucky to finish second.

That was enough for me. By game time I was a fervid Jets-hater. I had small bets spread among my friends, all of them on the Colts by varying margins of victory, and all of them intended to help send Namath, the Jets,

1

and the entire AFL back to the obscurity they deserved. What was the AFL anyway but a fly-by-night operation, a circus of bums and rejects from the NFL who couldn't play defense if you armed them all with grenades. Who had they produced? Clowns with names like Wahoo McDaniel or "The Hammer" or "Super Gnat." The NFL was proud, mature, conservative as old money. They gave us Graham, Tittle, Nitschke. They ran the ball down your throat and erected stone walls for defense. The AFL threw wobbly 80-yard passes till time ran out.

In 1969 I was a sophomore in college playing football, and I had not been raised to brag or show excessive confidence. Humility made one a good winner, and it reduced the edge after defeat. I didn't understand Namath. Guys like Muhammad Ali could brag and carry on. Ali was a black dude, a boxer, and boxers were different. But Namath was willfully thumbing his nose at something much more sacred. He was, I determined, thumbing it at us, at me. And he needed a lesson.

When the Jets proceeded to win Super Bowl III, 16–7, I didn't know quite what to do. Namath, the press wrote, had called "a near-perfect game," whereas sage and humble Earl Morrall had played roughly on par with a baboon. On one particularly gut-wrenching play he didn't even *see* Jimmy Orr all alone in the end zone, even though Orr was jumping up and down like a man on a trampoline. With a couple of very minor breaks and some just-average quarterbacking, the Colts still could have won; few people will deny that the Colts had more talent than the Jets. But they lost, and the implications were obvious. The Jet victory, stated sportswriter Edwin Shrake, "lifted an entire league out of its adolescence."

Despite such tributes, my view of Joe Namath did not change much. He had not risen; the NFL had fallen. The only comment of his I agreed with was that Earl Morrall would indeed play third string on the Jets. After that year I had little reason to think deeply about Namath at all—the next season the Jets would not make the AFL playoffs; in 1970 they would finish 4-10, their worst record up to 1975.

Still, an annoying truth remained: If you tell everyone you are going to do something and then you do it—you aren't bragging. Or if you are, maybe you're just being more heroic. Hadn't Beowulf sung loud and long in the meadhalls about snuffing out Grendel? Where did this idea of being humble come from anyway? Who said a winner should be clean-cut? The Colts had shorter hair than a road gang. Here was Joe Namath, wild and woolly, just twenty-six years old, blithely atop the sports world, just as he had predicted.

"He poses a question for us all," wrote Dan Jenkins in 1966. "Would you rather be young, single, rich, famous, talented, energetic and happy—or President?" I wasn't looking to be President, but like anyone else, I sometimes scanned the horizon for new heroes. Then in 1973 a teammate of mine from college, running-back Mike Adamle, was traded from the Kansas City Chiefs to the Jets. I'd been with Mike very briefly at Kansas City before getting cut, and one of our preseason pleasures had been discussing the weirdness of pro football. I asked him after the '73 season if there was a big difference between the Chiefs and the Jets. "It's unbelievable," he said. "Like night and day. You thought KC was strange —well, the Jets are a whole new ball game. It's so weird I don't even know how to describe it. But it has to do with being in New York, and mostly it has to do with Joe."

By 1974 the Jets were no longer a factor in hard-core professional football, at least as far as winning championships was concerned. In 1973 they equaled their worst record at 4-10, and through the first eight games of 1974 compiled a 1-7 mark. Joe Namath's personal notoriety, however, had not faltered.

"I was used to people gawking in general at pro football players," recalls Adamle. "But I honestly never thought I'd see the kind of reaction Joe got. Policemen had to hold back the mobs. Women screamed and cried and fainted. It was just like the sixties' mania for the Beatles."

Obviously Namath had moved into a realm far

removed from ordinary football—in fact, had been there quite awhile. "Being best in the world at what you do . . . is not enough," wrote Joe McGinniss in an article about unsung quarterback Sonny Jurgensen of the Redskins. "To make it pay, you must either do it with a winner or do it in New York." Namath had played on only three winning teams in his pro career, but he'd been in New York a decade. He had hosted *The Tonight Show* and escorted Raquel Welch to the Academy Awards. He had coauthored two books and starred in three movies. His personal appearance fee was $25,000. A female writer took a poll and found Joe to be a runaway as "America's sexiest sports personality ever."

Forces had combined to raise Joe into that vague, yet all-important world of fame, that stratosphere of the stars where nothing seems to matter except the fact that you are, indeed, *famous.* As early as 1970 Robert Lipsyte had written that Namath had "almost ceased to exist as a human being"; by 1975 only a wizard could have determined where the image left off and the man began.

A few things, however, were ascertainable. As a football player Joe ranked near the very top. He had won virtually every award possible, from being named MVP in the Super Bowl to first-team All-Pro. He was selected AFL Rookie of the Year in 1965 and was voted the Colclough Award in 1971 by the New England Writers as the most courageous player, following his return to action from knee surgery. In between he won the Hickock Belt and the George Halas Award and was voted a member of the all-time All-AFL squad selected by the Pro Football Hall of Fame.

As a passer Namath had few peers. During his three varsity years at Alabama, in which the Crimson Tide lost only three regular season games, Namath completed 230 of 428 passes for 3,055 yards, 29 TDs, and a 54 percent completion average. As a Jet rookie he completed 164 passes for 2,220 yards. Two years later, in 1967, when he was just twenty-four years old, Namath completed 258 of 491 attempts for 4,007 yards, more yardage than any pro quarterback before or since. In one game that season he attempted 60 passes and during another stretch completed 15 passes in a row, a record that stood for seven years. In 1972 he outdueled Johnny Unitas in the greatest aerial show ever presented in the NFL as the two combined for 872 yards in one game. Namath that day hit on 15 of 28 passes for 6 TDs and 496 yards, the third best yardage total in football history. His yards-per-completion average was an astounding 33.1.

As a complete quarterback, however, Namath has always been somewhat suspect. He never was an All-American at Alabama, as is popularly believed, and he made the all-conference team only once, his senior year. His interception totals have always been high (he has thrown 33 more career interceptions than TDs) and his agility limited. There are football analysts who claim that a great quarterback will guide his team to victories regardless of poor personal statistics. There are those who say that Namath is not a true leader, that in the Super Bowl it was actually the Jets' defense, with its four interceptions, and Matt Snell's 121 yards rushing that made the difference.

One thing that can't be argued is that football has made Joe Namath rich. "I believe you could say Joe is a millionaire," says his lawyer Jimmy Walsh with typical discretion. Indeed, if Joe has hung on to just a part of the money he has earned, he is close to *multi*millionaire status. His first contract in 1965, the contract that redefined the term "bonus baby" and left the sports world slightly ga-ga, was for $427,000.

Dick Young, the ever-vigilant *Daily News* columnist, investigated his wealth and broke it down thus:

Salary (1965)	$25,000
Salary (1966)	25,000
Salary (1967)	25,000
Option year (1968), renegotiable upward	25,000
Bonus (spread payments in future)	200,000
Lawyer's fee (10 percent)	30,000

One car (Lincoln Continental)	7,000
Brother's salary, scout (1965-1967) at $10,000	30,000
Second brother, scout (1965-1967) at $10,000	30,000
Brother-in-law, scout (1965-1967) at $10,000	30,000
Total	$427,000

How much scouting for the Jets Joe's family actually did is questionable, but the ruckus such extravagances raised was quite tangible. Frank Ryan, the quarterback for the Cleveland Browns, stated that if Namath was worth four hundred thousand, "I'm worth a million." Ryan, of course, wasn't, and Namath was worth several times that. His drawing power, as it turned out, was the rival of Ruth's.

Outside of Muhammad Ali, Namath still appears to have no equal as a sports commodity. In one of the most desperate attempts at "respectability" ever, the luckless World Football League attempted to sign a $4 million contract with Namath in the spring of 1975. It was a sign of both Namath's financial status and business acumen that he refused the offer. The WFL folded shortly thereafter.

As with most constant celebrities, controversy has been the glitter for Namath's marketable qualities of youth, success, and talent. It didn't hurt that his knees were fragile as glass or that he was Hungarian and from a small town in Pennsylvania. But controversy—staying out late the night before games, wearing $5,000 black mink coats, weeping over the fate of his restaurant, Bachelors III, shaving his legs for a panty hose commercial, growing a Fu Manchu mustache when facial hair was tantamount to Communism—those things made him famous. It seemed fitting that in the spring of 1975 Chester LaRoche, the founder of The National Football Foundation and Hall of Fame, football's shrine to college stars, would state that Joe Namath might never be inducted into the Hall. "Namath's a great player, but what's he done with his life?" asked LaRoche. "He hangs around saloons."

In 1974 Namath played out his option with the Jets,

leaving him free to go with another team or quit entirely, as he occasionally hinted he might do. But the Jets won their last six games of the season, finishing at 7-7, with Joe playing spectacularly down the stretch, hitting on 58 percent of his passes for 1,196 yards, 11 TDs, and only 5 interceptions. For the first time in five years he finished a season completely healthy. His teammates voted him the MVP. In the off-season Joe told the press he was eager to return, that the Jets could be on the verge of something big.

In late July he signed a two-year contract with the Jets for $900,000 ($450,000 each year) making him far and away the highest salaried football player ever and second in all of sports only to soccer's Pele, a man who had once been declared a national resource by Brazil.

The Jets won four of the five 1975 preseason games they played (the New England game was canceled because of the players' strike) and boasted a 10-1 streak as they headed into the regular season. Throughout New York there was talk that this could truly be the year, the Second Coming of Joe and the Jets. A few nonbelievers cautioned that there were still some basic flaws with the team, in the secondary and at the linebacking spots in particular, and perhaps second-year coach Charley Winner was too new on the scene, but their voices were lost in the bedlam.

Dick Young took a different tack, warning that the major flaw could be what most people considered the greatest strength: Namath himself. "I don't want you to go rushing out to buy your Super Bowl tickets," he cautioned in August, pointing out that despite Namath's "blue eyes" and "cleft chin" he was only the twelfth-ranking NFL quarterback in 1974, trailing Anderson, Stabler, Johnson, Griese, and Pastorini in the AFC and Jurgensen, Harris, Kilmer, Tarkenton, Hart, and Munson in the NFC. He also pointed out that "Nobody threw the ball to the other team more than Joey Baby last year." Namath had led the pros with 22 interceptions.

But this was just whispering in a wind tunnel. The fans, the press, the team members, the coaches—all

7

were ready for the juggernaut to roll. It looked like 1968 all over again.

I met Joe Namath before the Jets' final 1975 preseason game against the Redskins in Washington, D.C. The team was staying at the Shoreham Americana Hotel, and every player's room number was listed at the hotel desk except Joe's. That was fine except that his phone number was also a secret. How could I and my accomplice, a sportswriter for the *Washington Star,* announce our presence?

"I'm awfully sorry, sir," said the desk manager. "But our switchboard is already swamped with calls for Mr. Namath, many of the people claiming to be close friends and relatives. And there are girls prowling the halls. We just can't give out his number."

Eventually we managed to track down Frank Ramos, the Jets' public relations man, and he took our message to Namath, still without disclosing any numbers. Ramos returned and said that Joe would meet us in the lounge at nine that evening.

I had decided to write the book about Joe for a number of reasons, and not without some serious thought. One of the main reasons for doing it was that I still had not settled my personal feelings about Namath, something that seemed oddly important considering that I no longer played football and was at best a weekend fan. Another reason was that my friend Mike Adamle was a member of the Jets, wearing jersey number 1 and leading the team in sideline satire. The big drawback, I knew, would be what I was now experiencing—wading through the interference that surrounds a superstar.

We walked into the lounge at nine, and there sat Joe at the bar in a khaki leisure suit with an open-necked flowered shirt. He was drinking vodka on the rocks and joking with four black teammates. When he saw us he motioned us over and we introduced ourselves, shaking hands. My friend had come ostensibly on business, to write a column; but as far as Joe knew I was along for the ride, a freeloader. He had no idea I would be writing a book.

After a while Joe picked up the tab for everybody's drinks, not aggressively, but thoughtfully and with a surprising grace. The three of us went into the dining room, where we were joined by Joe's attorney, Jimmy Walsh, and another friend. For the first time I allowed myself to look hard at Joe's face. I was shocked by its instant familiarity: floods of newscasts, magazine covers, advertisements, movies, talk shows, and front pages intermingled with its features. When he smiled, his teeth gleamed white and even and dimples creased his cheeks. His pale green eyes counterbalanced the large, bulbous nose and swarthy complexion, and curly black hair covered most of his low forehead. It wasn't an aristocratic or young face—Joe was thirty-two—but it seemed to be the kind that would be noticed even without fame. A truck driver with Namath's features could probably count on a few second glances from hashhouse waitresses.

We ordered more drinks, and when Joe got his he recoiled in mock horror.

"What's this, water?" he cried to the table at large. "Take this back and get me a *real* drink."

The waiter, obviously confused yet eager to please, hesitated.

"I mean just put something in there. See if you can't fill it up or something."

Dick Schaap, the editor of *Sport* magazine, says that in his twenty years of covering sports only Joe and Ali have constantly been good copy. "I used to think the only thing I couldn't excuse was hypocrisy," states Schaap. "Joe isn't hypocritical—though Ali has become that way lately. But now I'll excuse *anything,* as long as it's not boring."

The waiter returned with a virtual tumblerful of vodka, and Joe smiled appreciatively.

Judging from the hundreds of thousands of words written about him, Namath has never been boring.

9

There have been Namath dolls and Namath hamburgers. Joe has received FBI protection because of death threats. He has been quoted in the press on religion, sex, politics, and most recently was featured in a nationally syndicated article with the epic headlines, "Joe Namath: Of Love and Life."

As we ordered our dinners I became aware of an attractive girl at the only other occupied table in the room. She was batting her eyes at Joe and only sporadically paying attention to her boyfriend next to her. Namath, with the tunnel vision celebrities can afford, took no notice.

He began talking about how late he had stayed out drinking the night before. "If I hadn't had a couple Michelobs before practice I never could have made it," he confided. I thought of my days at the Chiefs' training camp when veterans like Johnny Robinson, Lenny Dawson, and Mike Livingston would stay up half the night drinking beer, get up at 6:30 for breakfast, go to practice, eat lunch, and then play golf in the blazing sun before hurrying back for the afternoon session, followed by dinner, meetings, and more beer. It was a common thing in pro football.

The waiter brought us our dinner and more drinks. "These are from the couple over there," he said.

Joe looked at the other table and waved. The girl and her boyfriend waved back.

"I was with this girl the other night," Joe said. "I didn't even know what she looked like until the next morning, and I'll tell ya—she wasn't too pretty. But the thing was I'd had a good time, I kinda liked her. So before I left I asked her for her phone number. But she wouldn't give it to me. She refused."

Joe paused to take a drink from his wineglass. He had ordered three carafes of wine and wineglasses for everyone, but no one else was drinking.

"I told her I meant it, that I'd really like to give her a call. 'That's what they all say,' she said. And she just wouldn't give me her number."

Joe smiled, and one could tell the story interested him,

that he could see the inherent sadness in it and the put-down for his ego and still be pleased by the lady's pluck.

Shortly after that more drinks came to our table.

"From the couple over there," said the waiter.

Joe told the waiter to thank the people but that we really didn't need anymore.

A few moments later the girl walked by followed by her boyfriend. The boyfriend, obviously quite drunk, stopped and planted himself next to Joe. He thrust out his hand.

"I'm a Redskin fan," he grinned, as though we would find that hard to believe. "But, Joe, lemme tell ya. Yer the greatest."

His girlfriend was standing in the foyer looking decidedly nonchalant. After patting Joe's back for an embarrassing amount of time the young man stumbled up the stairs after her.

The incident, for all its banality, did not seem to affect Joe one way or the other. The table conversation drifted from bonefishing in Florida to Joe's knees to his recently purchased catfish farm outside Tuscaloosa. Joe listened carefully whenever someone asked a question or made a comment, and at one point he asked me what I did for a living. I told him I wrote frequently for *Sports Illustrated*. I noticed a change in both his and Jimmy Walsh's expressions. It wasn't till much later that I discovered they had a million-dollar suit pending against *Sports Illustrated* for what they felt was improper use of Joe's likeness on subscription cards.

Once again Joe paid the check for everyone, without any show. One of the serving girls came by and Joe thanked her for the pleasant meal. She said nothing, and this seemed to bother him. When she had moved away he muttered, "Those damn Japanese just aren't friendly." The girl, I felt certain, was Puerto Rican and hadn't understood.

At 10:55 Joe left for his room to make the 11:00 curfew. The next day was, after all, game day.

I pondered my first impressions of the man. One

writer working on a cover story for *Time* magazine in 1972 had been amazed upon meeting Namath. "He was nothing that I expected him to be, having read about him, and everything I expected him not to be," he stated in the publisher's memo. I was not sure exactly what the man had read, but it's hard to believe anyone could be "nothing" like you imagined.

In the course of the evening Joe had shown signs of sophistication, wit, and charm as well as touches of profanity, cockiness, lowbrowism, and nearsightedness. He had become a bit more opinionated as he drank. He was not one-dimensional. He was, I felt, simply more of a person than one might at first be led to believe.

TWO

The lamentable truth seems to be that Broadway Joe is fated to a career of a handful of brilliant successes and a pervasive sense of might-have-been.

—JONATHAN YARDLEY

It's the last day of practice before the last game of the 1975 season and seldom has any team sunk so low. Super Bowl talk died long ago, followed shortly by hopes of a conference championship, of a .500 season, of moral victories, of any semblance of respectability. The Jets won two of their first three games and one of the next ten. They sputtered, detonated, came apart like a car pushed off a mountainside—first a tire, then a door, then the entire body slipping off the frame like the husk of a nut.

If they lose to the surging Dallas Cowboys on Sunday, they will be the worst Jet team in history. "Lose?" choked one of the players yesterday. "We're wondering if they're gonna put a hundred points on the scoreboard."

There is a beaten look to the players as they walk onto the field, but it is covered as usual by a veneer of strained looseness. "I have never wanted to be out of a place so bad in all my life," says guard Garry Puetz, smiling and shaking his large, battered head. "Hey, when that final gun sounds, I'm gone."

The Dallas game is absolutely meaningless for either team, except in the coaches' jargon that all games are important to professionals. Randy Rasmussen, the left guard and one of the four remaining veterans from the Super Bowl, closes his eyes, thinking about the contest. "Shit, I can just see it. Dallas'll probably have their rookies in there going wild, trying to make all-world."

What is left for the Jets is very little—nobody wants to play, everybody wants to hop in their cars and go. John Riggins, the Jets eccentric fullback and recently announced Most Valuable Player on the team, at least would seem to have a reason to play. He has 943 yards rushing in 13 games and needs just 57 more on Sunday to become the Jets first 1,000-yard runner ever. But disillusionment hasn't been selective.

"It seems like a kind of ludicrous award this year, doesn't it?" he said when told of the MVP voting. And when grilled on the possibility of a thousand yards he stated that it might mean something in ten or fifteen years, but right now "I'm sort of tired of talking about it." In fact he seemed most pleased with a captain's hat presented to him in the back room of a bar that evening. On the peak was a small plaque saying, "1,000 or bust." John said he'd like to wear the hat out for the opening handshake.

It begins snowing as the Jets continue to wander out of the locker room, the sky taking on the thick oyster color that makes spatial judgments nearly impossible.

Though Joe had done his part in the collapse of the season, it was the defense and not the offense that had self-destructed first. The yardage-given-up and the points-scored-against were the match in the gas tank. During a six-game stretch in midseason Jets opponents had scored a total of 219 points, averaging 36.5 per game, a touchdown and a field goal per quarter.

The two elements, offense and defense, split up now as they always do, each aware of its role in the disgrace. The dullness of the day and the snow tend to obscure their presence, which they seem thankful for.

A number of the Jets are nursing hangovers, the result

of various celebrations the night before. The party I went to was informally tagged the "Last Tango in Point Lookout," Point Lookout being the small ocean community on the south side of Long Island where a dozen or so Jets live during the season.

There had been no real reason for the event, but I had found the Jets needed little reason to party. In fact, I had never seen a group celebrate as much as they did. In preseason they had adopted the motto, "Win or lose, we booze," and though their festivities often hinted more at suppressed rage than any pressing desire to be jubilant, they lived up to their words.

Last night Ken Bernich, a good-natured linebacker who stayed down the hall from me at the Hofstra dorms, spent part of the late hours asleep in a Point Lookout street. And Darrell Austin, the 260-pound wedge-breaker nicknamed the "Bionic Man" because of a plastic finger and other bodily aberrations, strummed his mandolin free of charge for the patrons of the two local bars. As he headed across the street from The Patio to Chicolino's he leaned heavily on me (I was accompanying on guitar) and winced each time he put pressure on his damaged right knee. It would need surgery, though he didn't know it at the time. "They know I'll give up my body for the wedge," he said earnestly, his last vestige of pride riding on that assumption. "It came out in the papers back home in South Carolina. They know I'll give it up."

The season had taken a cut of each man's heart, for it smacked more of a loss of courage than a lack of skill. In the second Buffalo game, with the Jets leading 23–17 in the fourth quarter, they needed one foot to ice the game. They couldn't get it. With the ball 80 yards away the defense needed to keep the Bills from scoring a touchdown in five minutes. The Bills scored in two.

In the locker room Namath looks at the clock now and sees that he should be on the field in exactly fifteen seconds.

His role in the debacle has been endlessly debated in the New York press, from his crippled knees to his aging arm to his suspect brainpower to his paycheck to, of course, his unwholesome habits. Dick Young has been clamoring for Joe to be put out to pasture for months. "You get rid of him," he wrote three days ago. "You rebuild heartlessly." Dave Anderson of the *Times,* always kinder, points out that the once-proud Jets' offensive line has allowed Joe to be sacked more times this year than any other QB in the league. Paul Zimmerman of the *New York Post* calls Namath a "statue who throws footballs, a $450,000 ornament." *New Times* magazine has gone so far as to feature Namath in their "Final Tribute," a column generally reserved for dead people.

The second hand is moving but Joe is having trouble getting into his green warm-up jacket. He is now thirty seconds late but he still has to lace one white shoe and tuck in his jersey. Jerome Barkum, the split end, flies past Namath and out the door. "C'mon, old man," he says, disappearing. Just last Sunday Joe was late for curfew before the San Diego game and was fined and benched on account of it. It was the first benching of his pro career.

Joe takes a quick look at his body, working from the toes up, making sure everything is where it should be. He starts to leave, comes back for his helmet, then looks up at the long table in the middle of the room where Emerson Boozer and Richard Neal are playing cards. Both are in street clothes, injured.

Boozer, along with Winston Hill, Rasmussen, and Namath, is a veteran from the Super Bowl Championship. He is black, handsome, well dressed, balding. At one time he was considered the fiercest blocking back in the league, capable of opening wide holes for Matt Snell and Bill Mathis or destroying blitzing linebackers intent on Joe's knees. Along the way he ran enough on his own to become the Jets' all-time leading ground gainer. Now a cane of polished wood lies under his seat.

"Hey, Boo," says Joe. "Come on out and practice one more time with us."

"No way," says Boozer, without raising his eyes from the cards.

"Go on out, Joe," says Richard Neal, throwing down a jack which Boozer pounces on. "How we s'posed to play cards, ya'll hanging around."

Joe leaves, but as he rounds the corner he turns out the locker-room lights, one of his favorite tricks. He is four minutes late.

Outside, no one seems to care that Namath is late, the coaches least of all. In fact interim head coach Ken Shipp's decision to punish Joe in San Diego was seen almost as insubordination on the coach's part. "For Christ's sake," said one of the players. "Why change things now?"

Joe picks up a ball and begins tossing it to tight end Richard Caster as the other players wander aimlessly about. They are dressed in their usual assortment of weirdness, although the cold has accentuated this a bit. Some are wearing gloves or ski masks; others have stocking hats under their helmets or long underwear dangling out of their pants. A few of the linemen have taped up their face masks so that they look like the cowcatchers on trains.

Drills start and the players run through the formations with as much enthusiasm as workmen laying sod. I wander onto the field and stand next to Jerome Barkum, Eddie Bell, and Lou Piccone as they form a small triangle and sing verses from Ray Charles's "Crying Time," snowflakes settling on their shoulders like epaulets. It is an apt song, for at the end of this season heads are going to roll. Ken Shipp and his staff will disappear, and from ten to twenty of the players will be discarded. Rumors are that even "the franchise itself," Joe Namath, may be asked to move on.

And why, I ask myself, aside from the fact that they are losers, is this such a strange team? I have come to know the players and like them—the Jets are without a doubt one of the friendliest pro organizations around— but something at the very core is twisted almost to sur-

17

real proportions. And it has to do, as my buddy Mike Adamle stated, with Joe Namath.

Ironically, Adamle was traded to Chicago, my hometown, three days after I joined the Jets in Washington, leaving me without my anticipated guide. But his reflections after a few months away from the Jets have become all the more beneficial, tempered by perspective. In a phone conversation he laid it out.

"I knew right off the bat things weren't kosher. In 1973 I walked into camp for the first time and all these guys were running plays, but the number-one quarterback wasn't there. Everybody's speculating about where he is, who he's with, how much money he wants this time. But nobody really gave a shit. They just took it as that's the way things are.

"And so you started to realize that if Joe could do certain things, there was really no way a coach could crack down on others without there being a terrible double standard. I'd just come from Kansas City where everything was so structured, everything had a place and a purpose, from the general manager down to this guy they called a 'strength coach.' But the Jets were at the opposite end of the spectrum. I mean, their general manager could have *been* the strength coach, for all anybody could tell.

"The difference between Hank Stram and Weeb Ewbank, the respective head coaches and GMs, was astounding. Henry, in his double-breasted Edwardian suits, was the Grand Exalted Imperial Stomper leading his boys out to do battle. And Weeb was this guy who was losing it, becoming more and more out of touch with his players. He was hard of hearing, you know, and you'd ask him, 'Weeb, we gotta wear ties in Baltimore?' And he'd say, 'No, no ties. Sudden death.'

"And Weeb sort of played along with the Namath thing. I think he found it humorous. I remember at this one exhibition game there were these two girls just hanging around to see Joe. They'd waited all day at the hotel, and then when the bus was leaving for the game they were there, and then at the game, and then afterward when we're getting back on the bus. They were begging to see Joe, and finally Weeb said okay, and he let them right on the bus. They ran down the aisle and kissed Namath, and they got to sit next to him for a couple minutes and talk and giggle.

"It was almost as though there were no rules on the Jets. Once Weeb started giving in and giving in—well, the precedent had been set. Kansas City sometimes seemed like a stalag from World War II—these huge signs saying 'UGLY FAT!' and the cement walls and all the weight machines—and there were times there when I just *knew* something had to be said. My function, I suppose, was court jester, team fool. [This was a role I knew Mike could work wonders with. Once at a Chiefs' team meeting he had dressed up in Hank Stram's coat and hat, climbed on a table and done an impersonation of the coach. So accurate were his mannerisms that when Stram entered the room he watched the entire performance without interrupting.] So then when I got to the Jets I was ready to carry on the role, but I got all screwed up. They didn't need a clown, they didn't need social comment. They needed Hitler."

Swimming had been taboo on the Chiefs, but right away Adamle decided to test the Jets. Before the first exhibition game he walked past the coaches in his bathing suit, and they asked him where he was going. He said swimming. They asked him to check the water, they'd probably be in in a minute. At Kansas City everyone had been made to wear the Chiefs' outfits to games —black blazers and straight-leg gray slacks. There was a $500 fine for offenders. Adamle reached a near state of shock, he claims, on his first road trip with the Jets.

"First Riggins got on the plane wearing a pair of shorts and suspenders and a bowler and all this turquoise jewelry, cowboy boots, and sanitary socks. Then came Steve Tannen in faded blue jeans and a work shirt, all tattered and hanging out of his pants, and penny loafers with no socks. Then came some of the black guys in dashikis and leather suits. I actually pinched myself to make sure I was awake.

"You could hang out in the bars, hustle waitresses—some of the coaches did that, too—grow beards, act crazy. I think that short of screwing somebody's wife right in front of them or killing the trainer, you could do anything."

As Joe whips passes to the receivers in his shoulder-rolling style that is virtually impossible to duplicate (attempting it makes one feel like a shotputter), he does not look like a man who would willfully disrupt a franchise. In fact, he isn't. His 28 interceptions, the most in the league this year, have done their share. But the other—the fomenting of chaos in the household—seems to have happened accidentally, without guile.

"Joe, I quickly realized, was *not* a nondiscipline ballplayer," Adamle continued. "As a student of the game he had no peer. But I think he just felt there was no congruency between certain rules and certain players' ability to function. In fact, he may have done some things just to that end—to show people there was no correlation. *He* could handle it. But I don't think he had any idea of the grand lengths things would come to."

Joe, in fact, appreciates discipline that leads toward victories, even if he constantly tests the limits of such rule. The only coach he speaks of with true reverence is Bear Bryant, one of the toughest taskmasters ever—and the only man to punish him severely for infractions. And when I asked him whom he'd like to see as the next Jets' head coach, Joe immediately replied Don Shula, another no-nonsense teacher. "I love this game," he says, a statement at least half the other Jet players can't make.

Practice ends and Mike Holovak, the Jets' director of scouting, approaches Joe with a sallow-faced high school quarterback, the son of a friend.

"Could you just give him some pointers?" asks Holovak.

Joe says sure. The kid, who is either very cocky or

scared sick, begins to fire away into the swirling snow. After several passes Joe stops him.

"Your motion is fine. But you don't have a good stance or dropback. You need to work on the basics. Here." Joe picks up a ball and then crouches down as though receiving a snap. He slaps the ball and dashes back eight yards, plants and pivots 180 degrees, the ball at shoulder height and cocked. It is a beautifully choreographed move that loses nothing from the fact that it is performed identically fifty times a day. Like a student confronting a Rubens, the boy has obviously assimilated nothing but the net effect. His next dropbacks are just like his first ones.

After a time the volunteer receivers go in and Joe, Holovak, the boy, and his father are left alone. Joe continues to talk, to clarify the components of dropping back, setting up, and scanning the field. The father and the boy will be able to say Joe Namath helped us, but it is obvious they had wanted something a little more dramatic, something like the secret to throwing last-second touchdowns or a blessing with holy water.

In 1966 Namath said, "I don't know *how* I throw the ball, and I don't remember anybody ever teaching me to throw it." But now he has written a book on the art entitled *A Matter of Style*.

"Jump rope, work on footwork, practice without a ball." He continues to lecture the boy, even as the group starts to head off. Eventually he is left alone by the back entrance to the locker room, pawing at the snow.

"I don't know why everybody went in," he says, looking around. "This is nice."

The snow is wet and soft, and there is no wind. Jerry Eskenazi, the sportswriter from the *Times,* walks up the sidewalk with his little girl at his side.

"This is Ellen," he says to Joe.

"Hi, Ellen." The little girl and Joe shake hands.

"You know, I never shake hands with a lady unless she offers her hand first."

The girl giggles and Joe brushes hair out of her eyes. "Looking forward to Christmas?"

"We're Jewish."

"Oh," says Joe. He looks out at the white field, then over at the parking lot, unwilling to leave.

"Good snowman weather in a while. Let's see how it packs."

He walks over to one of the tackling machines and scoops snow from the frame. He gets another handful from one inscribed, "I'm the Smart Dummy," and packs it into a ball. Jerry and his daughter say goodbye, and Joe stands with the snow in his hand.

He sighs. The last practice of a disastrous, horrible, ugly year—but the last practice, nevertheless. Once a few years ago Joe missed his tee-off time at a celebrities golf tournament. His partner, Willie Mays, had been furious. Joe made a formal apology. He hadn't done it maliciously; he had just overslept. Joe, in fact, never shows up late maliciously. Nor does he work out later than others for effect.

"Maybe I will build me a snowman," he says. "Get drunk and build one in the front yard. I remember that snow in 1967 when Jim Hudson and I got stranded in a single lane on the Fifty-ninth Street bridge and threw snowballs for a half hour before we backed all the way off the damn thing."

He chuckles and looks around for a target. Nothing beckons. He looks at his hand. "Guess I'll put this down Barkum's back or something," he says. Then he walks into the complex.

THREE

*The great man is too often all of a
piece; it is the little man that is a
bundle of contradictory elements. . . .
You never come to the end of
surprises he has in store for you.*
— W. SOMERSET MAUGHAM

On the afternoon that the Jets arrive in Kansas City
for their second game of the regular season in 1975,
Kerry Reardon is out in his backyard fiddling with the
lawn where it begins to turn into brush and timber. A
fifth-year reserve defensive back with the Chiefs, Kerry
is small, red-haired, and suitably Irish-looking. He is
scratching himself because he has contracted poison
ivy from previous such fiddlings. He is thinking about
snakes, which he doesn't like, and a mustache, which he
hasn't had the courage to grow, and about Joe Namath,
whom he regards as perhaps the most dangerous quarterback ever to face a secondary.

Kerry Reardon is not famous, nor will he ever be.
Fame is not something defensive backs acquire even
when it is deserved. Their lowly position in the pro hier-
archy is designated by the fact that only kickers, men
who see action four, possibly five times a game, are paid
less.

Still it is the defensive backs, faceless and poor, whose
play interweaves the closest with the celebrities. They
are the ones who play private games with the quarter-

back, shuffling in and out, faking zones, man-to-man, blitzes, staring each other down; they are the ones who determine whether his passes are caught or not, and they are the ones who run back his mistakes, his interceptions—the ultimate disgrace. Namath himself had played defensive back at Alabama, but only briefly. "The coach said I had too much talent to be back there," he says.

Kerry Reardon, who comes in as a fifth back on the Chiefs' prevent defense, is thinking about Joe and his talent and his fame, and how playing against Namath one is never sure where the one element starts and the other leaves off. Kerry is certain that last year Joe left the Kansas City stadium in an ambulance to avoid the crowd. "He must have loved that," Kerry says. "I would have."

For his own taste of glory Kerry has done a brief TV ad for a local bank. In it he mimics O. J. Simpson's Hertz Rent-a-Car ad, running through the bank at full tilt to show how fast deposits can be made. "I sort of felt like an idiot," he confesses, "but my wife Peggy owed this guy at the ad agency a favor." Of course, there was no pay involved.

But it is nice, in a certain way, for an anonymous defensive back to play against a famous quarterback. If nothing else, the opportunity to star is there. As Kerry points out: "It's really something I can get keyed up about. Like the guys were saying—you have so much more to gain than to lose."

Kerry and I had been rookies together at Kansas City, and at times during camp we had gone in to listen to the veteran defensive backs talk about the great quarterbacks. Squashed down with humility we listened silently on those occasions. "You could tell just by their expressions how they felt," says Kerry. "Johnny Robinson had survived by outthinking quarterbacks, by reacting as soon as or even before they did. But the word was that Namath was so quick with his release and so smart and so strong that there wasn't time for reaction."

All-Pro Emmitt Thomas, the wiry right cornerback,

had paid the fragile-legged Namath his ultimate compliment. "Joe is such a great player," he said, "I only wish I could give him my two good knees."

Reverence can only go so far, of course, and in 1974 in the Chief's 24–16 win over the Jets, Kerry had come in near the end of the game and intercepted one of Joe's passes. Kerry watched films of the Jets' first game this year against the Bills, a 42–14 defeat at Buffalo in a near-hurricane, but felt there was little he could gain from observing Namath and his receivers. "Everybody'd be standing there and all of a sudden some paper would go flying past about a hundred miles per hour. Nobody could throw in weather like that. Mostly it's his reputation you think about."

Defensive backs have different ways of preparing for quarterbacks. Cornerbacks, who play much of the time one-on-one—all alone with a receiver, a quarterback, and acres of grass—have the most varied methods. Some, like players I remember from college, did virtually nothing at all. They adopted the attitude that a little knowledge could be a dangerous thing. This was not as stupid as it sounds; indeed, pro scouts often say they don't want too much intelligence in a cornerback. Too much thinking—the "paralysis of analysis," as Coach Chuck Noll calls it—and you're beaten.

What a cornerback truly needs, Lem Barney once stated, is "a short memory." "The thing to remember," said Green Bay's Herb Adderly, "is that you're going to get beat. The question is, when you get beat, can you recover?" The answer, for many, is no. I, personally, was never the same after Mel Gray beat me in the 1971 East-West Shrine Game, and I wound up on the front page of a San Francisco paper, on my back, legs splayed wide like a wishbone, Dan Pastorini's touchdown pass frozen inches from Gray's belly.

For Kerry the possibility of such ingracious moments is countered by worrying; he is a profound worrier. During the 1971 rookie preseason at Kansas City, Kerry kept a list of every player on the squad and his chances of making the team. Rookies went to him to find out how they were doing. The list, a paranoid hedge against the dreaded knock on the door, was revised daily, and if Kerry said your chances weren't too good, you could pack your bags.

In that same 1971 East-West Game, Kerry was designated the punter on our East team as well as a starting defensive back, but it was the punting that really worried him. After one punt our defensive unit took the field, and as we lined up I noticed there were only three defensive backs. I started looking around and screaming, and then I noticed Kerry sitting nervously on the bench. He was absolutely engrossed in worrying about the fact that his last punt had gone just ten yards.

Defensive backs are a different breed, to be sure. If they had more size they might be running backs; more talent, wide receivers; more brains, doctors. To say they are high-strung is an understatement. Kansas City back Mike Sensibaugh once brought a dead snake into the Chiefs' training room. Safety Willie Mitchell, clad only in a jock, saw it, leaped through an open window, ran past spectators arriving for practice, tore down the sidewalk, and hid on the floor in the back seat of a team car, shivering with terror.

Defensive backs experience more anxiety and rage and less satisfaction than probably any other players on a football team. Dr. Arnold J. Mandell, a psychiatrist who studied NFL players for a year, noted that there is nothing else quite like being beaten on a pass. In an analysis of more than six hundred potential NFL draft choices, he found six men who were almost suicidally depressed. All were defensive backs. Depression, he wrote, "can put such men in constant danger of self-destruction."

"We have talked about covering a man perfectly all day and then suddenly being a bum," says Peggy Reardon, Kerry's wife and a former cheerleader at Iowa when Kerry starred there. "It's an understanding we have. And have had. But it's funny, so much of it's just in the defensive back's mind."

Still, there is much that takes place directly in front

of 70,000 people. Once against San Diego, Kerry missed a tackle on Gary Garrison and watched from the turf as Garrison romped into the end zone for a crucial touchdown. Kerry had been a wide receiver himself in college, and when he first switched to defense he thought it would be "all fun, only glory to come." Lying there he knew different.

"In those postseason college bowl games they let me play free safety, and it was like there was no responsibility," Kerry says. "All you could do was good. If somebody got beat it was the corner. It took me a couple of years to think about things—to realize the differences in positions, to know where help was coming from, where Lanier and Lynch were going to drop. Now I realize a free safety can get beat."

Despite his harmless looks, Kerry is a gutsy athlete. In time he began to relish the new challenge. "The competitive angle got to me, the fact that now things were reversed, that those guys were trying to beat me. It became almost a personal thing."

At dinner at a restaurant in the "old town" section of Kansas City, Kerry continues to think about Joe Namath and his receivers, Barkum, Bell, and Caster. "Those guys are good," he says. "I mean, Caster is a weapon of his own, but I don't know why the Jets never went after the Isaac Curtises and the Cliff Branches, speed guys. With Namath and his arm, that would have seemed like a smart thing to do."

It is something many people have asked, but discounting sheer speed the Jets have always had fine receivers. In the mid-1960s Don Maynard and George Sauer were consistent league leaders. Since 1970 Richard Caster has been one of the NFL's best tight ends. Last year the Jets' three starting receivers—Caster, Barkum, and David Knight—averaged 40 catches and 616 total yards apiece. Namath, the saying goes, makes good receivers.

Though he is not even sure how much he will play, Kerry is becoming so fidgety and distracted that he can barely eat. "He gets nervous, and then so do I," says Peggy. "Pretty soon I'll end up doing something stupid like forgetting my coat or locking the keys in the trunk."

"I remember seeing Jim Marsalis and Johnny Robinson and those guys just shaking before they had to play Namath," says Kerry, putting down his fork. "Shaking. He's just such a neat guy. Last year I got as close to him as I could in warm-ups. This year I probably will, too."

At the hotel where the Chiefs stay before home games, Kerry greets his roommate Barry Pearson, a calm, confident wide receiver who keeps Kerry loose. Kerry's old roommate had been free safety Mike Sensibaugh, but Sensibaugh's night habits had driven Kerry close to the breaking point. "He stayed up half the night, and even when he slept he needed lights and noise." Once in a fit of rage Kerry threw Sensibaugh's bed into the hallway. Now with Pearson, who invariably watches *Mary Tyler Moore* and then turns in, Kerry is at least assured of quiet and darkness.

The next afternoon as Arrowhead Stadium begins to fill with fans, I look out of the glass-enclosed press box to the field below, and, sure enough, Kerry is standing very near Namath, secretively watching him warm up. Even some of the veteran Chiefs are sneaking glances. Others, such as All-Pro middle linebacker Willie Lanier, don't have to look.

"I remember 1969 as plain as day," Lanier says after the game. "The Jets were at our forty. Namath dropped back and looked at Maynard, who's covered by Marsalis. Sauer's on the other side doing an out-and-up on Emmitt, and Emmitt's right on him, but all of a sudden Joe just pivots and throws because he *knew* where Sauer was, and that ball landed right over Sauer's left shoulder for a touchdown and I just said, 'Damn.'"

When the players are introduced, Namath gets the loudest ovation of anyone on either team. It is a display I will get used to by the end of the season.

The game starts and the Jets immediately run 80 yards for a touchdown without a pass being thrown. On their second drive Joe throws only once, to Caster for 35 yards, and then Garrett runs it in. On the sideline, Coach

Paul Wiggin of the Chiefs is moaning because no one expected the Jets to have any kind of a ground game.

On the Jets' third series Kerry comes in for the first time as Greg Gantt drops into punt formation. Instead of punting, however, Gantt throws a sideline pass to flanker Lou Piccone. For some reason Kerry has seen this coming and has already started running from his safety position. He arrives just as Piccone catches the ball, nearly decapitates the 5-foot-9 speedster, and holds the play to a one-yard gain. Using that break the Chiefs go in to score. At the half the Jets lead 23–14.

As the second half is about to start, I look down and notice that Kerry seems more agitated than usual. Then, when the Chiefs' defense takes the field, he lines up at the left cornerback position normally filled by Jim Marsalis. After the game Kerry would explain this mysterious occurrence.

"It was strange because when we got inside at the half I walked into the john with Marsalis, and for some reason we were right together taking a leak. Then I heard him go, 'Oh, no,' and I looked over and saw that he was pissing blood, just a little, but he broke out in a sweat and it scared him to death. I'd hurt my kidney the year before and had seen how black the urine can get when you're hurt real bad. I told him he better see the trainer, and he walked out, and then I went in and saw Tom Bettis, the secondary coach, and told him that maybe he should check Jimmy out because he was pissing a little blood. He went running out, and I sat down and started psyching myself up. I went to my locker and took out my punt return pads and put in some plastic things with no rubber at all, my defensive back pads. I was hoping to God I wouldn't be a dog."

In the third quarter the Chiefs play even with the Jets. Like a cat who sees a mouse on a distant wood pile, however, Namath is acutely aware that a new player is in the game. Once against Baltimore he threw an 80-yard TD pass over Rex Kern the moment the cornerback entered the game as a substitute. When asked about it later, Joe replied, "I saw that nice clean jersey and knew where I was going." But in this game he bides his time until late in the period.

On third down with the ball deep in their own territory, Joe splits Barkum to the left and sends Eddie Bell, the quickest of the receivers, on a streak up the right sideline. Kerry is with Bell stride for stride, as Joe spins and lofts a mighty pass 50 yards in the air directly at them. Suddenly I find myself remembering the time in practice when Kerry had wheeled and run 40 yards step for step with Jim Hines, a wide receiver trying to make the Chiefs but a man whose real claim to fame was a time of 9.1 in the 100-yard dash and the title of "World's Fastest Human." After that I began calling Kerry the "World's Fastest 5' 11" Redhead."

Kerry plays Bell like his dance partner and, at the last instant, outleaps him for the ball, catching it like an outfielder at the warning track. The moment he hits the ground he jumps up, tossing the ball to the ref and dancing and clapping for himself.

"Some inexperienced quarterbacks can make you feel like a fool by never looking at you," Kerry would say later. "But every time I peeked at Joe he stared a hole through me. He knew I was there and he had to throw on me."

In the fourth quarter Joe tries Kerry again on a critical third down when the Jets are trying to run out the clock. This time Bell runs a 10-yard buttonhook, but Kerry has anticipated the call and reaches around to knock the ball down, coming inches from a second interception. Still, the Jets hold on at the gun to win, 30–24.

In the parking lot afterward Kerry's parents and grandparents congratulate him. He looks over at the hundreds of fans screaming and pounding on the bus windows trying to get a closer look at Namath, and at Joe occasionally waving and grinning.

"I got as close as I could to him while catching punts and I could just see the steel impressions in his pants from the braces," Kerry says. "I said to Ed Podolak, 'God, look at his knees. How can he walk?' You can't help wanting to see how tall he is and that. And then how about when he got so mad at the ref and threw his helmet? I thought that was tremendous. Football players realize what a competitor he is, but the fans were probably shocked to think he has that much desire. They think he's just in it for the money and the glory."

Back in New York, Namath would remember Kerry Reardon. "He made some nice plays," Joe would say. "Especially on that curl at the end to Eddie. That could have been the ball game. The long one, well, that was a mental mistake. I just threw the fucking thing out there, figuring an interception's as good as a punt."

In the huddle in the third quarter Emmitt Thomas, who claims he remembers every pass Namath has ever thrown against him, had patted Kerry's back and said, "See, I told you you could play." Riding that crest of confidence, Kerry would start and play well for the Chiefs until getting injured against Dallas six games later on Monday night TV. The camera would pan to him on the bench, and when he looked up you could see the mustache he had been unable to grow while a substitute.

In the parking lot after the Jets' game, Kerry's wife and brother-in-law offer him a beer and tell him what a good game he has played. His brother Jerry shakes his hand. Kerry tries hard to keep his smile from getting out of control.

"Not bad for a five-eleven redhead," he admits.

FOUR

We may stop ourselves when going
up, never when coming down.
—NAPOLEON BONAPARTE

The New York Jets, in a sense, are not really the New York Jets. A more appropriate term might be the Long Island Jets, since for more than two years the Jets' training complex has been at Hofstra University in Hempstead, Long Island, some 25 miles from Manhattan and nearly as far from Shea Stadium.

Only defensive backs Phil Wise and Steve Tannen still live in the city. The rest of the players are split between such nonurban centers as West Hempstead, Mineola, Long Beach, and Point Lookout. Randy Rasmussen, with wife and family, lives the farthest away, driving 88 miles daily to and from Elmsford, New York, and paying for it. While most players are still removing their pads after practice, Randy will be toweling himself off; by the time they hit the showers he will be roaring down Fulton Avenue in a desperate attempt to beat the rush-hour traffic on the Cross Island Parkway.

One of the last people to desert the swinging life in the Big Apple was Joe Namath himself; and when he moved to a house on a tree-lined street in Garden City, Long Island, prior to the 1975 season, reporters dashed off the predictable columns. Joe was settling down; Joe was growing up; Joe, God help us all, needed peace and quiet. It seemed about right—the Jets, who had been in existence for thirteen years, and Joe, who had been at the helm for eleven, were ready for the suburbs.

"You wanna know why I moved," Joe says at a Wednesday practice. "Because of the traffic. You ever commuted? No? Well, believe me, it's a drag."

In relative terms, Joe is not that old. He's "no longer a spring chicken," says Rasmussen, but at thirty-two he is, for instance, several months younger than Mick Jagger of the Rolling Stones, and sixteen years younger than the near-mythical George Blanda of the Oakland Raiders. The "Garden City Joe" moniker is handy for a press that envisions him out raking leaves, but Joe doesn't buy it. "Hofstra is nice," he says. "The field at Shea was horrendous, and the jet planes flying over every thirty seconds made you punchy. But I miss Manhattan. There are many, many finer restaurants there and more ladies, too. You take a guy like Winston Hill, he's thirty-four; that's about ten years older than me."

Part of the problem for Namath is that on a football field, with his knees encased in their Lenox Hill derotation braces, his neck jutting from the front of his jersey like a crane's, and his shoulders rounded like a half-melted snowman's, he *looks* old.

There is also the fact that having accomplished so much so quickly, he seems to have been around forever. "Namath," wrote Dan Jenkins back in 1966, "is unlike all of the super sports celebrities who came before him in New York—Babe Ruth, Joe DiMaggio, and Sugar Ray Robinson, to name three of the more obvious. They were *grown men* when they achieved the status he now enjoys."

By twenty-six Joe had already won a Super Bowl, starred in a movie, retired from football, returned to football and, during the Bachelors III incident, wept on national TV. By contrast, Johnny Unitas played in his first Super Bowl at age thirty-six. He *won* his first Super Bowl at thirty-eight.

"He's changed," says Winston Hill, Joe's right offensive tackle and protector all these years. "But no different than anyone else." Most players contend that he is basically the same old Joe, friendlier perhaps and less flamboyant, but his actions reveal nothing suggesting character reversal. "Mellowed" is a word his teammates frequently use when describing Joe. As Rasmussen says, "If we go to the Super Bowl again, I don't think he'll stand up and 'guarantee' that we'll win."

Joe himself makes it plain that given the opportunity he'd move back to his old haunts on the East Side. "The way it is now, you just can't get in there," he says. "That damn traffic."

As for myself, I found short-term lodging in the Hempstead area virtually nonexistent. Elsie Cohen, the Jets' chatty, matronly receptionist who occasionally takes messages to the locker room by putting her hand over her eyes and shouting, "I'm coming," suggested I take a dorm room at Hofstra. "Quite a few of the players stay there," she said.

I found that hard to believe, but it was true. I got a room on the sixth floor of Tower F and found my floor-mates consisted entirely of Jets. All-Pro Richard Caster lived through the bathroom and across the hall. Corner-backs Delles Howell and Roscoe Word lived down from him, as did safety Bob Prout. On my side of the hall lived Leland Glass and James Scott, both flankers who had been injured and were sitting out the season. The reason the players gave for staying in the dorm was that it was cheap ($35 per week) and convenient. I noted to myself that they were all either defensive backs or receivers, but I had no idea what that meant.

From the top floor of Tower F, I could see the Jets' practice field, Nassau Coliseum, where the Nets and Islanders play, and on a clear night the top twenty or so floors of the Empire State Building far off across Queens. The Hofstra campus spread flat as an airport below. Later I would learn that this part of Hofstra actually had been an airport and that the parking lots were, as I suspected, runways.

At a Thursday practice on the first day of October the sun is shining and things look relatively good for the

Jets. "The pressure is off," reads the press release, meaning that the Jets have now won their first game of the season and things should start falling into place. No matter that the victory over winless Kansas City was salvaged by linebacker Godwin Turk stopping Jeff Kinney one yard short of the first down at the Jets' five with 54 seconds left. "We're cooking now," says Jazz Jackson.

The players are getting dressed, so I take a casual walk around the training hall. Laid out like a square within a square, the complex is designed so that the hallway begins and ends at the reception desk.

Starting straight ahead one goes past the assistant coaches' offices and equipment room, takes a left past the locker room, takes another left past the training room and player meeting rooms, then one more left past the press room where the hungry New York sportswriters are fed and lectured each Tuesday, past General Manager Al Ward's office, President Philip Iselin's office, Head Coach Charley Winner's office, and then back into the foyer. In the center square are the showers, handball court, soda machine, weight room, player personnel room, sauna, and sunken hot bath known as "the swimming pool." The entire building is carpeted and immaculate.

The walls of the hallway are hung with action photos of the Jets from beginning to present; circumnavigating them becomes a history lesson. In black and white and color the pictures show fumbles, touchdowns, ecstasy, and anguish; but more than anything else they show Joe Namath. Joe, barechested, with his arms around Weeb Ewbank and his dad; Joe standing in the snow; Joe peering out from behind his bench in 1965, his heavy-lidded, wise-guy's face a stark contrast to the short-haired, thick-necked men in front; Joe with his finger raised in victory, the bodiless hands of the Super Bowl crowd reaching out to touch him.

Namath's historical presence in the Jets' complex is so palpable—from the Leroy Nieman oil original inside the front door to the autographed glossies ready to be sent round the world—that it is a shock to see the real

35

thing walking down the hall munching on one of Elsie's cookies. Outside of museums or their own family rooms, few living men are so enshrined.

Charley Winner, short and trim, with blue eyes that will prevent him from ever looking mean, enters the lobby. He is a nice man and during the season he will occasionally call me aside to talk about irrelevant things—his daughter's tuition at the University of Missouri, the WFL, good meals, journalism. I often wondered what it was like for him, coaching a quarterback making ten times his salary, working under the burden of a living myth.

Charley had started under unfavorable conditions, being Weeb Ewbank's son-in-law, and midway through last year, with the Jets 1–7, he had nearly been ridden out of town. Then there had been that six-game streak at the end to smooth matters. The last frames of the 1974 highlight film showed him being borne aloft through the muck of Shea Stadium by players and fans alike.

"It's been great working with Joe," he says now. "The guy is such a great athlete. If he had decent legs there's no telling how good he could be. Hell, he used to run a four-six forty. In college he *carried* the ball two hundred times for fifteen touchdowns. And he's got this overall quickness, this hand-eye coordination that's just fantastic. He still sets up quicker than anybody in the league. And when he throws, bang, the ball's gone—*foom,* on a line. Or if he needs it, he'll just lay it out.

"And then there's his heart. Hey, he doesn't have to play this game. You know what I've seen him do? I've seen him get on one of our buses when it's crowded and some businessman or whatever will get up to offer his seat but Joe'll say no, that's okay, and he'll sit on the steps. He does things like that. One of his best buddies is this guy Hoot Owl Hicks, just an old shoe from down in Alabama. No, I'll tell you, I'd like to have Joe on the team as long as I can, as long as he's got that arm."

Out on the practice field the Jets' special team players are simulating the New England offense for the first-string defense. Joe sits on a ball placed on his helmet

36

and watches, his red "hands-off" jersey shining in the sun. On another field David Knight, the Jets' second-leading receiver last year, stretches his left knee, the one that was recently operated on to remove torn cartilage.

"What am I doing here?" he says. "I should be out saving the world."

At 6 feet 1 1/2 inches, 175 pounds, with hair as long as a rock star's, David looks out of place in a football uniform. Indeed, to the Jets he is something of an enigma —frail, handsome, intelligent, aloof, he reads Ayn Rand, shuns physical contact, and drives an old Volkswagen. His nicknames include "Hippie Weirdo" and "The Commie," but everyone likes him. His cynicism lacks malice or the strength to back it up. There is also the fact that when healthy he possesses the grace of a gazelle and hands, as one writer put it, that can catch eggs.

Right now he is depressed.

"Look at this, I can't cut to my right. I take these little stutter steps. Is it in my mind? I don't know. Why couldn't I be hurt up here?" He points to his skinny chest and then flops down to continue stretching and bending his leg.

I ask him about Namath's arm.

"You know, when I first came here in 1973 I told the press that the players in the pros aren't that great, just good college players, really. All except Caster and Namath. Caster because as big as he is he can run a four-five forty, which is about ten seconds faster than me. And Joe because of his arm. Look over there . . ."

J. J. Jones, the backup QB, is firing away, imitating Patriot helmsman Jim Plunkett.

"Joe throws a soft pass with the nose up, but J.J. throws with the nose down, which makes the ball heavy, it smacks your hands. And sometimes J.J. throws too hard. See . . ." The ball whizzes through tiny Jazz Jackson's hands, caroms off his helmet and hits cornerback Delles Howell in the head. "Joe throws like a lot of guys who throw floaters and get a lot of interceptions, but his passes have more speed. I guess that doesn't sound right. But when he's throwing good, the ball is fast and easy to catch."

Against New England on Sunday, with Hirohito, the Emperor of Japan, in attendance behind bullet-proof glass in the upper deck, Joe's passes are easy to catch. He hits his first 9 in a row and at the half is 13 of 16 for 201 yards. His arm and timing are uncanny: On one pass to Caster he waits for the tight end to make four fakes before hitting him for a ridiculously wide open touchdown. On another pass he hits Jerome Barkum on the fingertips at full extension in the end zone for a touchdown, even though Barkum is blanketed by two defenders.

The Jets win in a rout, 36–7, and aside from the fact that this is to be the high point of the season (which, of course, no one knows yet), there are three specific plays that seem important. Each, like the photographs in the hall, points to something larger.

The first play occurs on the Jets' first series. Namath hands the ball to Riggins, who goes right, breaks outside, stops, and suddenly decides to come back. As Riggins heads back toward Namath with pursuit thundering after him, Joe abruptly dives in front of 250-pound defensive end Tony McGee, who, taken by surprise, falls down. It is a rather ungainly attempt at a block, but it is a block nevertheless, and the crowd roars its appreciation.

This is the side of Namath, the competitive side, that has never failed to stir his teammates. Some quarterbacks would have stayed out of the way; others would have thrown the block for effect. Namath does such things without hesitating or evaluating, and not always wisely. When in 1971 he tried to tackle Mike Lucci of the Lions and ended up tearing the collateral, medial, and crucial ligaments in his left knee, many people questioned his sense of values. Namath was outraged. Weeb Ewbank shrugged. "Trying to tell Joe not to tackle is like trying to tell an old firehorse not to kick his stall when the bell rings."

But it is not the dramatic gestures that most impress

his teammates; rather it is the smaller, more mundane ones that catch their eye. "A lot of quarterbacks, they throw the ball too soon, but Joe never does," Emerson Boozer says. "He always waits until the last split second —until the rush is only this far away. And then he gets hit in the mouth. But he throws without ever thinking about possibly getting hit in the mouth."

The second notable event occurs on the play when Namath correctly reads Caster's elaborate, four-move, double zigzag, "QP" pattern and tosses an easy touchdown. The reason he was able to wait for the proper moment was that he had the time. And the reason he had the time was that his offensive line—Robert Woods, Randy Rasmussen, Wayne Mulligan, Garry Puetz, and Winston Hill—neutralized the New England pass rush.

"If you give a quarterback enough time," says St. Louis QB Jim Hart, "I don't care who he is. He'll kill you." The Jets' line has always tried desperately to give Joe, immobile and fragile as a vase, enough time—by whatever means available. In the first two series alone they were called twice for holding. The risk, invariably, is worth it. In the pocket, with three or four seconds working time, Namath is probably the most efficient quarterback ever to play the game. Without the time he is helpless.

The third important play happens after Namath has completed his first nine passes in a row and has dropped back for his tenth. Instead of throwing safe, he winds up like a kid in the punt, pass, and kick competition and heaves the ball 60 yards downfield in the direction of Jerome Barkum. It is intercepted, easily, and the Patriots take over.

Interceptions are one of Namath's biggest flaws; they point directly at his style, indirectly at his personality. He throws *long* interceptions, always going for the bomb. Some call it gambling, others call it greediness or a what-the-hell attitude. At Kansas City, even before Kerry Reardon's long interception, Emmitt Thomas had picked one off deep in the end zone; again Joe had been going for the cheap score.

Weeb Ewbank, who coached both Johnny Unitas and Namath, used to say both quarterbacks threw interceptions because they had so much confidence they would force the ball where it couldn't go. The fact is that long, fly-pattern routes used to work much better before zone coverages replaced straight man-to-man, the basic defense of the 1960s.

At the end of last year Charley Winner had finally gotten Joe "to take what the defense would give," to throw little safety-valve passes when the deep ones weren't there. "Overnight he became a more efficient quarterback," recalls Charley. "More efficient than he had ever been." But the mad bomber still lurks inside Joe, and at times it is hard for Namath to keep him under control.

The next week, Minnesota week, the sun is shining even brighter on the 2-1 Jets. They are now, as the press release states, "seeking a spot in the playoffs for the first time since 1969." Temperatures hover consistently in the 70s, and the Hofstra grass is soft and green.

In a chat with Charley Winner I mention that practicing during these days is probably a lot of fun. He looks me over. "Why don't you come out and run some patterns," he suggests. "With this forty-three-man rule, we have to use our kickers as receivers. Bill Hampton will give you some shoes and sweats. It'll save our boys' legs and give you some fresh air."

The thought of catching passes from Namath has me out by noon the next day. Unfortunately the thrower for the prep team is always J. J. Jones, or Al Woodall, when he is healthy, and it will be a while before I'll catch anything from Joe.

In the huddle I line up in the back next to Pat Leahy, the kicker, and Greg Gantt, the punter. The regular receivers are supposed to alternate, but I try to get back as quickly as possible after each route so I can say, "That's okay, Jerome, I got this one." Once the huddle is formed, everybody cranes as far forward as possible trying to decipher the lines and circles drawn on the flash cards held up by Jim Spavital, the backfield coach. This week

40

the prep team is running the Vikings' plays, and at various times I am supposed to be Jim Lash, Stu Voigt, or John Gilliam. Playing Jim Lash gives me a particular kick since we went to college together and I used to cover him every day in drills during the football season. J.J. seems to enjoy playing Tarkenton; periodically he smiles and says, "Watch Fran this time." Little Jazz Jackson wears number 44. This week he is Chuck Foreman.

On my first play I line up in front of cornerback Roscoe Word and smile at him. He doesn't smile back.

I had met Roscoe under curious circumstances the week before. At three in the morning he suddenly walked into my room.

"Let me use your phone, man," he said.

For some reason there was a phone in my room that worked. I didn't know who it was billed to or why it was there, but I used it occasionally without asking questions. I said okay. When Roscoe was done I asked him his name. "John," he said, and walked out.

A moment later he came back and asked what I was doing. I told him I was writing a book on the Jets. He started shuffling around the room, saying vague things about not telling on anybody "who, like, might be here today and gone tomorrow." Then he told me his name was Roscoe and that he had made the All-Rookie team last year at cornerback.

He started to leave again but stopped to tell me how lucky he was for a twenty-three-year-old black guy. "I got a 'seventy-four Regal, my wife's got a 'seventy-three Monte Carlo, and I got a forty-thousand-dollar house in Jackson, Mississippi. I don't dissipate because you can't do like that and play. Maybe Joe can. Not me."

He started to leave, then stopped again. "You know how some guys get cut and wait around camp to get picked up by another team? Me, I'll be home in a den where they can call me—not my mother's den, or my sister's, or my aunt's, but *my* den. What's your name again?" I told him.

"Rick, I feel good."

Periodically he would come in to use the phone after that, always very late at night. Once when the door was locked I could hear the knob turning slowly back and forth. "Just let a good thing be," he always said.

But now, he seems not to recognize me. Actually, as I gradually find out, all the players treat me differently when I am in uniform. Indeed, even by the end of the season, some of the Jets will still think I am simply trying out for the team.

In the locker room I have taken over injured Steve Tannen's cubicle, just down from Namath's. Joe's locker is in a prestigious position, situated near the exit and away from the crowds. The locker room's layout is shown on p. 43.

Occasionally I will simply stare at Joe, feeling like the writer who reported to his editor back in 1965 that Joe had "languid, incredibly light, yellowish-green eyes." He had then added a note saying: "I looked into them as carefully as is decent and they look yellowish-green to me. The sportswriters say they're blue. I'll be covering the exhibition game Friday and will check again then if you care."

Sometimes Namath's eyes look pink to me, and he appears very ordinary, his lower lip full of snuff, disheveled, homely. As Mike Adamle said, "You see him hung over a few times with Skoal dribbling down his chin and the magic starts to wear off."

The locker room itself is a rowdy place. Second-year linebacker Godwin Turk, 6 feet 3, 236 pounds, touted by assistant coach Buddy Ryan as "Too Tough Turk" and a certain All-Pro, leads in the shaving-cream, ice-down-the-back brigade. Namath himself enjoys watching the horseplay but generally remains out of the action. The jokes frequently get too strenuous, with players flying out the doors and wrestling over the tops of the picnic tables laid out for card playing. In one match Jazz Jackson gets run into the bulletin board and cuts himself badly enough to require stitches in his back.

Joe enjoys making wisecracks, and if he gets a good put-down in return, he chuckles with appreciation. If he

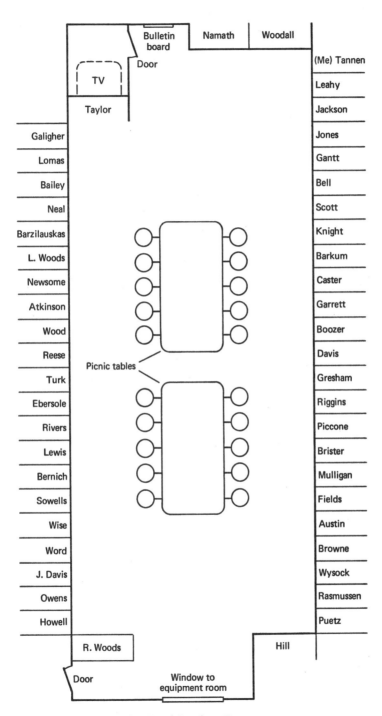

The Jets' Locker Room

is in a particularly feisty mood, he will pester someone who is too busy doing something else to get involved, and then on the way out he'll invariably turn out the lights.

Some of the older pros—Winston Hill, Emerson Boozer, John Ebersole, Billy Newsome—and most of the really large people on the team, such as Carl Barzilauskas and Jim Bailey, watch the mayhem from a distance, resignation in their attitudes. "I know this is close to the end of my career," says Winston Hill. "I see so many reoccurring things. Different faces, different guys, doing the same old things."

On the plane to Minneapolis on Saturday, Charley Winner talks about Fran Tarkenton, a quarterback much maligned when he was in New York with the Giants but now a superstar with the Vikings. In style, Tarkenton is about as far from Namath as two men can be. With an admittedly weak arm (at one time last season it was so sore he could barely throw thirty yards on a loop), he leads his team through craft, brilliant play-calling, scrambling, and guttiness.

The scrambling is the most obvious difference—Tarkenton drops back, looks, dodges, darts to the side, looks some more, ducks a lineman or two, and then decides whether to throw or run. And just as important, in fourteen years he has never been hurt. "In the pocket everybody would like to have a Joe Namath," says Charley. "But out of it they'd like to have a Tarkenton because he has two options on every play. A guy like that should be outlawed."

Shrewdness is the other Tarkenton trademark. "When I was coaching at Baltimore we called a safety blitz, and Walsh, our safety, nailed Tarkenton," says Charley. "Later in the game we called it again. Tarkenton was counting out the signals, and Walsh was getting ready to go, and without any hesitation in the cadence Tarkenton just looked right at him and winked."

In Minneapolis the press has built up this first-time meeting between Namath, the "world's most famous quarterback" and Tarkenton, "who may be the world's best quarterback before his career is over," as something of a spectacular. Officials at Metropolitan Stadium claim there hasn't been such a demand for seats since the Beatles came in 1965. "In all my years of coaching and playing I can't remember so many people I didn't know asking me if I could get them tickets," said Viking Coach Bud Grant.

For the Viking players the game has also taken on special significance. "It would definitely be some kind of an honor to dump someone like Namath a couple of times," stated left defensive tackle Doug Sutherland. Even Karl Kassulke, the ex-Viking safety, now paralyzed from a motorcycle accident, has reviewed his memories of previous meetings. "This was one miserable peon of a defensive back who just wanted to steal the thunder from Broadway Joe," he wrote in a pregame paper. "To see him eat humble pie is dynamite!"

The game itself is played under abnormally balmy skies in front of a standing-room-only crowd that roars each time Namath makes a move. Joe plays cautiously the first half, throwing quick flare passes to Riggins and letting the big fullback run over the contain men. Then, with a 7–6 Jet lead, Namath throws low to Richard Caster in the end zone, and middle linebacker Jeff Siemon intercepts to stop the drive. Again, it was an attempt at a quick score, a play Joe would later call "a real blunder."

In the end, however, the game is decided by the Jets' defense. Lacking veteran linebackers like Al Atkinson, who is on injured reserve, and Ralph Baker, who was released at the start of the year, they seem confused by elusive running-back Chuck Foreman. For the day Foreman catches a career high 9 passes for 105 yards and 2 TDs and runs for 96 yards and a third touchdown. With the Jets down only one point late in the fourth quarter, the defense lets Minnesota score easily to put the game away, 29–21.

Namath makes one spectacular play on a third down when the Vikings come at him with five down lineman and a double safety blitz. Throwing off his back foot with a man hanging onto his left arm, he hits Caster on the fingertips for 20 yards. "He has such tremendous strength in his wrist," said Bud Grant after the game. "Not many other quarterbacks in football could have made that play. Maybe none."

But few also could have made the play Tarkenton did in the first quarter when he dropped back, spun away from two tacklers, ran to his right, pulled out of Jim Bailey's arms, eluded Barzilauskas, and still completed a toss to Foreman for a first down. In comparison, Namath, with his straight dropback and hunched stance, resembled an arthritic old man.

Insult was added to the Jets' effort when the defense tried three badly concealed safety blitzes and was burned by Tarkenton each time, once for a touchdown pass to Foreman. "That embarrassed me," said Tarkenton afterward. "They should have known better."

After the game a flying wedge had to be made to get Namath out of the stadium safely. The Minnesota girls screamed, "Joe! Joe!" and held out scraps of paper, and all the fans were happy and glowing in the late afternoon sun. On the plane the Jets drank beer and played their tape decks, unaware, or uncaring, that the long slide had already begun.

FIVE

God will not look you over for
medals, degrees or diplomas, but for
scars!

—ELBERT HUBBARD

Joe Namath's knees. Perhaps the word should be capitalized, as in the name of a building or an institution: Joe Namath's Knees. Seldom is the man mentioned without some passing reference to the parts.

Joe's knees are his particular flaw, or weakness, or curse, depending on one's viewpoint. They have their equivalent in Sandy Koufax's elbow, Beethoven's ears, Fitzgerald's booze, Nixon's tapes, Achilles' heel. They are the obstacles that have limited him in his career, perhaps kept him from achieving his true stature; yet at the same time they have humanized him, made him at once more sympathetic and open to attack.

There have been other cocky pro quarterbacks. In his first year in the NFL Joe Kapp of the Vikings yelled across the line at the Los Angeles Rams: "Fuck you, Rams. You're not much. Here I come." But Kapp was more than simply confident, and there was little for one to identify with in his excesses. "I'm an animal," he said. "Is it normal to wake up in the morning in a sweat because you can't wait to beat another human's guts out?"

Likewise, the God-fearing, efficient quarterbacks tend to leave one uninterested. In the introduction to his book

47

Quarterbacks Have All the Fun, Dick Schaap explains why he hasn't included an article on Miami's two-time Super Bowl Champion Bob Griese by stating that Griese's "character reflects his play: no visible flaws. Perfection tends to bore . . ."

Namath's damaged joints have made him more fragile than he might have been, less the bratty kid than the vulnerable young man, the champion by setback, or at least the daring artisan who, as Robert Lipsyte says, "perceives that his value to himself depends on climbing out of the pit and making a life before all the juice is wrung out of him." Shakespeare himself never made a hero without a flaw.

"For the last ten years people have come up to me during the off-season and said, 'Hey, do you think Namath will play again?'" says Paul Zimmerman of the *New York Post.* "That's what makes him what he is —the fear. The fear that he might be gone, injured for good. It's a love-hate relationship, a life-death thing, it brings out the motherhood in people or brings out their own fears of death or whatever. The threat of danger around the corner is the guy's great appeal, the fact that he's on a tightrope."

For some people with their own infirmities Joe has become something of a patron saint. One devout Namath fan, a corpulent, middle-aged Connecticut woman who has not missed a Jets game for six years, went to her first game back in 1969 just to get "a look" at Joe. "I had always identified with him because of the way he played under adverse conditions with his bad knees," she told a reporter. "I've had adversity, too. I had polio in 1960 and was paralyzed from the neck down. I had to stay in the hospital for nine months and learn how to walk all over again."

Joe's fragile joints have given press gadflies like Dick Young unlimited opportunities to harp on his unfitness and to sound premature death knells; no New York off-season is complete without someone writing Joe off. Even fellow NFL players take Joe's knees into account when they consider the man. "I'll go for his head, his

48

chest, hit him in the nose, most anything to make the play," says All-Pro middle linebacker Willie Lanier. "But I won't hit his legs. Even if it were the only way, I wouldn't do it. You have to live with yourself."

Ernie Holmes, Pittsburgh's defensive tackle, notorious for playing at a point close to blind rage, admits he'll take down most quarterbacks by ripping their arms off if necessary. But with Joe he feels a special compassion. "He's handicapped. I wouldn't hit him low. That'd be like saying to him, 'Kiss my ass.' "

Despite the physical drawbacks, the degeneration of Namath's knees has closely paralleled his rise to fame. In the 1965 Orange Bowl, Joe came off the bench for Alabama and, though severely hobbled, nearly passed the Tide to an upset victory over Texas. Sonny Werblin, the owner of the Jets, was in the stands and saw the effect the quarterback had on the crowd. "I don't know how to define a star," the former show business talent agent said later, "but I knew Joe had what it takes when he limped off the bench that night and seventy-two thousand people moved to the edge of their seats."

Until three months before that Orange Bowl game, Joe had never limped to do anything. "Joe Namath is not the type of athlete who gets injured," said Dr. E. C. Brock, the Alabama team physician. "Just the usual scrapes and bruises, and when he gets these, he usually treats himself."

But then on October 10, 1964, in a game against North Carolina State, something happened.

"I remember it well," says Joe. "It was the fourth game of my senior year. We were undefeated and I was at my peak physically. It was a run-pass option to the right, and I saw I could get the three yards we needed by keeping the ball, so I cut to the left. My knee just gave out. Nobody touched me. Nobody was even near me."

Trainers carried Joe to the locker room and iced down his knee, which Joe claimed hurt him on each side and in the back. Two days later the joint was swollen enough to require draining. But by the end of the week, with tape and elastic, Joe could move about reasonably well.

49

"That was only the fourth week of the season and we were heading for the national championship, so I finished the year," he says. "Nobody was exactly sure what was wrong with my knee anyway. We knew something was torn after the blood showed when I had it aspirated. But at the time they didn't do arthrograms, where a doctor injects your knee with fluid and the fluid goes into the crevices of the knee and shows what is torn on X rays. I just made the best of it."

In the next two months Namath reinjured his knee four more times. Oddly, in not one of these incidents was he hit by an opponent. Against Florida State the knee gave way under circumstances identical with the first—as Joe was cutting upfield on an option. The next injury happened in practice the day before the Mississippi game when he came down hard after a jump pass. The final two injuries came before the Orange Bowl game in Miami; the first occurred when he stepped up into his car to unload his baggage, and the final one happened just three days before New Year's as he routinely jogged back to a huddle.

By this time it was apparent that something was badly wrong with the knee and that surgery would be necessary to correct it. Joe himself was aware of a new threshold in his life. "I never felt anything that hurt so much," he said of the five injuries. "I almost cried every time it happened."

He now looks back on his senior year at Alabama with a touch of regret. "Because I continued to play on my right knee while it was injured, it just tore up the insides of the thing. It destroyed my knee. I've had an arthritic condition for eleven years because of it."

Immediately after the Orange Bowl game, with Joe's monstrous contract signed, Dr. James A. Nicholas, a New York orthopedist, entered the scene. In 1954 he had been a member of the surgical team that operated on the war-damaged spine of then Senator John F. Kennedy. In 1960 he had become the team physician for the New York Titans of the fledgling AFL and had stayed on when they changed owners and became the

New York Jets. As a sports physician Dr. Nicholas's reputation was just beginning in 1965; within ten years he would have founded the prestigious Institute of Sports Medicine and Trauma at Lenox Hill Hospital in Manhattan and would be a consultant for the New York Knicks, Rangers, and Cosmos as well as the Jets. Magazines now do personality profiles on him; *Esquire* has claimed that "he may well be the most important doctor in sports today."

In a sense Dr. Nicholas's rise to fame has paralleled Joe's, or, rather, Joe's knees. Indeed the physician now knows more about those two joints than he does his own, having operated on them four times. In January of 1965, however, he wasn't sure he wanted to get involved.

"I was worried, in fact I was horrified," says the muscular, fifty-four-year-old doctor. "When the Jets drafted Joe it was my impression that he had a simple cartilage problem. Actually he had a very unstable knee; it was very seriously damaged. I went to Sonny Werblin and told him he'd better look for another quarterback; I wasn't sure Joe would make it. We held a press conference and I remember it being a very low point in my life. I had to tell everyone how serious things really were."

When Dr. Nicholas cut into the knee in an operation that was covered feverishly by the news media (there were even photographers in the operating room), he found the medial cartilage was shredded and crumpled into a wedge, damage that kept the knee hinge from closing completely and made Joe's season-long performance all the more amazing. He removed the entire cartilage and a small, fluid-filled cyst he discovered behind the knee. He then shortened a stretched inner ligament by folding it back on itself in a pleat, and put in several stitches. The operation was long, an hour and thirteen minutes, and Dr. Nicholas hoped that it would be successful.

When Namath, who suffered the indignity of having nurses hoist his eyelids to look at his eyes while he was still unconscious, awoke, Dr. Nicholas made him immediately begin raising and lowering his right leg.

Strength, said the doctor, would be the key to recovery.

Despite fears, the operation and rehabilitation were a success; Joe was voted AFL Rookie of the Year twelve months later. But that was hardly the end to his knee troubles. Soon the right knee would need another operation, a "complete reconstruction" this time, and the left knee would require two cuts of its own.

"For three weeks prior to that first injury I'd had a charley horse on my thigh," says Joe. "And the only theory we could figure was that the bad blood from the thigh went down to the knee enough to weaken it, and when I made that cut it just didn't hold up."

Actually, doctors found Joe had a problem that made his injuries almost predictable. Called "marked recurvatum of the knees," in layman's terms it means that Joe's legs bend slightly back and outward at the knee, an unnatural curvature that weakens and relaxes the ligaments and makes them unusually susceptible to injury. Many colleges, in fact, will not accept otherwise qualified athletes if they have recurvatum.

Dr. Nicholas, who has developed a twenty-one-factor sports-comparison chart, which includes an athlete's mental, physical, and environmental traits, says that Joe shows up as a basically loose-type player. Loose athletes are agile but susceptible to torn ligaments, he notes, while tight athletes are stronger and more prone to fractures.

"Mark Spitz had a hyperextensibility which helped him in swimming," says Dr. Nicholas. "Joe has the same thing. Tarkenton does not, nor Blanda, nor Hadl. Ali, on the other hand, is loose; he would probably do well at basketball. Hyperextensibility means that you can get more offset movement to develop power and more gymnastic ability. It has to do with rhythm and grace of movement."

It also has to do with injury, since loose-jointed people frequently put their bodies in vulnerable positions. For this and other medical reasons, Dr. Nicholas developed his famous Lenox Hill derotation brace. Originally designed for geriatric surgical cases rather than football players, at a research cost of $70,000, the brace consists of two pieces of steel with a patented mechanism that allows the knee joint to rotate only in its normal axis. Each brace along with its straps weighs sixteen ounces and must be custom built for each wearer.

It wasn't until after the 1971 injury to his left knee and his fourth operation that Joe finally agreed to wear the derotation brace. It was another year still before Dr. Nicholas could talk him into wearing a brace on each knee. "We told Joe at the very beginning in 1965 that he'd have to wear a brace," says the orthopedist. "But he wouldn't wear the one we had designed. He was young, he didn't want to be encumbered."

Watching Joe strap the braces on before a game, it is not that hard to understand why. They are frightening hunks of metal that squeak when he walks and drastically reduce his mobility when he runs. He loses at least two tenths of a second in the forty and a great deal of cutting speed. "He can't dodge, can't rotate," says Dr. Nicholas. "Cuts have to be rounded; that's why we can't use the braces for basketball."

Jim Bailey, the Jets' right defensive tackle, tried a similar brace recently but took it off almost immediately because it was so painful. "If Joe had been wearing those braces from the beginning, I don't believe he would have gotten reinjured," insists Dr. Nicholas. "I had my doubts at first, but I've seen him take direct blows on his knees with them on and not get hurt."

Knee braces could not have helped the rest of his body, however. In his career Joe has suffered numerous concussions, sprains, dislocations and fractures. He missed nine games in 1970 because of a broken wrist and ten games in 1973 because of a separated right shoulder, perhaps his most serious injury ever, since it was not certain that he'd be able to throw again.

After the 1973 injury, Stan White, the Colts' linebacker who ran Joe down on a blitz, came into the Jets' locker room to apologize. "I really felt bad," he said later. "Not just that I did it, but that anyone did it." White's tackle made him somewhat famous, nevertheless, and for the rest of the season that particular Baltimore blitz was known throughout the league as the Namath Blitz.

Pain is the one element that has been consistent in Joe's career. I asked him one day if his knee hurt him all the time. "It doesn't hurt right now," he said matter-of-factly. He was sitting and his knees were stretched in front of him. "It does when I run, though, or walk around, or move. Just about every movement."

Joe is a notorious noncomplainer—"He's as tough as they come," says Jet trainer Jeff Snedeker—but injuries have changed him. He has come to accept his braces and his hobbling gait. "He's willing to compromise now," says Dr. Nicholas. He has also become more reflective.

"When I'm sitting by his bed and he's in pain and he's talking about his future, that's when I learn from him," says Dr. Nicholas. "After his shoulder separation I remember he expressed doubt for the first time. He wasn't sure if he could get his arm back. He said he might quit. He is very careful now—he alway wears his braces, he exercises, he follows advice, he watches his weight. He is very much aware of his body and being cured by his body. He never wants to take pain killers."

Injuries have also made Namath realize what football means to him. Before the 1970 season he claimed he really didn't want to play anymore. Then he broke his wrist, missed most of the season, and came back the next year full of enthusiasm. "I've discovered that I really miss not being able to play," he said. Then in the first exhibition game of 1971 Joe tore ligaments in his left knee and the ever-ready Dick Young wrote that "this could be it for good."

Namath has always measured himself through pain. His favorite game, for instance, is not the Super Bowl or his six-touchdown performance against the Colts, but the brutal Oakland game for the 1968 AFL Championship. "It was such a tough game physically, that's why it was so important," he says. "In the first quarter I got a concussion, in the second quarter I dislocated a finger, at the half I got a shot in both knees and a shot in my finger. I was feeling really bad physically, everything hurt. But to be able to come back from pain and not quit, to be able to grit your teeth and say, 'Dammit, they're not gonna get me, they're not gonna finish me off,' that's satisfying."

In his dazed condition Namath was still able to lead the Jets to a 27–24 come-from-behind victory. Two weeks later the Jets won the Super Bowl. "It's the same thing now," he says. "There's less satisfaction from those games where you don't get touched, where it's easy, where you know you haven't reached deep down. When you're physically hurt it's hard to work your mind properly. But that's the added incentive. It's something I learned in the hospital after a couple of operations. Hell, those things are serious—Mack Lee Hill died during a cartilage operation—but you just tell yourself to be tough, that your back's to the wall but it's not gonna kill you."

Joe's teammates recognize his stoicism. "Joe would never say anything like he wished he had better knees," says safety Phil Wise. Richard Caster even sees Joe's toughness as a subconscious impulse toward self-destruction. "They say that deep down inside true gamblers are really looking to lose, not win. Who knows? Maybe Joe is searching for that one big, final injury." For its part, the press continues to goad him with what-if questions. "I've said this since I first came to the pros. If I hadn't gotten hurt I'd have gone to Vietnam and probably gotten killed," answers Joe. "I was drafted and if I'd been healthy I'd have been in the service."

Namath also suffers from another, less publicized injury, a torn left hamstring that has hobbled him nearly as much as his knees. That injury occurred while Joe was water-skiing in Bimini. "The towrope snapped and my hamstring just rolled right down," he says. "That's why I can't run. I can't extend the leg more than six or eight times without it weakening. I mean, there's the hamstring, that thing, right there in a knot, a ball." He points to a grapefruit-sized lump on the back of his thigh.

At the end of the 1974 season, Hoot Owl Hicks, Joe's buddy from Tuscaloosa, brought up some University of Alabama game films from Joe's senior year. It marked the first time Joe had seen the films in a decade. "I looked at myself and, jeez, I could *move,*" he says. "The first game of the year against Georgia I ran for five touchdowns; two of them got called back, though. The next two games I scored two or three touchdowns in each. They weren't sneaks either, they were bootlegs and options. I was leading the country in scoring."

At times Joe's noncommittal attitude erodes and he shows genuine hurt over his limitations. "I know I can't do what I could before," he snapped at one reporter recently. "So what!" It was widely printed that Joe visited wounded servicemen in Vietnam a few years back, but though he did tour Japan, Guam, and the Philippines, he refused to go to Vietnam. He felt the men would resent him. "Those guys had been fighting over there for so long and here I come—Big Joe, 4-F because of my knees, a hot dog from New York."

In the second game against Miami this year, Joe attempted to run five yards for a first down. It was a pathetic display—a slow jog with a racing dive at the end that fell a yard short. Joe, in utter disgust, slammed the ball to the turf and received a five-yard delay-of-game penalty. "A man has pride," he muttered after the game.

It was pride that led him on his famous bootleg the year before against the Giants, a play that almost singlehandedly ignited the Jets to their six-game winning streak. In that game the Jets were behind by a touchdown with time running out. The ball was inside the Giants' ten and Namath had called Boozer off tackle. "I'd studied the films," Joe recalls, "and I knew in that situation their linebacker liked to close fast. The play I'd called was a good one, but when I got to the line I knew the right thing to do was to keep it. I didn't tell anybody. Boo had a heart attack. He thought he'd fumbled."

The entire team nearly had a heart attack when they saw Namath staggering, alone, around left end. "Lord, it looked like he had a broom up his ass," recalls Dave

Knight. "It must have taken him ten seconds to go five yards. Two defensive backs saw him at the last second, but Joe put his hand up and they just stopped." Namath claims the gesture wasn't "Stop, I'm in," but a "very casual protective move." On film it looked like "Stop, I'm in." "The thing is," says Knight, "our record was one and seven at the time. He could have gotten killed. But that tied the game and then we won it in overtime. The league would probably fine a guy if he ever cheap-shotted Joe."

People—the press, teammates, critics—have a tendency to worry about Namath's future. This season in particular, as his infirmities become more obvious and the team sinks further into oblivion, words such as "pity" have begun to appear in Namath write-ups. Joe acts astounded by such postures. "It's really stupid for people to feel sorry for me. I'm happy, I've got my health. It's just silly."

Dr. Nicholas agrees. "This whole 'tragic hero' element, I feel, is unfair. Joe's knees are not as bad as they are alleged to be. They are not crippled old man's knees. I know a sixty-year-old tennis player who plays daily on a knee like Joe's left one. The right one has some arthritic changes, but they are moderate, and if Joe doesn't get any new injuries he can function for many, many more years in a normal life. Can he jump on a trampoline? No. Should he ski downhill? No. Could he cross-country ski if he wanted to? Yes. He can run without the braces right now."

Dr. Nicholas mentions that one day spent taking care of high-speed auto accident victims or war-injured, both of which he has done aplenty, will convince anyone that Joe's injuries are "elementary." "People say he is so brave and courageous. In my opinion that's nonsense. Seventy percent of all pros have had knee surgery by the time they are twenty-six and, with few exceptions, all the quarterbacks. Joe is far from being the most beat-up quarterback. Dick Wood played five years and had more injuries than Joe. Norm Snead has had as many operations as Joe. Charley Johnson has had seven.

Quarterback is a vulnerable position—for anyone."

As a physician Dr. Nicholas sees the degeneration of the body, particularly the knee, as part of the game, a cumulative deterioration affecting all athletes—ballerinas and football players alike. "Olga Korbut, the gymnast, has been in the hospital seven times because of her knees. Julius Erving, at twenty-four, wears two braces. Ben Hogan has a worse knee than Joe. Emerson Boozer does. There is no crucial age for deterioration—in many athletes the discs in the back begin degenerating at age twelve.

"The reason Joe's problems have become famous is because he is in New York," explains Dr. Nicholas. "Look at me, I get into *People* magazine because I'm in New York. That's the nature of communications."

The orthopedist suggests, as have others, that the knee damage may actually have been a blessing for Namath in that it made him concentrate on other facets of his game. "He might never have developed his pinpoint throwing accuracy," says the doctor. There is also the fact that Joe gets paid well for his work and that Joe has, as he says, "more or less conditioned myself to the whole damn thing." In midseason a reporter asked Namath if he might not miss his agility when he was finished with football. "I don't think so," he replied. "I think I'll be able to do everything I want to without running."

From Dr. Nicholas's viewpoint, Joe's knee troubles are far from discouraging. After comparing frames of Joe in action this year and in past seasons, Dr. Nicholas has determined that Joe's dropback is nearly as quick as it was in 1965, an amazing retention.

"Vince Lombardi called football a game of violence as distinct from brutality," he states. "Brutal to me means exploitation. It's not the ideal to achieve something at the expense of something else, if it's preventable, but you have to decide if you want to take someone out of physical activity that is risky at the expense of his ability to achieve. To me, letting Joe continue on with the things he is doing is allowing him to achieve the wholeness of his being."

Dr. Nicholas talks about the artificial knees that are being developed and about the days ahead when athletes will wear braces before they need them. Seeing Joe after a normal game, his knees bloated and wrapped in ice bags, a grimace on his face, one wonders about the sacrifices behind such developments. And the limits of achieving wholeness. Still, on a good day, Joe's knees do not look that menacing. The scars are thin and brown and symmetrical.

"His future just depends on how he takes care of his body," says Dr. Nicholas. "Joe likes to fish. You don't need knees to fish."

*Being called an intellectual next to
Namath is like being called a
weightlifter next to Truman Capote.*
—DICK SCHAAP

"The people that own this house, the doctor is about
eighty-four and his wife is seventy-five. Everything in
here is theirs, except the TV [a small portable on the
kitchen table] and the bed in my room. It's an old-timers'
home," says Joe.

I lean back in my chair and observe the furnishings
in the kitchen—a baby chair, mops, cooking utensils,
yellow walls, yellow tile floor. Through the doorway I
can see the living room, the old floral-covered furniture,
candles on the walls, gilt-edged pictures, a grandfather
clock in the hall. Joe's two-story house is off a tree-lined
street in Garden City in a quiet neighborhood just ten
minutes from the Hofstra training camp. It is about
10,000 miles from his old llama-rugged, mirror-
festooned swinger's pad on Manhattan's upper East
Side. I lean back to look out the window, and abruptly
the chair leg gives way with a crack.

"Richard Neal broke the lock off the door," says Joe,
rummaging around looking for something in which to
spit a growing mouthful of tobacco juice. "And he broke
the bed upstairs. Roscoe broke that chair over there.
Don't feel bad if you break something. This house was
not designed for men to live in, I don't think."

I feel good just being allowed in the house. As a rule Joe despises the press, with the exception of a few friends such as Dick Schaap of *Sport* and Dave Anderson from *The New York Times.* He also has days, even weeks, when he is off-limits to anyone from any medium—days when he sits on his stool in the locker room and radiates don't-ask-me-what-I-think-because-I-won't-tell-you vibrations. To be asked into his inner sanctum, especially with the way the season is going, seems to me like a major coup. But then Joe has been in a good humor lately, granting interviews to high school newspapers, even answering inane questions from a reporter doing a feature on player notebooks. His hubcaps were stolen the other night at Penrods, a nearby disco, but Joe only shrugged. "I used to do a little of that, myself," he said.

He walks out to put on some music now, and I get up for some ice cubes. The freezer half of his refrigerator is empty except for a pint of Baskin-Robbins 31 Flavors ice cream, two pizzas, and several Milky Ways. The other side contains virtually nothing—some wine, grapefruit juice, a beer or two. Inside the door, however, resplendent in their green labels, are twenty or more cans of wintergreen-flavored Skoal snuff.

I had asked him the other day if a person could get high on snuff, as I'd heard. "Not when you been dipping as long as I have," he said. "Here, try some." He threw me a can from the supply in his locker. "Just take a pinch like this and put it like hah, inside huh lip." In pictures taken on the field, Namath frequently shows up with a puckered, jut-jawed expression usually interpreted as the old wise guy's face, though in reality it is just a clump of snuff in front of his teeth. Likewise, numerous shots purporting to show him drinking on public streets actually show him holding a half-filled spittoon cup.

I placed a cud behind my lip, and immediately the fine-cut shreds of tobacco spread throughout my mouth like wildfire, filling me with much the same sensation as drinking from a beer can filled with cigarette butts.

Apparently the thrill of smokeless tobacco comes easier to men who spend a lot of time outdoors, for nearly all the Jets dip or chew. Indeed, the wastebaskets in Weeb Ewbank Hall are coated with plastic baggies to receive the incessant volleys of juice.

"When I first came to the Jets a few of the guys got me started," says Joe, letting a trickle slide into his cup. "Gene Heeter, the tight end, and Mark Smolinski, a running back, mainly. But it was in the rule book that you weren't supposed to chew, there was a fine for it, so these guys used to hide their stuff all over the field. And rather than use chewing tobacco they'd dip snuff because it was easier to hide. Finally, there were so many guys wanting to chew, and so many guys chewing on the sly, that we went to Mr. Werblin. He didn't think it was a fair rule, so Weeb got lenient on it and nobody bothered us again."

In those days, back when so many of the patterns for the future Jets were incubated, Joe's relationship with Sonny Werblin was more like one between two drinking buddies rather than player and president, and what Joe wanted soon became what Sonny wanted. And what Sonny wanted generally became what Weeb wanted, whether he wanted it or not. It was Joe's voice that got the snuff law rescinded, just as it was Sonny Werblin who sometimes paid Joe's fines for him.

"I used to smoke, too," adds Joe. "I smoked for eight years through high school and college. Then I quit on April 12, 1967. I remember that because I made this five-year bet for ten thousand dollars with a woman down in Miami. The way it happened was I was sitting with this lady, Liz Whitney, of the Whitney Stables, and she said, 'What are you doing smoking?' I said, 'Well, I'm gonna quit as soon as training starts this year.' She said, 'You should quit right now.' Then she turned to my mother, who was sitting there with us, and said, 'Mrs. Namath, you should quit too. It's terrible for you.' My mother said, 'I'll quit when Joey quits.' So I said, 'Okay, I'll quit.' Then this other lady, Connie Dinkler—ever hear of the Dinkler hotels in Atlanta and Louisiana? Well, she says,

'You can't quit without me.' So it became a real bet. We had contracts and everything made up for ten thousand dollars to be paid if any of us started smoking."

Were the contracts valid? "Nobody collected," says Joe. "We all quit. I've made some money and spent some money but I sure wasn't gonna throw away ten thousand dollars. Legally, I don't know if it would have been binding, but morally it sure would have. Hell, they're my friends."

Friends are important to Joe. He doesn't always pick the best ones, but he sticks by them like a faithful dog. When word got out in 1969 about all the Mafia hoods and street thieves hanging out in Bachelors III, the East Side bar of which Joe was part-owner, NFL Commissioner Rozelle demanded Joe sell or quit football. Joe quit—in a tearful exit broadcast live over TV. Though he was back within the month, and his share of the lounge sold, his point had been made. "It's a matter of principle," he said repeatedly.

"Joe is a very moral person, which would surprise most people," says Dick Schaap. "There is no great intellectual or psychological depth there, but there is a great honesty and loyalty, an unusual loyalty. And I think he has the conviction that all his friends would be the same to him if they were the fortunate ones. I find that hard to believe, but he doesn't."

In her book, *Namath, My Son Joe,* Rose Namath Szolnoki states repeatedly that her boy, Joey, never told a lie. The book, of course, is fantastically biased, but it points out that Joe's morality, however naive or contradictory it may be, is something he has remained reasonably faithful to through the years. Before the second Buffalo game this year I overheard a Hofstra University reporter interviewing Namath for the school radio station, asking him what he knew about groupies. "Only what I read," Joe said seriously. "I've never had personal contact with a groupie. In the many cities that we play in and the many travels that I have, I've never had that experience so I don't know anything about it." I thought perhaps Joe would burst out laughing, but his expression remained stony. Whether he felt a truthful answer would have been too hot for the student station or whether his definition of "groupie" was something at variance with the common one, I couldn't tell. But I was certain that in his mind he had said the right thing and had not told a lie.

It is well known among reporters that Joe will never denigrate friends or teammates, even when deserving. "He never says anything bad about anybody or talks behind anybody's back," says Steve Tannen, "and that's a very good quality."

"I live and let live," Namath told *Sports Illustrated* in 1966. "I like everybody. I don't care what a man is as long as he treats me right. He can be a gambler, a hustler, someone everybody else thinks is obnoxious, I don't care so long as he's straight with me and our dealings are fair. I like Cassius Clay, Bill Hartack, Doug Sanders and Hornung, all the controversial guys. They're too much."

But Namath also expects others to be equally as lenient. "Don't ever say anything bad about one of Joe's friends," the sportswriters warned me as soon as I got to the Jets' camp, "because he'll never forget it."

Cosmo Currie is an old Manhattan friend of Joe's from the days when Bachelors III was going strong. He runs a hair-styling salon at 795 Lexington Avenue just across the street from the bar (now renamed The Tuppence), and he remembers the times when he'd go over to the place at noon and stay there till four in the morning, "dropping hundreds like they were nothing." He treasures his friendship with Namath.

"What a nice guy Joe is," he says. "What an easy touch. He couldn't say no to anybody. Oh, man, people didn't just ask him for ten bucks, they asked for a thousand. You can't imagine all the people that owe him money."

"He's always picking up tabs," says Dick Schaap. "He's not cheap in any way, and for his old friends he'll do anything. But he doesn't have conspicuous consumption himself. The apartment he had in New York was very expensive, but what's he gonna do, live where he's gonna get mugged? He doesn't go around buying Rolls-Royces, he certainly doesn't buy expensive clothes. Somebody gave him that Cadillac he drives. And another thing is that he is unfailingly nice to people who need it, like old women and ugly girls, much nicer than he is to an attractive model or a healthy-looking guy."

"I remember one night at the club this girl who was very ugly and fat came in," says Cosmo Currie. "She was from out of town and her car had been towed away. She was almost crying and Joe asked her what was wrong. She didn't know she was talking to Joe, she just wanted help. Joe told her to settle down, that she'd need fifty dollars to get her car back because that was what the fine was for those things. He asked her how much she had and she said fifteen dollars, really crying now. So Joe gave her thirty-five out of his pocket and told her to forget about paying it back."

It was considered somewhat humorous by Namath friends and foes alike when in June of 1973 he turned out to be the only sports figure named on Nixon's infamous "enemy list," the sheet of citizens deemed dangerous by the Watergate-era administration. "It's a little crazy," Joe understated when he heard the news. Indeed, for a man of Joe's simple tastes, a man who admits he gets chills every time he hears the national anthem played because it reminds him of "where we are in the world, in life," the inclusion verged on the absurd.

As one might expect, Joe is intensely patriotic, with political leanings that sometimes hit right of center. At our first meeting, a time when Patty Hearst was still at large, I asked him what he thought of the fugitive heiress. "What has she got?" he scoffed. "So what if she can stay loose. What does that prove?" Somebody jokingly asked Joe what he would do if he found her on his bed when he went back to his room. "I'd call the police," he stated. "Damn right, I would. I don't go for that stuff. I believe in law and order."

Most of Joe's beliefs spring from his roots in the steel mill town of Beaver Falls, Pennsylvania, from his family and their strict teachings. One of his standard refrains is that nothing came easy in Beaver Falls, that his three older brothers were constantly pounding on him, showing him right from wrong. Integrity, he says now, was the reason he ended up at the University of Alabama.

"Maryland and Alabama were the only two schools that offered me legitimate scholarships, no under-the-table money or things like that. Initially that stuff excited me, but after a while they turned me off—the schools offering three or four hundred dollars a month, offering my father things. There was no doubt we could have used the money; my mother and everybody in the family was working. But one day my brother Frank, who went to Kentucky, came to me and said, 'Joe, if you go to one of those schools offering fringe benefits you're part of the cheating and not only that, they can turn around the next day and cheat you, too.' He set me straight.

"My first choice was Maryland, but I couldn't get in because I flunked the college boards. You needed a seven hundred and fifty, and the first time I took the test I got a seven forty-six, and the second time I got a seven forty-eight or something. So the head coach there, Tom Nugent, called Alabama and told Coach Bryant that I was still loose. He called that same day and asked me if I was still interested. I was totally depressed and I just sort of mumbled, 'Yeh, yeh.' So that night a coach flew up and the next day we left for Alabama, even though I'd never even visited the campus. We went straight down there to Tuscaloosa, and, well, I hated it . . ."

It has been well recorded that Joe's arrival at Alabama created culture shock for both the boy and the school. The school was hardly accustomed to Yankees—Joe says there was one other Northerner on the football team the entire time he was there, and he was from Virginia—and, of course, Joe was unusual even by Pennsylvania standards.

"I guess you could say I was a novelty," he continues. "I didn't dress like them or talk like them or anything. It was strange—them in white socks and loafers and khaki pants and me with my peaked beret—they didn't have hats like that anywhere down there. I had some sharkskin pants, too. And back home it was stylish to have a straw hat with a pearl in it, so I had one, and in Alabama they hadn't seen anything like that.

"That first year I tried to quit I don't know how many times. But I couldn't even quit, I didn't have enough money to get home. It was just too different, coming from the background I came from, brought up in a predominantly black neighborhood. Most of my friends were black. At Alabama it was nigger this and nigger that, and there just weren't any blacks. I got in some pretty heavy discussions with guys early and I didn't like it."

Joe was ostracized rather heavily that first year and earned the nickname "Nigger" for his racial views. But his football prowess soon became apparent—at one practice that fall Bear Bryant had Namath simulate kickoffs for the varsity by throwing ninety-yard passes into the end zone—and gradually Joe made friends and learned to like grits and pecan pie. His passion for the South now is unbridled; he even speaks with a drawl when it suits him, and he claims the greatest thrill he's ever had in sports was the day his Alabama teammates elected him team captain.

The thing he still does not like is the trauma he went through defending a racial view that came so naturally to him. "You know, I don't *try* to hang around with anybody," he states. "Other people, there's always some of them have hassles or hangups, but I don't get into that. I get the hell out of the way. I don't *like* hassles."

Joe, by his own definition, is not a "forward person, not someone who believes in offering advice. "Joe is very observant," says Steve Tannen. "But he doesn't initiate things. I think, for instance, that it would be hard for him to get up in front of a crowd and give a speech or go on a lecture tour."

In the Jets' locker room Joe remains aloof from most of the action. He watches things and seems to enjoy it when players approach him to talk, but he also seems

67

wary, as though even on the Jets there are people who want to get close to him because of his name. When he does talk he tends to avoid matters of depth.

"When you talk with Joe," says Tannen, who was once his closest friend on the team, "you talk about what you did last night, this buddy you knew, golf, how it was really neat being in front of a studio for the first time. Broads, parties, cards—locker room conversation."

The fact that one must deal with Joe's celebrity status as well as the man tends to keep a few teammates away. David Knight, for instance, estimates that he has spoken to Joe twice in three years. Going out with Joe to public places is the same as going out with a Hollywood idol. "People are so aggravating," says Roscoe Word. "They come up and hang on him and beg autographs. Once in St. Louis we were playing this machine in a bar and a girl comes up to Joe and says, 'My boyfriend thinks you're a jerk.' For no reason at all. Even at his house the doorbell rings a hundred times, and fifty times it's kids who run away."

Currently Joe's closest friends on the team are black —Roscoe Word, Richard Caster, Richard Neal, Phil Wise. They go drinking at some of the local taverns and occasionally charter a boat for deep-sea fishing in the Atlantic. "Joe finds himself very much at ease with us right now," says Caster. "It's developed a nice feeling." Still, there is no real commitment on anyone's part. Says Caster, "It may be somebody else next year."

Joe's avoidance of responsibility in relationships is a very deliberate thing. He speaks of the "bad feeling" he gets in his stomach from getting too wrapped up with people or places. "I am not settled down anywhere," he states adamantly. "I don't have any obligations, no wife, no family. Do I like it that way? Hell, yeh. That's the way I want it because that's the only way I know I can be comfortable inside."

The closest he has come to a serious relationship with a lady is with his current girlfriend, Randi Oakes, a slender blonde model who took her first name from her hometown of Randalia, Iowa. The two have been dating off and on for five years, and most of Joe's friends tend to believe they are in love. "We are in love," says Joe. "But we're both gone a lot and we both have different aspirations, so it works out pretty well."

Marriage is still out of the question. "I have no desire at all to have children," Joe says. "That's not putting them down, I love children, I have eighteen nieces and nephews and one great-niece. But I personally don't look forward to having my own child, I really don't."

Joe still sees a wide variety of women, and he is aware —his know-nothing statement about groupies notwithstanding—of his immense appeal to them. "I've learned to understand what that's all about," he told *Life* magazine in 1972. "They're caught up in the excitement of what they think I am, what they've read and heard."

"The Namath groupies come in all ages," explains Mike Adamle, who used to observe such things closely. "There are teeny-boppers and stewardess-types but also a lot of thirty-five-year-olds all made up with lipstick and black beauty marks and mesh nylons and eyelashes that look like Morticia's out of the *Addams Family*. Of course, it varies from city to city. That's more a Baltimore-type crowd. In Tampa we'd hit the blonde halter-top crew. I'm sure the girls dressed the way they thought Joe would appreciate. They all knew he was a ladies' man."

Just tonight before we came to Joe's house, Joe had a meeting with a girl fan. Eddie Bell brought her to Bill's Meadowbrook Bar across from the practice field. "I don't know anything about it," Bell shrugged. "She was outside and said she wanted to be taken to Joe." The girl was perhaps nineteen, maybe younger, and she sat next to Namath saying scarcely a word while he had a beer. When we left, he took her back to Hofstra and, placing her on the sidewalk, gave her a hug and a small peck on the forehead, like a father seeing off a child. The girl then turned and scurried back to her dorm, obviously satiated.

As a slayer of the opposite sex, Namath is scarcely as vain as one might expect. In the locker room when the fleet of hair-dryers starts up, Joe sits on his stool drying his head with a towel. When he wants to look nice he'll wear an off-the-rack suit; during the week he wears jeans, Puma track shoes and, generally, a red velour zip-up shirt.

Once, after he'd worn the velour shirt for nearly two weeks in a row, I asked if that was his only one. "No," he said. "Actually I have two." Occasionally he uses some witch hazel on his face, but not once the entire season would I see him use cologne—though the locker room was stocked with Fabergé products he had donated—or a comb. "Joe," sighs Gilbert, the head stylist at Cosmo Currie's, "he just doesn't care too much about his hair."

As we are chatting at his kitchen table, the phone rings and Joe goes to answer it. It is Randi, just back from some television work on the West Coast, asking Joe to pick her up at the Garden City train station.

I leave shortly after that, and as I'm driving back to the sixth floor of Tower F, I think about quarterbacks. I had been one myself, for one year as a senior in high school, but the experience left an indelible impression on me. Being a quarterback gave me a feeling of power and self-sufficiency and, eventually, a sort of unquestioning self-confidence that I don't believe I've experienced since.

Namath, at thirty-two, has been a quarterback in various forms for nearly a quarter-century. His personality has been defined by the role; it would be impossible to separate "quarterbackness" from the rest of him. Just trying to imagine him at another position is proof enough.

But I wonder what it is, aside from his arm, that has made him such a *good* quarterback. Dr. Arnold Mandell, the California psychiatrist, has determined that there are two basic kinds of successful quarterbacks—one being the religious, "assurance from on High" type such as Roger Staubach, and the other being the "naturally arrogant man who does not feel bound by the rules governing other men." This type, states the doctor, makes his own rules: "He exploits the environment in a tough, tricky way and with very little compunction. Such men have run their talents and capacities to incredible self-advantage with no apparent anxiety or guilt. The Joe Namaths . . . fit well into this category."

The question that arises is *why* don't such men feel anxiety, and further, what role does intelligence play in their makeup?

Namath's IQ is perennially debated by people who say he is dumb and people who say he is smart. Those who say he is not smart point to his academic record, his shallow life-style and the fact that he once scored 104 on an IQ test administered by a pro scout. Those who say he is intelligent point to his shrewdness and his skill at calling and analyzing a football game. One believer is backfield coach Tom Bettis of the Chiefs, who says, "Namath is brilliant. He read our 'Nickel Caster' defense immediately. I'm not sure anybody else could have."

Still others make the point that whatever Namath's IQ is, it is not something that can be gauged in a normal fashion. "The guy went straight from being a star in Beaver Falls to being a star at Alabama to being a star in the pros," says Steve Tannen. "Nobody ever asked him what he thought about the new tax laws, what he thought about the UN, what he thought about Zionism. He's never needed to read or know things in the way intelligence is usually measured."

What Joe does have, everyone agrees, is "street sense" —that, and the amazing ability to focus on the intricacies of his chosen sport. As a pure student of the game, for reading defenses and picking up crucial subtleties, he has few peers. "Sometimes I think maybe he haphazardly stumbled onto a way of doing things and it turned out to be the best way," says Richard Caster, whose own IQ has been measured at a whopping 143.

Tannen, also known as a heavy thinker on the Jets, sees it differently: "I think Joe is like the person who designed the transistor radio. Maybe that guy can put a transistor radio together better than anyone, has an intelligence for that, but does he know what 'ten factorial' means, does he know why the King of England sent his daughter to marry the King of France?"

The specificity of Namath's intellect has been cited by many. As ex-Jet receiver coach Ken Meyer put it: "Joe's football intelligence must be in the genius range."

Philosopher George Santayana once described intelligence as simply a "quickness in seeing things as they are." Namath is incredibly quick at recognizing field situations, frequently pointing things out to his receivers and linemen and coaches before they are readily apparent. Motivation plays a big factor here. "You have to want it bad," says Coach Charley Winner. "You can find geniuses on any skid row and average intellects as presidents of banks. It's what pushes you from inside."

Dr. Nicholas, who believes Namath is intelligent beyond common sense and quickness, points out that Joe has, for instance, learned a great deal about medicine and the anatomy of the knee. "Things he's interested in, he learns." But on his sports performance chart, which breaks skill down into various components such as discipline, alertness, and creativity, Dr. Nicholas notes that learning capacity may be highly specified for a given sport, thus distinct from any known definition of IQ. "For example, I've tried to sight-read on the piano for ten years," the doctor states. "But I can't do it. It may be symbols we're talking about."

What Joe definitely has, Dr. Nicholas declares, is something called "football intelligence." But what exactly that means, he's not sure. "Defining that," he says, "is our work for the next twenty-five years."

SEVEN

I don't mind being an offensive lineman.
Really.

—RANDY RASMUSSEN

While driving the Jets to the airport for an away game late in the season, the hired bus driver gets confused, makes a wrong turn, and quickly loses all sense of direction. He begins to drive in circles and before long is passing through Garden City, just a few minutes from where the excursion began. Finally two or three of the players come forward to aid the helpless man, and while they are talking, one of the reporters who rides along with the team points out to a companion that Joe Namath lives just a block or two away. Hearing this, Wayne Mulligan, the Jets' center, pushes forward in his seat.

"Is that where he lives?" he asks.

"Yeh," says the reporter.

"No kidding. Is it a big house?"

"Not really."

"What's it like?"

"Looks like old people live there."

"What is he, incognito?"

"You're his center."

"Hey, all I do is hand him the ball. After that he's on his own."

This, of course, is not true. An offensive lineman for the Jets may not know where Joe Namath lives or what he does in his free time, but he does know what Joe does on a football field—when and where and how—and he knows that, while there, Joe Namath is never on his own.

Namath is the prize—for the other team. "He's like a fish bowl placed on a one-legged table in the middle of a gang war," says David Knight, who can make such observations from the safety of his flanker position thirty yards away. It is the line's duty, their very livelihood, to make sure no water is spilled, God forbid the entire structure should crash to the ground. "It was different when I was in college," says guard Randy Rasmussen. "Everything was sprint out or roll out, no straight dropback. The quarterback wasn't a valuable property. He could be replaced."

That is definitely not the case with the Jets, where a Namath sprint-out is as rare as lips on a chicken and replacement is out of the question. "I remember how excited Weeb Ewbank used to get about Joe's safety," recalls David Knight. "In my first exhibition game as a rookie in 1973, Joe threw an interception and Weeb went nuts, he was so worried about somebody taking a shot at Joe. So on the sideline he got all the rookies together and told us that if Joe threw another interception we were all supposed to run out there and protect him. All of us."

Sadly, Joe did not throw any more interceptions, and sports fans were deprived the thrill of seeing twenty-five members of the same team all playing at once. The offensive line probably wouldn't have enjoyed it if it had happened, so imbued are they with the sense of anonymity that comes with their role. "One of the Cleveland Browns once told me," Jerry Kramer wrote in his book *Instant Replay,* "that if he ever had to go on the lam from the law, he'd become an offensive lineman."

Paul Zimmerman got his big break as a cub reporter for the old New York *World-Telegram & Sun* when he was sent to write about the 1960 NFL Championship game between the Green Bay Packers and the Philadelphia Eagles. An ex-lineman himself, Zimmerman spent the day interviewing guards and tackles and centers rather than the "important" players—halfbacks, receivers, and quarterbacks—and when he filed his story his editor nearly lofted him out the window. As penance Zimmerman spent two more years on the high school beat, the point being that not only do offensive lineman have nothing to say, but nobody wants to hear it even if they do.

Who, the rhetorical question goes, would want to be one of these wretches in the first place? Who could survive on a steady diet of drubbing forearms, gouging fingernails, one- and two-handed head-slaps, kicks and bites and karate chops—all this absorbed silently, without acclaim or individual statistics and, essentially, without retaliation.

"Well, let me destroy a false rumor right now," says Randy Rasmussen by way of an answer. "Offensive linemen are born, not made. I had a stamp right on my forehead." Indeed, offensive lineman do seem to be formed from the beginning. "If I ever actually carried the football," says right guard Garry Puetz, "I believe my dad would kill me." An offensive lineman's personality must suit his role or else he will suffer horribly from attempting to control his aggressions. Former Jet guard Dave Herman was said by some to have been too excitable for the disciplines of his position and might have been better suited as a linebacker or defensive tackle. "I disagree," says Rasmussen, who played with Herman for seven years. "Way deep inside he was one of us."

Of course, most offensive linemen started somewhere else—few of them had the single-mindedness of purpose to become human punching bags from day one. Their calling swiftly catches up with them, however. Darrell Austin wistfully recalls the season in junior high when he played fullback and scored three touchdowns. At the start of the next year the coach had him penciled in at offensive tackle. "Son," said the coach, "if you're a fullback, the woods are full of 'em."

Namath, as the fragile commodity behind the beasts of burden, feels strongly about his line. With his appreciation and respect, however, goes a touch of thankfulness for his own position. He makes it clear he would not have played football if he'd had to play as an offensive lineman.

"I don't think I could have tolerated it," he says. "When I was at Alabama I used to watch the linemen go through their drills, and I used to thank the good Lord that I was a quarterback. I remember we had this one thing called the 'Kill or Be Killed Drill,' where three guys got in a circle and when the whistle blew they just started fighting, literally fighting—kicking, slugging, anything. When I first saw the drill I asked the secondary coach, Gene Stallings—he's with the Cowboys now—I said, 'Coach Stallings, *what* is going on over there?' He said, 'Well, Pat'—Pat James, one of our line coaches—'he's got a new drill he figures'll toughen the boys up a bit.' I'm looking over there and three guys are fighting and one guy hits another and then the other two are fighting and one of the guys goes down and the whistle blows. Two walk away and one stays there on the ground. He's out, got kicked in the mouth. They move the drill ten yards and proceed again, and the trainers went over and took care of the guy on the ground. I said, 'Oh, Lord, thank you that I'm not a lineman.'"

But did Joe question the merit of such drills? "No sir, because I knew it sure as hell made 'em tougher, the guys who survived." It must have, since Alabama lost only four games in three years, and Joe, at 207 pounds, outweighed some of his linemen by as much as 25 pounds.

Now with the Jets he is openly solicitous of his blockers' welfare. Once, when one of the defensive players grabbed left tackle Robert Woods in a good-natured bear hug and Woods began complaining about his stiff back, Joe rushed into the melee. "Don't hurt this guy," he pleaded. "His back is my back."

Before the November 16 game with Baltimore, Garry Puetz found a note in his message box that read: "Give me a call or we'll settle this on Sunday—John Dutton." John Dutton was the Colts' 6-foot-7, 270-pound defensive end who had nearly decapitated Joe several times in the earlier Jets-Colts contest. Puetz, assuming the note was a gag, tossed it aside. Namath picked it up and ran after him. "Puetz!" he cried. "Get on the phone, boy."

To a large extent, as the offensive line goes, so goes Joe; and as Joe goes, so goes the team. In 1974 when the Jets streaked to six consecutive victories, the line allowed only 19 quarterback sacks, second best in the NFL; in the 1968–69 Super Bowl season they allowed only 15, lowest in all of pro football. By the end of the 1975 season, the Jets had allowed 34 sacks, fourteenth worst in the league. Seven of those dumpings came against Baltimore and set a new Jets-Namath record. "I don't know what went wrong this year," says Rasmussen. "We didn't block well and we didn't mix the plays well, and then there was overconfidence and the strike and that big opening loss to Buffalo. It may have been the coaches' fault or the lack of leadership. People just lost heart. It was a cumulative thing."

The Jets' line, any line, begins with its center—the only lineman to have physical contact with the quarterback. Wayne Mulligan, a seven-year veteran obtained from Chicago via St. Louis in the 1974 preseason, is a player like Dave Herman in that he frequently seems troubled at his position. "Centers don't get enough recognition," he says constantly, though he knows things are unlikely to change. He threatens more aggression than the other linemen, particularly when "assholes start head-slapping. That's when I'll get 'em back," he states.

The other linemen are notoriously sloppy dressers—reserve center Joe Fields wears baggy gray pants, black basketball shoes, and white T-shirts; Rasmussen wears work clothes; and all Winston Hill would have to do to be mistaken for a giant derelict would be to lie down in a gutter with a brown paper sack. Mulligan, on the other hand, wears three-piece suits and monogrammed jackets. On one finger he sports a large sparkling ring with diamonds set in the number 50, his jersey numeral since he started playing center.

His greatest show of vanity, though, trifling as it is by usual standards, is his pair of low-cut, white game shoes. All the other offensive linemen wear the klutzy, old-fashioned black models. "Who's gonna look at us?" asks Garry Puetz. "We're just fat slobs. If they see my black high-tops maybe they'll think it's Bronko Nagurski back from the dead."

In his pro career Mulligan has snapped for numerous quarterbacks, including Jim Hart, Charley Johnson, Pete Beathard, and Gary Cuozzo. With Namath he feels more secure than with any of them.

"To work things right you have to have confidence in each other," he states. "You can't be worrying about the snap at all. It has to be just a reflex. At St. Louis with Charley Johnson something was wrong, and we fumbled a lot. I hated that because how can you block somebody when you're moving out listening for the crowd to go 'Aaaaggh!' because the ball's loose? Joe and I, though, we've only fumbled twice in two years. We mold together. For instance, a lot of times against a four-three defense I have a dual responsibility where I have to check the middle linebacker and one of the outside linebackers, which means I actually pull back as fast as I can, even cross my feet and run back, because if the outside linebacker is blitzing I've got to get there fast. But unless you're really confident in the quarterback you have to be more casual pulling out. With Joe I can be moving my whole body, twisting every which way, but we still connect."

Getting their snaps down wasn't much of a problem, he adds. "We didn't really talk about it. He knew I'd been snapping a long time, and I knew he'd been taking them a long time. He just got underneath and made a few grunts and took it on 'Go' until we had it. The way I do it is I hold the ball lengthwise in my right hand so that the point is heading downfield. And when I snap, the wrist and arm turn naturally a few degrees, and the ball comes up at a slight angle. I always make sure I have the air valve in my hand so that when I turn the ball he doesn't get anything except the ball with the laces up, ready to throw.

"Joe puts his right hand on top and the left next to it and down. You can tell the difference in quarterbacks just by the feel of their hands. Joe seems to get underneath more, but he doesn't apply too much pressure because I don't like that. And he doesn't pull out too soon. You can startle yourself a bit if that happens and you snap the ball up there, right in your crotch, with nothing to catch it.

"I have a problem sometimes snapping to J.J. because he's got bamboo shoots for fingernails. I think he cuts them about once every eighteen months. But there's nothing too tricky with Joe. A couple of times I've stepped on his feet, and for a while there I was getting knocked back into him. That, fortunately, was not in a game but in practice. That was from Barzilauskas. His rookie year he forgot we only play one game a week. I think after he knocked Koegel into Joe a few times, Joe finally got mad and told him to settle down."

Warren Koegel, a twenty-six-year-old journeyman center cut by New York before this season, was the Jets' starting center for exactly one game—the season opener against Kansas City in 1974 when Mulligan was out with pneumonia. But he remembers that game as clearly as a newsreel; it was one of the high points of his life.

"The first time I snapped to Joe in practice I didn't think much of it," he recalls. "I'd already snapped to Stabler, Lamonica, and Blanda at Oakland, and Pastorini and Plunkett in college all-star games. But then in that game I realized that here was Joe Namath, and I was actually handing him the ball. He was in total control. On the very first play of the season Robert Woods jumped offside. In the huddle Joe just says, 'We're gonna get it right back. On three.' At the line he does his, 'Hut, HUT! Hut,' in that real high voice, and sure enough the Chiefs jump offside and we're first-and-ten again.

"Then later, we had a play called and Curley Culp jumped into the gap between me and Puetz. Joe checked to this fullback dive called P-Ten, and I saw the same thing just when he did. But I was thinking so hard and I was so excited that I snapped on one instead of three, and we only got two yards. Joe looked at me and said, 'Don't worry.' On the next play he audibled again, this time a pass, but he pulled out on one instead of two and I held on to the ball. He looked at me afterward and shrugged. It was like, 'Hey, it's over with. We'll get them this time.' Then on the very next play he threw a touchdown pass to Caster. It was dynamite. I got hurt after that game and didn't play anymore, but Joe told me I did a good job. I'll always remember that."

Next to the center are the guards, Puetz and Rasmussen. Puetz is the youngster, just 23 years old, 6 feet 3 inches, 275 pounds, crafty and full of laughs. Against New England he had a simmering feud going with linebacker Sam Hunt. Finally, on a play that was all but over, he took a running start and blindsided the linebacker, knocking him over the pileup like a sack of potatoes. Hunt came up swinging and was immediately ejected from the game. "Oh, I just waited for the right time like a good offensive lineman," said Puetz.

He is perhaps more impetuous than any of the other linemen. After the Jets' 43–0 loss to Miami, I saw Garry drinking in a Point Lookout bar, and I commented to him that he looked rather keyed up. "Let me see your drink," he said. I handed it to him and he bit off an inch of the rim, chewed it up and swallowed it. "I don't know why I did that," he said, returning the glass.

After games Puetz is beat up. His arms are stained with huge, brown bruises and his fingers dotted with gouged-out holes. His neck is swollen and there are twin, bleeding cuts on each side from his shoulder pads. Frequently he will wander in circles around his house, moaning, or else pass out fully clothed on his bed. "I used to be six-four," he says. "Now I'm about five-eight."

His pains are typical and relatively short-lived. He was ecstatic about being drafted by the Jets when he graduated from college, and he deeply enjoys blocking for Joe Namath. He also enjoys making light of his responsibilities. "Joe gives me good protection," he told a visiting reporter. "I'm getting beat and he falls down and everybody stops beating on me."

But the jokes are just a cover for the meticulousness and loyalty of a true offensive lineman. After the San Diego Monday night game he was in a rage. "Do you know what that number seventy-two said to me during the game?" he cried. "He said, 'Psst, give me a sack. Let me get through to Joe.' I said, 'What?' He said, 'Gimme a sack. I'll give you a six-pack of beer.' Three plays in a row he did that. I told Joe Fields and we were gonna take his knee out. The guy was actually serious."

The other guard is Randy Rasmussen, a nine-year veteran with freckles, sandy hair, and legs like ship timbers. As a farm boy in tiny Elba, Nebraska, he learned discipline early and says now that if the Jets ever get close enough for another Super Bowl try, "We'll win, or they'll carry me off dead."

In high school he played eight-man football. ("One year we had sixteen players on the team and it was the talk of the town—we could actually scrimmage.") But since the school couldn't afford films of games, he couldn't get a scholarship to the University of Nebraska. He ended up at tiny Kearney State instead, and when he was drafted by the Jets he nearly died. "I was petrified. I didn't know anything about Joe Namath or the Jets or New York. I'd hardly ever been out of Nebraska."

His first pro season was a tough one because he was immediately forced into a starting position because of an injury suffered by regular guard Sam De Luca.

"I had a lot of trouble with any kind of a pass rush that first year," he says. "But my biggest problem was with the guys who used the grab-and-pull technique, guys like Dave Costa of Denver and Buck Buchanan of Kansas City. I didn't know how to give ground and they'd just throw me out of the way. The first time I played Costa he got to Joe two or three times with the ball and about six times without the ball. It was terrible. And then before the next game with Denver the line coach told me that if Costa got to Joe one time he was gonna have me hanging from the goalpost after the game. I told him he'd *better* hope Costa didn't get to Joe because sure as shit he'd be hanging right there with me. Fortunately, Dave Herman was in his prime then and he could handle anybody alone, which gave John Schmitt, our center, a chance to help me out."

Through that year and the next, the Super Bowl year, Rasmussen began to appreciate Namath's skills as a playcaller and a field general. His respect quickly grew to open admiration.

"Back in those days Joe called ninety-five percent of his own plays. In the Super Bowl he checked off fifty percent of the time, sometimes just saying in the huddle, 'Check with me.' That's how I knew he was in control. He was reading the defenses, taking what was there. Weeb just let him go. Nobody helped him unless he asked for it. And that's how it has to be—he's got to get a feel for the game, work it out himself. I *know* he'll call the right plays. But this year they sent in a lot of things and that broke his train of thought. He'd say, 'Who the hell called this?' But we'd still have to run the play."

It was Joe's famous "guarantee" of a Super Bowl victory four days before the game that really catalyzed Rasmussen's opinion. "At the time I thought, jeez, Joe, just keep your mouth shut. But before I knew it I'd reexamined what was going on—everybody had—and we realized we all felt the same way. We'd seen the films, we *knew* we could win. Joe just said it, was all. And the thing is, the papers played it up like he was wisecracking. But he was serious as can be."

Playing off the shoulders of the guards are the tackles—the hulks who take their beatings from probably the most devastating players on the field, the defensive ends. For the Jets the tackles are third-year-man Robert Woods and elder statesman Winston Hill. Of the two it is Hill who is by far the more interesting, for in his history is interwoven the history of the Jets and in his makeup is the essential makeup of all offensive linemen.

At thirty-four he is the oldest player on the team, an eight-time All-Pro whose longevity and skill are exceeded only by his consistency—since 1963 he has played in 181 consecutive games for the Jets. At 6 feet 4 inches and close to 300 pounds, he is round and virtually shapeless, a brown snowman who fights the poundage the way his old 350-pound teammate Sherman "Battle of the Bulge" Plunkett used to. Winston wears a skin diver's wetsuit under his practice uniform, stating that it "might be harmful for somebody with solid muscles, but not me," and judiciously wipes all moisture from the scale before he climbs on.

As a rookie he was released by the Colts and was apparently finished with football. He phoned Denver because they had shown interest earlier, but when he made the collect call they refused to accept the charges. "They said they were busy," remembers Winston. "My stomach was already down to the ground, and then it went below the ground." Eventually he joined the Jets as a free agent, starting the procession of unheralded offensive linemen who have made good with the team; of the five 1975 starters only Robert Woods was drafted above the eighth round.

It was Winston's quick feet—he was a state high school tennis champion in Texas—that won him his job, and it was his personality that kept him there. "I was cut out to be an offensive lineman," he says. "I have never been the aggressor. I have never been reckless. I am a counterpuncher. I don't take chances. That is why I've never been hurt in thirteen years. But also I have this belief that an individual should do as much as he can, and when he can't do any more there is no need to get excited. For an offensive lineman, perfection means doing away with as much emotion as possible."

Because his parents warned him that "the height of happiness can only be matched by the depth of sorrow," Winston made a goal of avoiding both. After the Super Bowl victory, when his teammates were out celebrating, he went to his room and watched television. "I tried not to feel anything special," he says. So smooth has he tried to make his life that once when his car was sliding out of control toward an approaching semi, he merely said, "Lord, forgive me for my sins," and relaxed. Fortunately the car stopped inches from the truck, and Winston calmly drove on his way.

Despite his lack of excitement and his statement that "if everybody were like me you'd probably have a losing team," Winston has been a stellar performer for the Jets. In 1968 he soundly whipped Oakland's Ben Davidson in the AFL Championship Game, and in the Super Bowl he manhandled Ordell Braase, the Colts' much-heralded right defensive end. "Braase had intended to play some more years," says Winston, as close to boasting as he'll ever get, "but after the Super Bowl he just retired. I know I wasn't responsible, but it was quite fitting anyway."

Religion, as for many football players, has been his opiate. "It's like we're running around a track with weights tied to our feet," he says in one of his semi-mystical explanations. "The weights are symbolic of social pressures, ego, accomplishments, embarrassments, happiness, everything that we have. My relationship with God takes all these things away. I only have to account to Him."

At times, however, it helps to account to Joe. Namath himself realizes the good fortune of having Hill in front of him. "A lot of people don't realize that Winston is one-on-one all the time, what a burden he has. But after you've been under pressure with a man as often as we have, you learn who you can count on. Winston is one."

One of Winston's principal tactics in keeping his man occupied and away from Joe is talking to him. Indeed, on the field he becomes a veritable talk-show host, asking questions, shaking hands, telling sly jokes, anything to distract his opponent. "I like to ask somebody a question and then when he's answering, jump on him," says Winston. "Once I asked Roy Hilton how his wife was and he was saying, 'Oh, fine,' just as the ball was snapped. On the next play he looked at me and said, 'Hey, you don't even know my wife.' "

Holding is a tactic all offensive linemen use. The rules are so vague that a line *must* hold to remain competitive. "Holding penalties are arbitrary," says Wayne Mulligan. "Like a cop giving out tickets."

Some cases, of course, are more blatant than others, particularly in desperate situations—when a yard is vitally needed, when a linebacker is blitzing, when a quarterback stands alone, unprotected.

With Namath, holding becomes more than a strategy, it becomes a necessity. As a straight-dropback passer unable to move away from his pocket, Joe is vulnerable even to the least creative charge. "He's different in that you always know where he's going to be," says Vern Den Herder of the Dolphins. "You can take a charge you wouldn't be able to take on a normal quarterback," states Baltimore's Fred Cook, who leveled Namath twice in the October 26 game. "You can zero in."

The stress this puts on the Jets' offensive line is awesome. Mike Adamle says bluntly that opposing defensive lines "would rather play against the Jets than anybody else." And even cautious Winston Hill, who states above all that he is no one to "sit in judgment of Joe or any man," will mention that it would be nice to have a Tarkenton-type scrambler behind one, "more for what the defensive linemen *cannot* do than for what the offensive linemen can do."

The burden has been passed down from lineman to lineman like a family flaw. "Jerry Kramer was telling me after our Super Bowl win about the pressure of being the defending Super Bowl champions," Dave Herman told *Sports Illustrated* in 1972, "but I told him that playing in front of a white-shoed quarterback taught you all you had to know about pressure."

Not surprisingly the Jets are known by opponents as the "holdingest team in football." This angers them a bit. Rasmussen, labeled an "octopus" by Pat Toomay of Buffalo, says it's all a bum rap handed down because everyone figures the Jets must do something illegal to protect Joe. "Man, every time the refs hear we're coming to town they start throwing flags," says Puetz disgustedly.

But the truth is they do hold. And they will admit it—with explanations. "With Joe you have to be perfect," says Mulligan. "A lot of times you'll actually be in control of a guy, riding him out, but if you get too close, Joe goes down. Sure we hold. We have to." Puetz, in calmer moments, will even admit that there are a lot of ways to do it without "making it obvious," and that he has even considered putting stickum on his hands for better grip.

When flagged for holding, the Jets seldom protest—even when it happens, as it did this year, three times in one series. There is, indeed, a virtual holders' code for the offensive line. "I don't think anybody ever told me outright, but it was kind of an understanding," says Rasmussen, recalling his rookie year in 1967. "If a guy started beating you, the first thing you did was grab him and tackle him. Take fifteen but don't let him get to Joe. It was just a thing, well, you'd see somebody else tackle somebody and you *knew.*"

The Jets' linemen expect others to be tolerant of their predicament. Winston Hill even likes to explain to his opponents *why* he holds them. "You probably would have killed my man back there if I hadn't grabbed you," he recently told Pittsburgh's L. C. Greenwood. And once several years ago he held an opponent often enough that the man went into a rage. "He called me names and said, 'Dammit, don't hold me again or I'll kill you,'" says Winston. "I was walking back but when I heard him say he was going to kill me I grabbed his arm and said, 'Listen, tell me not to play this game or not to do anything. But please don't tell me not to hold again.' He cracked up."

The responsibility of protecting a half-million-dollar quarterback is a big one, and the mistakes are costly. Winston admits he has "special" feelings when Joe gets hit, but he has prepared himself for such events by learning to cross things out of his mind. "It's a protection I developed early," he says. "I have the ability to cast things aside."

Not so with Randy Rasmussen, whose failure to read Stan White's blitz two years ago nearly ended Joe's career. "It was a play-action pass, third and short, and I thought they'd be in a short yardage defense," he recalls. "They weren't. When White blitzed I didn't read it fast enough. Joe saw him coming and ducked and got rolled onto his shoulder, separating it. It just made me sick. It was the worst experience I've ever had in football. Joe never said anything about it to me, and I've never said anything to him. Nothing needs to be said, believe me."

There are good parts to blocking for Namath. Some of the light from his shining star naturally falls on his line —such as the Arrow shirt commercial they all participated in with him last fall—but there are also the more cerebral pleasures of functioning together as a unit. Explains Rasmussen: "Sometimes I come up to the line and I know what the call is and I know it won't work because of what the defense is in. And then I'll hear Joe check off and I'll know he's thinking the same thing. Sometimes he'll call a new play and it will be the same one I'm thinking is the right one, and it's almost like you're talking back and forth in your mind. Sometimes he'll call a play and I'll have to examine the situation, and then I'll say to myself, 'Yeh, I see what you're talking about, Joe.' And now Puetz and I are starting to get this thing between us—I hear Garry make a call and I know what's going through his head, what he's seeing. I can hear him and Winston talking and I get the whole picture, and then to have Joe check off to the right play just as we all recognize it . . . it's the greatest thrill there is."

None of the offensive linemen are actually close to Joe, but that, as they point out, is more a case of their own peculiarities rather than any bad chemistry. "We don't get involved too much," says Rasmussen. "Offensive linemen don't speak unless spoken to."

Their big relationship is with each other, as foot soldiers bound by common wants and suffering. Faceless and spartan, their pleasure is directly related to the value of that which they protect. Warren Koegel started in exactly one game as a Jet but that was enough. "No matter what happens," he says, "I'll always have the thought that I played against the best and that I played in front of Joe Namath."

EIGHT

*Does football keep you from growing
up? Oh, my God, yes! One hundred
percent yes! I've even heard guys
who I thought had no minds at all
admit that.*

—DAVID KNIGHT

*People have started asking me if
we've got any talent on this team.
Well, I tell them, if we start winning
games we'll have talent. But since
we're getting beat to death, no, we
don't.*

—JOE NAMATH

Greg Gantt, a second-year man from Alabama, is the
Jets' punter. He is not an overly congenial person, being
somewhat humorless as well as fiercely defensive about
his kicking—last season he averaged a miserable 35.9
yards per kick, second worst in the NFL; this year he is
doing little better. His outlook in most matters is pro-
nouncedly gloomy. In the locker room his unathletic
build separates him from the others; indeed, in 1974 a
visiting physiologist found him to have the highest fat-
to-muscle ratio of any player on the team. While Mike
Adamle was still with the Jets he kidded Gantt constantly, calling him an "imposter," accusing him of killing and impersonating the real Greg Gantt who had

averaged 48.7 yards per kick his senior year at Alabama.

On the plane home from the Vikings game, Gantt smolders with outrage. He has just had the first punt of his career blocked, and he is telling several members of the press how he feels about it. "I've ruined my job," he states. "I've had to look up and walk around and sacrifice my average. But I'm not doing that anymore. I'm just going to kick, and if they can't block, that's their problem."

The "they," of course, is the line, a group Gantt occasionally refers to as "plant brains." Although the rush was heavy, the problem was not entirely the line's blocking. "Shit," says Wayne Mulligan. "Gantt takes four steps and moves up ten yards. He's got to learn to punt like everybody else in this league."

Namath, who has been sitting quietly a few rows behind Gantt, listens to the punter venting his frustrations to various writers. After a few minutes he comes forward and takes Gantt by the arm. "Don't be talking strategy or anything with these guys," he says somberly. "They'll start things, start writing things to cause dissension. Those bull-shit writers like Zimmerman, Fox, and Young, what they're trying to do is write something today so people will come back and buy the paper tomorrow. That Zimmerman is one of three or four people in America who I don't talk to, and that's because he prints so many goddamn outright lies."

Gantt shuffles his feet and looks penitent.

"I'm telling you," says Joe.

With the record now back to .500 and the toughest part of the schedule yet to come, there is reason to be cautious. The Jets, Joe seems to understand, are not a unified team. Small divisions can quickly become big ones in such an atmosphere. And now for the first time injuries are starting to play a decisive role. Jerome Barkum, Phil Wise, Richard Neal, and middle linebacker Jamie Rivers have all missed games, and many of the other players are limping or have not yet recovered from surgery.

Football, of course, means dealing with pain. "The

only meaningful explanation is if you don't get completely incapacitated, you play with some hurts," says Viking quarterback Tarkenton, who has played in 200 straight games. But a player's tolerance to injury, that nebulous term "pain threshold," is something that is always subject to inspection and doubt. Thus, a player with a broken bone is usually less anxious than a player with a bad muscle pull because treatment and recovery time for his injury are standardly accepted.

Already Charley Winner feels the frustration of waiting for his players to tell him when their bodies feel "all right." "When I was playing we didn't have all these fancy machines for rehabilitation," he says, grumbling. "If you sprained an ankle, you just ran on it."

Players like Darrell Austin are easier for him to accept. As a reserve guard and chief wedge-breaker, Darrell has both the stoicism of an offensive lineman and the recklessness of the classic bomb squadder. Each week in just a few seconds of playing time he manages to make several spectacular plays and nearly kill himself. Known as the "Bionic Man" or "Colonel Austin," Darrell's ability to recover by the next Sunday comes from what Namath refers to as "your bloodline and the way you've been coached."

Darrell was born and reared in the tiny hamlet of Union, South Carolina. His first job was delivering newspapers by horseback, and he recalls shooing cattle off the local runway so the airplanes that took him on college recruiting trips could land. Toughness was a virtue in Union, and Darrell never complained about the huge helmet scar developing on the bridge of his nose (he eventually had plastic surgery for it) or his fingers that were constantly breaking. "This finger here is plastic inside," he says, pointing to a digit that is fat and stiff as a roll of quarters. "When I'd just had it fixed I was down at Myrtle Beach helping a guy change tires, and the jack slipped and the car scrunched these three next to it. I just looked at them and said, 'Shit,' and went out and had another beer." One season in high school he played both baseball and football with a collarbone so severely fractured that when it was finally operated on a one-inch section of calcified bone popped out. "The football coaches down there are crazy, and they don't like you to be hurt," Darrell says. As recently as last season, when he was a rookie with Denver, he ran on a broken leg for a month because the trainer didn't think it was a serious injury.

"Football is a thing you want to be *able* to get out of someday," says Richard Neal, who is recovering from an ankle sprained on the pitcher's mound at Shea Stadium. "You want to be able to do the things you like to do. Right now, I'd like to sue Shea Stadium, but apparently I signed away all my rights on my contract. I guess they could pave the place and make us play on it. But what I mean is, a guy like Mike Reid, an All-Pro, quits the game so he can play the piano. He loves his music and he's worried about his hands. We're all gettin' beat up, man. Look at these things. . . ." He holds his hands out and they are almost as battered as Darrell Austin's. "After your first year or two, football loses its beauty and becomes all violence, man."

Something that was not considered a problem until recently is the fact that the Jets are relative strangers to each other. On the plane from Minneapolis, Charley Winner sat writing names on a piece of paper and suddenly discovered that since his arrival with the Jets two years earlier, over thirty new players have joined the team. The reason for the cuts and trades has been to bolster weaknesses—notably to add size and youth—but there has been a remarkable lack of concern over the loss of intangibles.

From last year's team thirteen players are gone, among them both stabilizing veterans and rah-rah types. "I almost quit when I heard Adamle was traded," says Riggins. "I thought if that's how they can treat somebody like Mike, I don't want to play this game." It is obvious to all that the delicate esprit de corps that developed in the 1974 streak has vanished. Not only that, but certain divisive elements have been added. Running-back Carl Garrett, for instance, has been a disciplinary problem on every NFL team he's been with. "In the future we will definitely deal more with personalities than we've been doing," General Manager Al Ward admits.

Another notable development is that for the first time in Jets history there are more blacks on the team than whites—26 to 17. In itself this means little except as an indication of a continuing trend in sports—in 1965 the Jets had only 10 blacks. However, for Charley Winner, who was once involved with racial problems as a coach at St. Louis, it is a matter of at least subliminal concern. The turmoil on the Cardinals was something he inherited rather than started, but he is understandably wary of the New York press pinning him down with labels, and he seems afraid of using too much discipline on black players. His hesitance, unfortunately, only adds to the overall confusion. "Charley's a nice man," says Jazz Jackson, who got his nickname because people said he was always "jazzin' around." "But he's the one person won't ever call me Jazz. It's always 'Clarence.' I kinda wonder about that."

At the Saturday practice before the Miami game, rain pours down, making the field as slippery as glass. The Jets splash and slide about like children. Namath throws knuckleballs and screwballs to some of the receivers, chuckling with glee when they can't hang on.

John Riggins wears a green garbage bag as a raincoat and has stuck his double chin strap behind his helmet so the snaps stand out like antennae. An agile, bruising runner at 6 feet 3 inches, 230 pounds, an unselfish performer and an articulate speaker, Riggins is nevertheless considered somewhat of an oddball. This is mainly because of his penchant for wearing bizarre, mismatched clothes and strange hairdos, his classic performance coming in 1973 when he started the season with an immense Afro, clipped it to a Mohawk, and later shaved his head bald.

Al Woodall is Riggins's closest friend and claims that John does such things solely to spoof people. "He's a quiet guy and not really interested in getting attention.

It's like he's saying to people, you think I'm really weird so I'm going to show you how weird I am by getting a Mohawk, but I'm not really weird because I know why I'm doing it."

Woodall explains that Riggins is not in the same class with Mike Battle, the Jets' legendary wild man of 1969–70 and a onetime pal of Joe Namath.

It was Battle who once leaped completely over a tackler en route to a touchdown, thus helping bring about an NFL rule forbidding hurdling, and it was Battle who once lay down in the center of a busy Manhattan street for ten minutes to prove that he wouldn't get killed. "I'm not enough of a psychologist to know why Battle did the things he did," says Woodall. "But he was insane. He'd drink a beer and eat the glass. He was only a little bigger than Knight, but he was a barroom brawler. He had a scar across his nose where he'd been hit with a bottle, and the knuckles on his hands were enormous. There was one situation I know of in the city where he and his wife started a fight with the wrong guy, and Battle got the shit beaten out of him. His wife was strange, too."

Charley Winner is not worried about the feelers protruding from Riggins's head right now as much as he is worried about the weather conditions for the game tomorrow. "They're supposed to have the tarps out," he says. "But who knows. It's ridiculous to be here in New York and have to play on a field like Shea. They can't even sod over the infield because the Yankees finish four days before our first game and it takes sod two weeks to knit. And then there's that wind . . ."

The wind is indeed a powerful force at Shea, swirling over the stadium walls and howling in through the open end at speeds frequently above forty miles-an-hour. The resulting turbulence, says *The New York Times,* creates "updrafts, downdrafts, cyclonic-like swirls that bubble and churn all over Shea—at field level, high in the stands, and places in between." Namath, who has had to throw half his career passes at Shea, is particularly affected whenever he throws deep, as he likes to do, for then the ball is assailed from all directions. "You can have this place," Terry Bradshaw told anyone who wanted to hear after the Steelers played the Jets in late November and Bradshaw completed only one of seven passes in the first half. "I don't know how Joe has survived it."

After practice I take a drive out the Meadowbrook Parkway to Point Lookout, the tiny seaside village where two thirds of the white Jet players live in small, rented bungalows. "It's nice and peaceful out here," one of them told me. "I don't know why none of the black guys live here. Maybe they won't let them in."

Gulls cry, the rain slants across the empty streets, waves beat on the docks. It is a scene far removed from the cosmopolitan images one associates with New York teams. In their living room, roommates Joe Fields and Darrell Austin lie on the floor watching afternoon TV. An old and terrible movie fades into *Batman,* but neither of them seems to care. Pro football players have a tendency to become superficial very quickly. "You don't grow up," says Garry Puetz. "You don't *have* to grow up."

"It's easy just to put everything aside and say, well, I'm playing ball and making money," says Richard Caster. "You just go out and fool around, buy records, watch TV. It happened to me a couple of years ago, but then I started feeling embarrassed. I mean I wasn't even reading the paper, something my grandfather told me to do when I was just old enough to read. It's amazing, but just that little bit, reading a newspaper, is something that can separate you from a lot of dudes."

Part of the problem is that many of the players never lose the feeling of transience that comes with the sport —from trades and injuries and having to make the team anew each fall. Most of the Jets do not even live in New York after the season, having brought no more belongings with them than can be conveniently dumped in the trunks and back seats of their cars.

At the Patio Lounge, Garry Puetz shoots pool with Pat Leahy, the kicker. Between games they watch the sparse traffic moving in the rain. Many days pass much like this one.

After ordering another beer Puetz comes up with his bit of wisdom for the afternoon. "Mulligan definitely must have wanted to be a running back," he states. "There's no reason for any lineman not to wear high-top shoes."

On Sunday the rain still hasn't quit, and the field at Shea has become a quagmire. Joe's first pass bounces off the fingertips of Carl Garrett for an interception, and from there it's all downhill. The Jets' defense becomes invisible, allowing Miami to score at will, and the Jets' receivers use their hands as though covered with mineral oil rather than water. Joe throws six interceptions, tying a personal record, three balls hitting his own men first. The Jets are humiliated, 43–0, their worst loss in a dozen years.

After the game I run down to the locker room, following the thundering herd of writers as they push and elbow their way through the exiting fans. I'm beginning to recognize the men now—smiling Larry Fox of the *Daily News,* efficient Jerry Eskenazi of the *Times,* gloomy George Usher of *Newsday,* and the leader of the pack, 6-foot-two, 250-pound Paul Zimmerman of the *Post,* a truly astounding individual. During the games I find it difficult not to watch Zimmerman rather than the field, for he is a study in compulsion and intensity the likes of which are seldom seen outside a grandmasters' chess game or, one suspects, a war room. Watching him devour a cigar, scribble microscopically in four different inks, or jerk binoculars to his eyes like a marine saluting, one recognizes instantly the movements of a fanatic. So meticulous are his notes that whenever a statistics announcement comes over the PA, the rest of the writers await his comment. "Namath, in the half, four of ten for seventy-four yards," barks the announcer. Pause. "Namath, four of eleven for seventy-seven yards," says Zimmerman, and everyone writes it down.

Today, when the locker room doors are opened, I walk

straight into the dressing area. The rest of the reporters must first get their standard losers' quotes from the coach, but I have no such responsibility. I walk over to Namath's cubicle and ask him how his knee feels. "Aw, it's just the usual," he says as he finishes wrapping an ice pack to it. He has on plastic clogs, but aside from those and the ice bandage, he is naked. He hunkers down on his stool, spitting tobacco juice into a cup, and waits silently for the press. They are not long in coming. Two men shoot around the corner and stand in front of him. Several more run over, and soon the area is seething with reporters, note pads held high, microphones dangling like bait, everyone squirming and eeling for better angles.

By not bracing myself I have gotten pushed out of my position all the way into the back of the room. But it makes no difference—the ritual is always the same. The questions come, basic ones, for everyone knows Joe will not answer indelicate queries. Joe looks at the questioner and decides what to say. If it is someone he doesn't like, he may look at the floor and say nothing. Zimmerman listens but asks nothing. Joe hasn't spoken to him in six years. When he is done talking, Joe will stare at his cup for a while, scratch himself, and then say something like, "I gotta take a shower." He'll then walk into the shower room and stay there until the locker room is fairly well cleared. Except for occasional times when he is in a playful mood, this is the basic Namath postgame interview.

On Tuesday a few of the Jets are feeling the effects of the lopsided defeat. "Oh, for the life of a defensive back," says one of the players. "That and ten cents won't get ya a cup of coffee," states Rich Sowells, the much-victimized left cornerback.

After being forced to run with the ball and then fumbling to set up a quick Miami score, Greg Gantt is now practicing his punts while taking only one step. The most distance he can manage is a wobbly thirty yards.

Jamie Rivers, who is still favoring his right ankle, walks around asking players if they're coming to his retirement party tomorrow. "Cut it out, Jamie," says Al Woodall.

"Why? The way I feel right now?" asks Rivers. "I should quit."

In the weekly Bible meeting held in the offensive-film room, Brother Herb, the black minister, attempts to give the eight gathered players some spiritual guidance. He tells a story about a centipede and a frog in which the frog asks the centipede how it can walk when it has so many legs to control. The centipede, who has never considered such a question, dwells on the puzzle so much that finally it can't walk. The parallel, apparently, is that the Jets have been analyzing themselves too much, that they would do better to play with more spontaneity. By the end of class the group is discussing Peter and his role in the foundation of the Church. "Delles Howell just made a good hit and we saw it on film," says Winston Hill. "Is that the same as saying, 'Delles, upon this type of hit I will build My Church? My Team'?" The players discuss this and decide that yes, that is the case.

By Friday, however, things are fully back to normal. Riggins, who has an injured toe, has painted all his toenails red. "He had one black one and he didn't want to bus," says J. J. Jones.

There is the usual pandemonium in the locker room: Eddie Bell tames Steve Reese with a chair and a towel, Godwin Turk shakes his wet hair on a group of card players, David Knight howls over his fan mail—a single letter from another person named David Knight. In everyone's locker two "Joe Namath Model" Arrow shirts have mysteriously appeared, gifts from one of Joe's many product endorsements.

After practice most of the players go across Fulton Avenue to Bill's Meadowbrook for a session of kangaroo court, a custom that was started last year after the Jets were one-and-six. "If anybody showed any spirit or enthusiasm, or if he started talking about how we could do better, then he had to stand trial," says Puetz. "Mark Lomas was the judge. We had several moves to impeach

98

him but they always died. The problem was that no matter how well guys used to plead their cases, they were always found guilty. This year we've already nailed Boozer because it said in the paper he was crying before the Buffalo game. The prosecutor said there were tear stains on his jersey, so we fined him."

Joe regularly attends the court sessions, and though he says little, he seems to enjoy the camaraderie. Last year he was among the first to stand trial, being charged with and found guilty of contributing to "interstate theft" for throwing so many interceptions. Linebacker Rich Lewis came to the Jets on waivers from Buffalo shortly after that, and because he had once intercepted one of Namath's passes, Joe charged him with "theft of services" at the next court session.

Today the major case is against trainer Jeff Snedeker for shirking duties.

"Who has come to the training room early only to find the doors closed?" bellows prosecutor Jamie Rivers.

Everyone yells, "Me!"

"Who has been made to sit in an ice-cold whirlpool?" Rivers asks.

The players scream in unison.

"Who has had to suffer through one of Snedeker's famed 'Asper-rubs'?"

Beer bottles are pounded on the bar.

"I rest my case," says Rivers, sitting down.

Snedeker attempts a defense but cannot be heard over the cries of "Guilty."

Mark Lomas, a defensive end out for the season with a torn Achilles tendon, stands up, rapping his gavel. "I sentence Mr. Snedeker to buy every player a beer at the next trial, with the exception of Mr. Namath, who, because he is the only one who receives the benefit of your full treatment, shall buy you a beer."

Joe chuckles from his seat in the rear where he is sipping a cup of coffee and gumming a wad of snuff. After the trial a few of the players stay on to play a word game, the loser of each round being forced to down a double shot of cheap bourbon. Godwin Turk quickly loses four rounds, and when he misfires on a fifth, he stands up and shrieks, "God day-yum!" Caster pours him the drink and hands it to him as everyone chants: "In the mouth, past the gums, look out stomach, here it comes." Joe has remained at the table simply to watch, and as the players laugh and fall over each other, he simply smiles and sips his coffee and spits in a cup.

The Baltimore game two days later on October 26 proves conclusively that the Miami pasting was not a fluke. Again things begin wrong, this time with Eddie Bell giving the invocation and asking the Lord to help the Jets "beat Buffalo today, October twenty-ninth." Carl Garrett then fumbles twice on the first two series, and each time the Colts score. After that the Jets' secondary disappears and the offensive line turns porous as screen, allowing such nonhousehold names as Fred Cook and Mike Barnes to drop Namath a record seven times.

Still there is a time late in the game when the Jets have pulled to within striking distance at 38–28, with the ball second and one at their own 20. Namath tries one bomb to Barkum that falls incomplete. Then instead of playing safe, he heaves another one to Caster on the other side. That falls incomplete also, and on fourth and one Steve Davis is stopped short of a first down. Lydell Mitchell scores for the Colts on the next play, and the game ends at 45–28.

"It was Joe's play," said Charley Winner afterward of the third-and-one call. "He was taking a chance to get on the board."

Under the circumstances, however, Namath played remarkably well. Despite some awesome blows to his upper body from the Colts' rushers, he still managed to throw for 333 yards, including a club record 91-yarder to Caster, and 3 TDs. In the locker room he displayed numerous arm and chest contusions as well as a badly bruised neck. Mike Barnes had given him that one on a late hit after which Namath had leaped to his feet and verbally assaulted the 6-foot-6, 260-pound defensive tackle.

In the Colts' locker room, Barnes, an admitted quarterback-hater who grew up just thirty miles from Namath, claimed he simply couldn't stop in time. "Joe called me a 'dirty little punk,'" he smiled.

For Charley Winner the loss was another confusing blow, because the disintegration of the offensive line meant the dam was leaking everywhere. "It's easy for these guys, with their ability, to be pro football players," he said, his blue eyes turning gray with frustration. "It isn't easy for them to be above-average players on an above-average team. Somehow, some way, I've got to get this across."

NINE

Joe's got it made. It's sickening. I'm glad he's got it made, you know. But it's still sickening.

—LOU PICCONE

The other day on the radio I heard a man say that a million dollars just isn't what it used to be. And that's so true.

—JOE NAMATH

In Miami before the November 9 Dolphins game, Lou Piccone edges into the hotel swimming pool, stiffly, because his legs are thick with knots and bruises. In the nearby lobby Joe Namath prepares to take a limousine somewhere. Throngs of fans follow his every move, begging him to autograph this or that or pose for a picture.

"Nice weather," says Lou, sinking in to his chest. "Joe comes down here and he's got it great." Lou paddles out a few feet and then returns to the side. The swim, he says, is for therapy. Absentmindedly he thumbs a nostril, a move that makes him sneeze. He laughs at himself. "Look at me. I don't even have enough money to pick my nose properly."

Lou Piccone, wide receiver, halfback, return man, bomb squadder, age 26, 5 feet 8 1/2 inches, 175 pounds, from West Liberty State College, is never going to be a star. To keep his name out of the papers all he needs to do, as the saying goes, is stay out of jail. Nor is he alone on the Jets as an obscure, low-paid bit player. He has good company in such as Bob Prout, Willie Brister, Gordie Browne, Joe Fields, Jerry Davis, George Hoey, Ken Bernich, and several others—none of whom will ever know the excesses of ten-point type or a six-figure contract.

Every NFL team has players like Piccone, hardworking, marginally talented, expendable special teamers and backup men. But no team has the contrast between them and their betters as do the Jets; no other team has a Joe Namath earning thirty-five times more than a teammate.

Lou Piccone doesn't always laugh about his financial status. Sometimes it is difficult for him and his peers to understand the difference between what they earn and what Joe earns. Concepts such as "gate appeal" and "charisma" have a tendency to lose their meaning, particularly after a player realizes that simply having Joe on the team doesn't guarantee wins. Each player can point to some way in which he feels just as vital to the Jets as Joe; in Piccone's case it is the fact that he returned more kickoffs for more yardage in 1974 than anyone else in the NFL. Further resentment comes from the old chestnut, true or not, that there's only so much in the till, that what one person gets, somebody else doesn't.

Nevertheless, the Jets have traditionally accepted their fate without bitterness. At the end of 1975 a reporter would ask John Riggins if it bothered him that he could gain 1,000 yards rushing and still earn only one-quarter as much as the quarterback who threw 28 interceptions. "Logically it should be upsetting," shrugged Riggins. "But then, this really isn't a logical world." First-year general manager Al Ward, who has decided to maintain the time-honored "Joe is special" concept, admits that in negotiations quite a few of the Jets will point to Joe's salary as a reason why theirs should be similarly inflated. "But I haven't talked to a player yet who will persist," he adds. "They finally just accept that Joe is different, that they're not like him."

Lou Piccone is a gutty, intense athlete who, as he says, just wants "to earn what I deserve." He doesn't compare himself with Namath, though he feels that with proper promotion from the Jets he could be a star, too. "I'm small, I'm Italian, I can beat any safety in the league. The fans would have to love me," he says. He and Namath kid each other a lot—Joe referring to him as a "little piece of minestrone," Lou calling Joe "old bag-of-nickels nose." But the contrast between the two makes real communication virtually impossible.

Because he couldn't get the $35,000 he wanted this season, up from his 1974 contract of $16,000, Lou is playing without a contract. Besides taking a serious physical risk, he receives the mandatory 10 percent pay cut for playing out his option. Also deducted from his salary is the $1,500 fine he incurred for walking out of camp in protest earlier in the season. Just as Joe Namath is unquestionably the highest-paid player in all of pro football, Lou Piccone is unquestionably the lowest paid. The fact that they are on the same team and share the same basic goals makes for a unique relationship.

One night over a lasagna dinner Lou related the story of his unlikely football career, at times becoming so emotional that the volume needle on my tape recorder buried itself. As a description of the nonglamorous side of the sport and as a counterpoint to Namath's journey, the story seemed quite worthwhile.

"I guess I started out as your basic wayward youth from New Jersey," said Lou. "Vineland, New Jersey, to be exact. I wasn't into crime or anything; actually I was more like an alcoholic. My high school buddies and I would booze it up on the weekends and then go into Philadelphia and dance our heads off. We did a lot of traveling around like that. Football and track were the only things that kept me from going into a complete stupor.

"My pa wanted me to go to college but I didn't want to. I wanted to pursue the streets, hang out, make a buck shooting pool. I was a great pool shooter, I had a high run of eighty-three balls. But my dad finally got me to take the college boards, which I totally messed up after drinking a quart of scotch with two buddies at eight in the morning. I sat there at my desk making patterns, and when it was all over, AA wanted me but no colleges did. Eventually this school called West Liberty State in West Virginia accepted me, but that was mainly because I was an out-of-state student and they could sop up my dough, really rip me off. There was no scholarship or anything.

"So I got there and I went out for the football team and the first year I never played and the second year all I did was return punts. That was kind of funny because I used to wear glasses—I was fairly blind and catching a football was not one of my better skills. Every time I'd drop back, the coach would hide; he couldn't stand to watch. But I did make some fantastic runs, zooming right into the middle of huge crowds. That was because I didn't know what a fair catch was; nobody'd ever told me there was such a thing. I didn't really play high school ball and I'd never followed football too much, so I just didn't know the rules. Then one day a teammate says to me, 'Lou, Jesus, why don't you fair catch, you take such a beating?' I said, 'What do you mean?' He said, 'Didn't you ever see a guy put his hand up and wave it around? It means nobody can hit ya.'

"But even after that I still didn't like to fair catch. I mean, running back kicks was the only thing I was doing in the games. Besides, people loved to watch me return balls because I was a crazy man. So, anyway, my junior year the coach told me I'd start playing a lot more and I got real excited. I called my parents and told them to come to the opening game to watch me. Then as the game's going on I'm just standing around on the sidelines getting frustrated because I'm not doing anything, as usual, and my parents have driven seven hundred miles to watch me play. With two minutes left and us way behind with no chance of catching up, I hear the coach say, well, we better put Piccone in so we can say we played him. I'd been pacing the sideline the whole game trying to get in, and up in the stands my parents and my brother and my girl are watching. That really hurt me. So the coach called my name, and from the corner of the bench I flipped him the biggest bird he'd ever seen and yelled, 'Fuck you! You go in!'

"After the game I went into the locker room and took off my equipment and went up to Leo Miller, the offensive coach, who's about six-feet-three, two hundred forty-five pounds, and I said, 'Leo, you see this equipment, you see this ball? Well, you can take this equipment and this ball and your whole football team and jam it right up your ass!' I walked out and he chased after me and I was waiting for him to say something to me because I wanted to punch his face in because I had so much frustration inside me. I wasn't playing, I didn't have a scholarship. Nothing. I was right in his chest yelling, 'Fuck you, Leo! And fuck you some more!' But by this time my dad had walked in and he finally calmed me down.

"Well, later the head coach called me and asked me to come back out, which I eventually did. And then the next year I started playing halfback and I did pretty well. I even got about eight hundred dollars off on my tuition. It got to the point where other teams started trying to hurt me to get me out of the game, which I guess was sort of a compliment.

"When I graduated I just started teaching sixth grade back at home figuring I was done with football. Then I got a call from this guy who was starting a semipro team in Youngstown, Ohio, and he wanted to know if I'd like to come up and play. I had to think about it, but then I decided, well, if that's the only place you'll make it as a pro, you might as well try. So I went there and we were having time trials and everybody figured I couldn't be fast because I was this little white guy. But they put the clock on me and I beat everybody they had—black, white, or maroon. But still everybody always started ahead of me, no matter what. It was like he's just a poor little creep, he doesn't need to do anything. In the meantime I had to work as a carpenter because I was only clearing forty-one dollars a game, and I wasn't able to save anything.

"The team almost went undefeated that year, though —I think we were twelve and one—so when it was all over I wrote to all twenty-six NFL teams asking if they might be interested in me. I got twenty-six replies, all of them saying no. But I started working out on my own, two and three times a day, and that summer I drove over to Washington for the Redskins' free-agent tryout.

"I walked into the stadium and there were five hundred people milling around—big fat slobs, weirdos, guys on lunch break from McDonald's, hippies—a complete zoo. I knew in a crowd like this, being five feet, eight and a half, and white, from a school like West Liberty State, I didn't have much of a chance. But I was running pretty well and somebody told me and a few other guys to stick around after the workout. So I sat up in the gym for a couple of hours with my father. After a while things started getting quiet, and I was wondering what was going on. I went down to the locker room and beat on a door until this coach came out. He said, 'What's up?' I said, 'What do you mean, what's up? What's up with you? How long are we gonna have to wait around? I might have to go home sometime, ya know.' He said, 'Well, okay, you can go home.' On the way out I passed George Allen, the head coach, he's about six-feet four, and I realized that the man had not even seen me, that I was a nonperson.

"I went home and a little later I drove to Philadelphia for the Eagles' free-agent tryout. So here we go again— JFK Stadium, four hundred and fifty bodies, fiasco time. My cuts were off that day, but I thought I was catching the ball pretty good. I also turned in the second fastest time of the whole group. Then when I was back returning some kicks with a group, a man comes up and says, 'Take a powder, you're gone.' I said, 'What?' He says, 'Goodbye, we've seen enough.' I couldn't believe it. What the hell is this? Here I am trying to find out if I can possibly play pro ball, and nobody's given me any kind of athletic assessment whatsoever. So I decided to go see Boyd Dowler, the receiver coach, and get his opinion. I asked to talk to him and the girl told him a Lou Piccone was here. 'Lou who?' he said. I said, 'A player from the free-agent tryout,' so he let me come back. I told him all I wanted was an honest evaluation of my talent. But after talking to him for a while, I realized the man did not even know I existed that day. Then he told me a nice story about his brother. He said his brother wanted to play professional football, and at one point he was out chasing after footballs, and Boyd said, 'Well, can you make a decent living doing what you're doing?' And his brother said no and hung it up. In other words, that was a nice way of telling me to hang it up.

"But I couldn't quit. He didn't actually tell me I couldn't play; he only told me I wasn't on his agenda for the day.

"So after that I contacted the Jets, and they had this nice man named Dick Connors who was conducting pretraining workouts on Sundays up in Bridgeport, Connecticut. I went up there and ran some four-four forties and he said, 'Hey, you can fly.' I was living pretty much hand to mouth at the time, driving my old black 'sixty-six Plymouth, and when Dick got me a job as a counselor at Joe Namath's Football Camp, I was really happy. I figured Joe could maybe assess my talent better than anybody. So I went to his camp, and every afternoon Joe would work out throwing passes to the counselors. Pete Athas, a defensive back for the Giants, was there, the very first professional I'd ever run against. And when I beat him a few times, beat him bad, I felt great. But actually I was pretty intimidated, I was awed. I'd never seen passes like Joe was throwing, beautiful passes. Another kid up there, Joe threw a ball and split his fingers wide open, and he had to get a bunch of stitches.

"Anyway, from there I got invited to the Jets' training camp in July. The first day in camp I ran the forty and just smoked everybody they had—Bell, Caster, everybody. I was doing four-threes and they said the watches must be wrong, that this was impossible. I was wondering what I was doing there myself, with All-Pros and huge guys and everything. I was trying to relax but it was difficult—the terminology, these passing trees, and all this other new stuff. Ken Shipp started yelling at me because I didn't know what was going on; he started trying to intimidate me, using me as a whipping boy. I remember one day we were upstairs for a meeting and everybody was drinking Coke, but I didn't have any because you weren't supposed to drink upstairs. So when the meeting's over everybody leaves and I'm downstairs and this kid comes down and says Coach Shipp wants to see you. I run all the way back up to the room, and you know what he wants to tell me? 'Pick up the cans,' he says. At that point I wanted to emaciate his face, but I didn't do anything, I just picked up the cans.

"So then it's Saturday morning and we've been in camp a few weeks and we're having our first big scrimmage. I've gotten a little bit of press and people have started to wonder who this fast little white boy is, this nobody who can really burn. I'm pretty excited because I figure this is my day, this is where I show them I can hit and block and tackle—all the contact stuff we haven't been allowed to do yet. I'm standing in the end zone, dressed and ready to go, getting loose, and Mike Martin from the front office comes up and tells me Weeb wants to see me. So I run over to Weeb and he looks at me and says, 'We have to let you go.' I said, 'What?' He said, 'We have to let you go.' I looked at him real hard. 'You gotta be kidding,' I said. 'Let me explain,' he said. 'We can't keep you because of the numbers thing. We do think you can play pro ball, but not right now. It might be good if you went to the minor leagues for a while.'

" 'What is this, a goddamn joke?' I said. 'I've *been* in the minors. You bring me here for two weeks, let me work out, then let me go without even letting me scrimmage. You've never even seen me hit somebody. All we've been doing is this mamby-pamby don't-touch-anybody bullshit. How do you know if I can play football? You've got to let me scrimmage.' 'We can't let you scrimmage,' he said. 'If you got hurt, we'd have to keep you.' Finally, I realized it was futile. I went into the locker room and proceeded to throw everything I had all around. I was beating doors, just fucking crazy. I split my hand open where I destroyed a locker. If they'd only let me scrimmage and then cut me, it would have been different.

"I hung around for a few days, not knowing what to do. Nobody showed any interest in me. Once again I figured this is it, the end of the line. After a while, though, I signed on with another semipro team—this time it was with Bridgeport in the Atlantic Coast League. I ended up doing everything for them. I played wide receiver, running back, tight end. I played on all the special teams. I washed the clothes and drove the bus. Then after the season the Jets decided they wanted to sign me. But they were still treating me like a nothing, they only offered me the bare minimum. Eventually I did sign, just because this was finally a chance to get paid something. You gotta remember, I'd been out of college now for quite a while.

"So this time in preseason camp I didn't hold anything back. I caught fifteen passes, I hit people, I played special teams like a bitch. I remember there was one play in particular that I made the team on. We were playing the Giants, which is always a big rivalry, and they had this nine-two sprinter back for a punt. I was flying down the field on coverage and I didn't break down in time and this guy catches the ball, sidesteps me, and takes off. He made a fool out of me. I fell down, but I got back up and started chasing him from behind. He had a head start but I started catching up to him. Somebody peeled back and threw a block at me, but I went up and over it, crashed into the returner, knocked him into some pursuers. He fumbled the ball. I got up and recovered the fumble. All in one play.

"So I made the team and Mike Adamle and I became the special team demons. The 'Mic and Pic Show' is what Zimmerman called us. We did all sorts of things. One day before a game Mike and I were looking at each other, and there was this can of shoe black just sitting there. Mike picked up the brush and put a big black cross on my chest and said, 'Banzai!' I put a cross on his chest and said, 'Banzai!' and from then on we were the Banzai Brothers, wedge busters.

"Don't get me wrong, I'm not a crazy idiot. I don't go out there recklessly. I try to treat everything as a skill. I'm not like Mike Battle, where you just let your body go, or even Adamle, who I think had a tendency to be like that. Some guys may have a little-man complex but I don't. It doesn't bother me to be little. You're only as little as your heart. One day before we played the Bears, Weeb told me that their players were very physical and would try to intimidate me. I said to him, 'Listen, nobody in this game can intimidate me, and the day that they can I'll quit.'

Last year against the Giants I was returning a kickoff and somebody missed a block in the wedge, and this guy named Pedigrew, about two hundred and sixty pounds, came through untouched. He hit me at a full gallop as I was hurdling somebody, and I just fucking disappeared. He destroyed me. It was the hardest lick I've ever gotten. I was laying on the ground and I could hear seventy thousand people oohing and oh-my-God-ing. I looked up and Pedigrew was smiling at me, and I said to myself this big jerk isn't going to get the best of me. I didn't get up, I jumped up. I looked at him and I ran off the field and I laughed.

"Then I came back this year for negotiations and Al Ward, the new man, only offered me twenty thousand. I said wait a minute, Al, let's not play games. I'm a pro now. I've been in the minor leagues. I've paid my dues, man. I led the league in returns last year. You're new this year and you've never even seen me play and here you are trying to make a fair offer. I told him to go watch the game films and I'd talk to him later.

"After I had a good camp he brought his offer up to twenty-two thousand dollars. I said where's your head? This is ridiculous. Don't you understand that I paid my dues, that I've already played two seasons making forty-one dollars a game. You never sniffed a jock in your life and yet you're trying to tell me what I'm worth? So I walked out of camp and I went over and sat at Bill's. After a while some of the players started coming in and ordering drinks. Riggins was sitting on one side of me and Namath was on the other and they started talking to me. You gotta understand that both of these guys are making pretty good money; Riggins hasn't had his thousand yards yet, but he's doing okay, and Joe Willie, he's making his jack. And now they're telling me to be patient, to come back to camp and take what I can get.

"Namath was saying that you can try to buck the system but that the system won't take that kind of stuff. You can't beat it, he says. He was trying to make a point but he was just antagonizing me. I said, 'What do you know about it? When was the last time you were down and out and didn't have enough money to pay your bills? Nobody pays my bills for me. I'm not a star like you. You're making four hundred and fifty thousand this year, and that's about ten times as much as I'll make in my whole career. But you're trying to tell me what I should come back and play for?'

"Then he looked at his knees and said something about all the abuse he takes. He does take a lot of abuse, but so what? 'When was the last time you played for forty-one dollars a game,' I asked him. We were drinking schnapps and things were getting pretty heated. He was hitting me in this sore spot, and it got to the point where I was ready to come off my stool. But then we both sort of let it drift. After that Riggins said that I should want to be part of this team because we had a chance of going to the Super Bowl. 'I'd play for nothing,' he said. 'Well, that's exactly what I'm doing right now,' I told him. I didn't come back to camp until a few days later after Adamle and Galigher and a few other guys talked me into it.

"See, the point is not so much the money as it is a matter of establishing respect. In this game respect is denoted by money; that's the only correlation you have. As it's turned out I'm getting sixteen thousand minus ten percent, which is fourteen thousand four hundred, minus the fifteen-hundred-dollar fine, which makes a total of twelve thousand nine hundred before taxes. That's less than your average garbage collector earns. Do you know what my paycheck was for the St. Louis game? Twenty-five dollars and thirty-eight cents. I was so crazy I didn't know whether to laugh or cry. Phil Iselin had come into the locker room one day and he said to me, 'What are you doing here? I thought you'd be in Jersey picking tomatoes.' See, New Jersey is noted for its tomatoes. I said, 'Maybe that's what I should be doing, Mr. Iselin.' So then when I got that check, I looked at it and I gave it back to John Free, the business manager. I said, 'Pay this to whoever gave it to you'—I was trying to keep cool and not lose my head—'and you tell him to buy a bushel of Jersey red tomatoes on me. If he can buy it with this.'

"On the bus I was laughing hysterically to myself. This is when I think I got closer to God. I said, 'If this is the way You want to humble me, by making me a pro and giving me twenty-five thirty-eight, okay.' That night in the game I almost lost my only testicle. I'd lost the other one in a childhood accident, and that night when I got hit over the middle on a return I thought I'd lost the other one. I looked up and said, 'God, if You have a plan for me, all right, I'm just gonna keep on.'

"I'm playing out my option now so maybe I can go somewhere where I'll be appreciated. Being associated with Joe and being on the Jets really doesn't mean anything to me. I can't even sniff Namath's candy wrappers. He don't care. He's laughing all the way to the bank. People say they pay him so much that they have to start skimping in other places. Well, I don't give a damn if the man makes forty million, that has nothing to do with Lou Piccone's allotment.

"My pop's been trying to talk me into taking what they're offering. He told me not to buck the system. I told him I'm not bucking the system, I'm just trying to get paid for what I do. I gotta live with myself. So now, well, maybe nobody will want me. Maybe I'll be through playing football. I don't know. But I'm willing to take the risk, I've been gambling all my life.

"The problem is I don't have a backlog of funds. I haven't even been making seventeen thousand for the past years; I've been making peanuts. Now I'm in the professional ranks and I'm supposed to live like a professional and carry a certain image. You're supposed to have enough money to do certain things, especially if you're on the Jets. But I can't do them. I can't go into business, I can't live in a nice place. I can't even pay my college debts; I still owe four thousand at the college. I don't want to borrow any more.

"You know, sometimes I wonder how all this happened. And I think to myself that it happened just because I wanted to see how far I could go, because I wanted to be a pro football player and not just a guy on the streets of New Jersey."

(In June of 1976 Piccone signed a one-year contract with the Jets for $33,000. "I'm satisfied—sort of," Lou said. The negotiations had been conducted by Namath's attorney Jimmy Walsh. "I got Jimmy because I felt he could help me off the field as well. I've been thinking about entertainment, you know. And besides, I got sick of talking."

When Piccone had tried to peddle himself after the season, he found that some coaches in the Jets' own division had never even heard of him. "I'll stay here for now," Lou said. "It's a new organization coming in and Joe Willie's throwing the ball nice. I don't resent Namath; I never did. If I ever get where he is, I don't want somebody like me saying, 'Hey, this guy's taking the food out of my mouth.' ")

TEN

*Sure Beaver Falls is dirty. But it's
not that dirty. You couldn't ask for a
better place for a sports-minded boy
to grow up.*
—DOM CASEY

*I think people like Joe because
they can see the boy in him. He's an
honest-to-goodness real American
boy.*
—JOHN NAMATH

Entering Beaver Falls, Pennsylvania, population 14,-
500, from the east side of the Beaver River in late December is not a visually stimulating experience. Dirty
wisps of snow blow past low buildings and clustered
two-story frame houses covered over with brown brick
shingling. Smokestacks protrude from factories, and
boards cover the windows of numerous old stores. Below, the river is gray and silent. It is soon obvious that
Beaver Falls, here in the hill country fifty miles north-
west of Pittsburgh, is graced with neither real beavers
or real falls.

In his first book done with Dick Schaap, Namath ti-
tled one of the chapters "There Are No Coal Mines in
Beaver Falls" to help clear up that myth as well. What
there are in Beaver Falls are steel mills. The Babcock &
Wilcox East Works at the north end of town is probably

the largest. It stands not far from Geneva College, the school from which Namath and some chums once "borrowed" some game jerseys, a caper that earned them several hours in the local police station. Railroad tracks encircle and cross the town, and several small trestles bridge into the hills, one of them being the famed structure from which Namath once hung while a freight train thundered overhead. The downtown area, a brief section along Seventh Avenue, has been laced with bright Christmas ornaments and tinsel; and the holiday shoppers appear to move cheerfully, as though generally pleased with the town's appearance. When Joe's mother painted a bleak picture of Beaver Falls in her book *Namath, My Son Joe,* the locals did not take very kindly to her work. But the basic industrial ugliness is there for all to see—the washed-out features, the lack of imagination emanating from the old, dark buildings. The wooded hills and the river are the lone touches of grace; one can imagine the countryside at least being colorful in the fall.

At the bottom of a hill at the south end of town sits the trim two-story frame house where Joe grew up. The neighborhood is shabbier than the rest of town—literally "the other side of the tracks"—a blend of warehouses, junkyards, and tall, narrow houses. The Namaths haven't lived here for years, although the family hasn't completely left town. Joe's three brothers still live in the area, as do his divorced parents, both of whom have remarried.

John Namath, Joe's sixty-seven-year-old father, lives across the river in New Brighton in a small brick house of suburban design. He likes to entertain his guests in his basement where he has proudly fashioned a game room with a bar and a puck bowling machine and carpeting composed of stitched-together remnants. The walls are dotted with photos of Joe and the other sons and grandchildren, and except for a few outlandish-sized football trophies, the room could be anyone's anywhere in middle America. A strong-featured, swarthily handsome man with silver hair brushed straight back and what appears to be a perpetual suntan, John Namath is unquestionably a picture of the way his son will look thirty-five years from now.

The Namath clan first immigrated to America from Hungary around 1909. John Namath, then just a baby, remained behind with his grandparents and an older brother and didn't rejoin his family until he was thirteen. Arriving in Beaver Falls he learned that the family name had been changed from Németh to Namath and that he wasn't to speak Hungarian anymore. "Learn American and learn it right," ordered his father. At fifteen John had a doctor change his birth certificate so he could legally quit school and get a full-time job. "I didn't have any fun in school because my parents wouldn't let any of us kids play sports," he says. "They always told us, 'We didn't raise our children to be cripples.' "

He got a job as a "heater boy," instead, heating rivets for the Penn Bridge Company. That began a forty-seven-year career in the steel mills—thirty-two years of which were spent in "hot mills," where the metal was cast and shaped in the presence of blazing furnaces. He recalls with pleasure the day his seniority allowed him to move away from the blast and become a "roller." "A piece of nine- or ten-foot steel pipe would drop into your trough and you'd have to stretch it and roll it out to maybe twenty feet," he says. "Rolling was still pretty hot and you were on your feet all the time, but you were the top man." In 1970 he was forced to retire early because of a worsening case of emphysema. "I'd quit smoking two years before," he recalls, "and when I asked the doctor if it was the cigarettes that caused the emphysema, he said, 'No, John. It's all that damn dust and steel dirt you been breathing for so many years.' "

A good-natured yet stern man who was never afraid to wallop his boys if necessary, John Namath molded his sons as best he could. He admits now to being "perfectly satisfied" with the way Joe has turned out. He even seems to have helped formulate some of Joe's more famous philosophies. "Before he went to Alabama I gave Joe some advice," John says. "I told him, 'Son, there's lots of pretty Southern babes down there. You don't have to pick one right away. Be like Jesus, just love 'em and leave 'em.' That's what I said. I'd have done the same thing. Any red-blooded American boy would have."

John Namath's decision to move his family to the lower side of Beaver Falls into a predominantly black neighborhood was one of the major developments in Joe's life. Until his parents were divorced in 1955 and Joe and his mother moved to another section of town, Joe's companions were virtually all black. At one point Joe even took to smearing his face with brown shoe polish to better resemble his best friend, Linny Alford.

"My family came here from another country," says John Namath, "and I've always maintained that we could have been just as black as anyone if the Lord had wanted us to be. Something else I found out was that when we lived in the white neighborhood, if I didn't go out in the yard and pick up all the bikes and balls when I got off work, they'd be gone the next day. Down there on Sixth Street with all the colored kids coming and going, if they saw a basketball out in the gutter they'd pick it up and put it on the porch. Never stole nothing."

From his association with blacks, Joe began to develop style, a natural sense of "cool." "The way we were rubbed off on him," says Butch Ryan, one of Joe's old buddies. "He picked up our slang. He started liking soul food. He grew up just like us." At Alabama, Joe was something of a mystery because he used words like "man" and "dig it" and sported a toothpick during scrimmages. Even at Beaver Falls High School he maintained his style: in one of the varsity baseball photos, Joe slouches forward in the front row, his eyes hidden behind huge sunglasses.

As a youth Joe was full of "devilment," as his elders liked to put it. This delighted Mr. Namath. "I wanted him to be cocky and confident and mischievous. And that's just how he was," says his father. A natural sense of caution and self-preservation kept Joe from getting too carried away, however. He was slyer than he was pushy.

"Sometimes I liked to give people trouble," Joe recalls. "But I wasn't a fighter or anything like that. When I went to dances I never hung with the guys who were looking for trouble. Hell, I had three older brothers and an older sister and some mighty strong disciplinarian folks, and they didn't like the idea of me being in that kind of trouble."

"He was the kind of kid who would shove somebody and then say he didn't do it," says Dom Casey, Joe's Little League and American Legion coach. "I remember one time we were playing at New Brighton and Joe was pitching and the kids on the other team were throwing pebbles at him. Joe ignored them for a while, and then he went into his windup and whaled the ball right into their dugout. Both teams emptied onto the field, and the umpire and everybody came out. Joe starts saying how the ball slipped. He's shaking his head and wiping sweat off his hand, putting on a great act. Hell, he had to throw damn near straight sideways to get the ball there."

The fact that Joe's father worked in the mills had a marked effect on the boy, particularly when Joe considered such a life for himself. "The mill work always sort of bothered him," recalls John Namath. "I remember one hot summer day I came home from work and Joe was in the driveway washing the new Lincoln he'd just gotten for signing with the Jets. It had been a hard day for me because at the mill you have to wear long underwear under your clothes to keep from getting scorched, no matter what the weather is, and, of course, you always get covered with dust. Joe saw me and he put the hose down. 'Come here, Dad,' he said. I went over there and I guess I looked a little haggard, which is how you get sometimes. 'Your eyes are all sunken in,' he said, 'and you look really pale.' Then he asked me if the work was awful hard. I said for him it would be, but that I was used to it. 'Dad,' he said, 'I can set it up for you so you won't have to work anymore and you'll have money for the rest of your life.' He begged me to retire. 'Joe,' I said, 'you don't owe me a thing. I'll retire when the time comes.' But I could see the mill life wasn't for him."

Cosmo Currie, Joe's barber friend from the swinging days at Bachelors III, remembers that sometimes in the midst of an elegant bash Joe would come up to him and say, "Cos, this is what I've always wanted." Money and its potential always meant a great deal to Joe, from the days of stealing pop bottles and hubcaps till the present. "Something that truly helped me achieve peace of mind was making money," he says now. "I couldn't be happy without it. Looking back on the way I was before I had money, I certainly wasn't happy. I had a lot of stress and a lot of wants. Money eliminated that."

Though sports would ultimately be Joe's ticket out of Beaver Falls, at the beginning it was just for fun. "From the moment he was big enough to hold a ball, he was always playing some game," says Mr. Namath. "Even in the winter he'd have four or five pair of socks rolled into balls, and he'd be shooting them and they'd be lying all over the damn house."

Athletics weren't shoved at the Namath boys but they were encouraged. As a youth John Namath had been forced to hide his sports equipment at a friend's house. He vowed then that his children would never suffer the same indignity. Indeed, in time the Namath household came to resemble a sporting goods store, so filled was it with balls and bats and mitts. "I went into hock a few times, but I made sure they always had the best equipment," John states.

Little Joe (and he was "little"—no more than 5 feet, 115 pounds as a high school freshman) joined his first competitive team when he was eight, a steel-union–sponsored baseball team for nine-year-olds. Already he had shown his natural gifts as an athlete, but according to his father he had not yet developed the famed Namath confidence. "That first night he came down to the back porch wearing his new uniform and I said, 'Well, that looks very nice, son.' He just sat there and then he said, 'Daddy, those other kids are so big and they're so much better than me, I know I can't make the team.' I said, 'If you're sure of that, then you'd better turn in that uniform so some other boy can use it.' Then he said, 'Oh, no, I can't do that.' So I said, 'If you don't have confidence in yourself you should quit. You should feel that you're better than anyone out there, or else don't play.' He said, 'Well, they're all so good.' 'You're just as good,' I told him. 'You can hit, you can field, you know where to make the plays. We've been going over all that stuff for a long time.' He sat there awhile and then he said, 'Okay, I'll try.' And sure enough he made the team and was better than anybody out there, even though he was the youngest boy in the league."

For a while Joe's confidence depended solely on his father's approval. When he was pitching in Little League he developed a habit of turning around after each pitch and looking for his father in the stands. "Finally, I would just drop him off at the park and tell him I had to go over to the union hall on business," says Mr. Namath. "Then I'd leave and come back and watch the game from left field where he couldn't see me."

It quickly became obvious that Joe had not only the physical skills but also the mental capabilities to become a good athlete. Lying around the Namath house were numerous sports-oriented games, and one of Joe's favorites was an electric football game. He and his brothers played it constantly, and whenever Joe scored on a long pass or held off an attack, he would leap up and scream, "I got you! I got you!" and dance around the room. "He had that game figured out," says his father. "Same as he had those electric baseball and basketball games figured out."

One of Joe's best friends in the early years was Butch Ryan, a black neighborhood kid a year behind him in school. An outstanding athlete in his own right, Butch followed Joe as the Beaver Falls High quarterback and led the team to its second straight undefeated season. He works now as the assistant football coach at the high school and during the winter coaches the girls' basketball team. After a Saturday practice he sits on a bench in the dingy orange and black gym and recalls the pickup football games he and Joe used to play as boys.

"Our team was usually made up of neighborhood kids," he says. "So it was almost all black guys except for Joe and maybe a couple of Italian kids. Joe always seemed to play quarterback, for some reason. I don't know why except that maybe we blacks couldn't really identify with that position. There was no hassle, though. Joe was kind of spoiled, really; he had all the best balls and gloves, and he always seemed to have money and nice clothes, but he wasn't selfish at all. We used all his stuff. And then he was really good, even back then. He was fast, he had monstrous hands, and he never lost his poise.

"By the time we got to high school he had learned to make incredible fakes with the ball. I remember at least three times his senior year the refs called back touchdowns because they had already blown the play dead because they didn't know who had the ball. Joe could be tough, too. I remember his senior year we were playing Ambridge and both teams were undefeated. Joe separated his left shoulder just before the half, and I went in for one play at quarterback. He came right back in, and even though he could barely take the snap, he threw about a fifty-yard touchdown pass on the next play. He played the whole game without being able to raise his left arm."

After the Jets won the Super Bowl, the high school retired Joe's jersey, number 19. Joe had picked that number because it was Johnny Unitas's, his hero, and he liked it very much when people called him "Joey U." Football, however, was far from being the only sport he played well. Bear Bryant has called Joe, not the greatest quarterback he's ever coached, but "the greatest athlete." Dr. Nicholas claims that Joe is the classic "natural athlete," a player who could excel at "anything requiring eye-hand coordination, agility, or dexterity." As proof he points to a bowling contest he and Joe had several years ago in which, without practicing, Joe rolled consistent 215s and 220s.

In high school Joe was the only white starter on the varsity basketball team. His style of play was dramatic if nothing else. He could easily palm the ball, pumping it in and out of an opponent's face before shooting, and he could dunk behind his head—a rare feat for a white, 6-foot-1 seventeen-year-old.

When Beaver Falls hired a new coach for Joe's senior season, he didn't take kindly to Joe's antics. "Joe liked the razzle-dazzle playground kind of ball," says Butch Ryan. "Coach Lippe liked ten passes before a shot." After being yanked from a midseason game for showboating, Joe and a teammate walked off the floor and never returned.

Joe had already been named to *Scholastic Coach*'s prep All-American football team along with Dick Butkus, Tucker Frederickson, Ernie Koy, and John Huarte, but some observers felt that baseball was actually his best sport. Upon graduation he was offered $20,000 to sign with the Baltimore Orioles. Later the Chicago Cubs raised the ante to $50,000. But by that time Joe was safely ensconced under Bear Bryant's big arm at Alabama, and his baseball days were over.

John Namath always felt Joe should have continued with baseball. "You could see him more as an outfielder than a football player," he says, "because of his size and his terrific natural swing with the bat." One Little League game in particular convinced Mr. Namath of his son's talents.

"I got to the game late, so I asked a man what was happening and he said, 'Well, there are no outs, the score is tied at three-all, and the bases are loaded. But don't worry, because they just brought the little Namath kid in from left field to pitch, and he's got ice water in his veins.' The man didn't know me, so I sat down to watch. Joe struck out the first boy. The next guy hit a grounder back to Joe, and he threw him out. Then up came this big kid named Walton, who later played pro football with the Giants. He was an enormous size, and whenever he hit the ball he knocked it a country mile. So Joe threw him a ball, then a strike, then a ball, then another strike, which Walton swung at and missed. Joe rared back and blew his next pitch in there, and it cut the plate and Walton stood back and the umpire said, 'You're out!' Well, Walton was so mad he grabbed his bat and threw it over the railroad tracks down into the river. It was beautiful. So now the score is tied and Joe was the last man up for his team with nobody on. He hit the ball over the boxcars in left field for a home run."

Parental pride may have gilded that performance just a bit, but others will vouch for Joe's skill. Dom Casey, his American Legion coach, says that Joe played the outfield "like an infielder" and that he had an "absolute cannon" for an arm. "His senior year in Legion ball he threw out eighteen players at the plate," says Dom. "Sonny Werblin once asked me what it was Joe did best in baseball, and I told him Joe could charge a ball and make the play at home better than anyone I'd ever seen. A pro scout saw Joe throw six balls on a line without a bounce from left field to the plate, and he said he'd never seen anything like it. Joe could also hit. I remember seeing him hit back-to-back home runs at least four different times. He did have a little trouble with curves, it's true, but a Cubs scout told me that with two weeks practice he could start Joe in the majors."

Throwing baseballs, his coaches agree, is what molded Joe's passing skill. "Those nine years on the diamond taught him how to 'shoot' a football out there," says Dom Casey. Another factor that enabled Joe to become an exceptional thrower was his build. Though his mother constantly harassed him to "sit up straight," Joe's stoop-shouldered posture was not an act. Rather, it was a unique blessing. Dr. Nicholas calls it the "most impressive thing" about Joe because it allows him to have a ball cocked and ready for release without bringing it as far back as normal athletes. "I've studied this by plotting as many as four hundred points on films," says Dr. Nicholas, "and I've found that because Joe is round-shouldered his release from the back position takes only about eight hundredths of a second, the same as Johnny Unitas, who was also round-shouldered. Al Woodall's release, for instance, takes about ten hundredths of a second. That extra two hundredths is very important on a football field." Indeed, swift defensive linemen can move nearly ten yards in one second, one yard in a tenth of a second, and more than half a foot in two hundredths of a second. If one adds to this the momentum of a flying forearm, it becomes obvious that for a dropback passer a quick release can mean the difference between a completion and a concussion.

Joe's father was always very cautious with his son's arm. He used to rub it down in the evenings after Joe had burned some in over the home plate Mr. Namath had anchored in the street. At baseball games he refused to let Joe throw curve balls, and once when he saw that Joe was "limping with his arm," he yanked him out of a championship Little League game. "After that I wouldn't let him pitch anymore," says Mr. Namath. "His arm was too good to ruin that way."

As Joe's talents developed, so did his competitiveness and his sass. "Kids from other teams just loved to ride Joe," says Dom Casey. "But mostly they were jealous of the things he could do." It infuriated them that Joe could be so crafty yet never get caught. In one baseball game a player hit a ball that appeared to skim over the outfield fence, bounce off a second wire fence, and carom back to the base of the first fence. "Everybody thought the ball had gone over but Joe stuck his hand under the fence and called the umpire out to look," recalls Dom Casey. "He told the ump that the ball had landed in front of the fence and got caught underneath. The umpire believed him and made the hitter go back to second base. When Joe came to the dugout, a couple of our kids told him that it sure looked like the ball had gone over. 'Well, it did,' said Joe."

Joe soon learned how to use his acting ability in other situations. Once when stopped for speeding on the way home from a game, Joe instructed one of his passengers to screw up his face and start moaning. Joe then convinced the policeman that the player had a broken jaw and he was rushing him to the hospital. Another time when a group of Beaver Falls boys stayed in the dorms at the state teachers college in California, Pennsylvania, for a baseball all-star game, someone complained about vanishing linen. Before the players were allowed on the bus, an official made them all open their suitcases. Joe opened his and there lay six or seven neatly folded towels. "Joe put his hands on his hips and said, 'I wanna know who the hell put them in there!' " says Dom Casey. "He acted really mad. I knew he was lying. But he did a very good job at it."

When a situation called for quick thinking, on or off the field, Joe could usually rise to the occasion. Toward the end of his senior year in high school, Joe began sporting a goatee, and on a recruiting visit to the University of Miami, Head Coach Andy Gustafson, a stern, conservative man, questioned him about it.

"Mr. Namath," he said, "excuse me, but what's that thing under your chin?"

"Aw, we got a Christmas play back at the school," Joe replied. "And I'm playing the part of Christ."

Rich Niedbala, a reserve quarterback at Miami, was in the room at the time, staring out the window because he feared the confrontation. He told Dom Casey that when he heard Joe's answer he nearly fell through the glass, particularly because the coach believed Joe. "I knew then and there that anybody who could think that fast was destined to be a great quarterback," said Rich.

By the time Joe was ready to leave Beaver Falls he had become a leader. The role was not his by choice, but as Butch Ryan says, "Even with his foolishness we believed in him, because he was so damn good." On a smaller scale, Joe had already begun the type of boasting that would shock the sports world in January of 1969. He told locals how good he was and how many points his teams could score; once he even told his football coach that the team would not have to punt even though they were faced with third down and long yardage. On the next play Joe completed a long pass and the team went on to score.

"Joe boasted a lot like that," says Butch Ryan. "One week I remember we had an open date, so we all went up to watch New Castle play because we were playing them the next Friday. New Castle is a heavy betting town, and we were sitting with our orange and black Tiger jackets right in the middle of a bunch of bookies. They started asking us how many points they should give New Castle against us. Without hesitating Joe said, 'Give 'em thirty.' All the bookies roared because New Castle was a damn good team. Joe meant it, though. The next week we won by thirty-five.

"See, most of the things Joe boasted about he knew damn well he could do. I don't remember him ever not backing up what he said. In baseball he could throw guys out from the fence, and he could hit home runs past the railroad tracks into the piles of shale out there. But he also knew that he had great teams around him. In football we had two tremendous ends—Tom Krzemienski, who went on to play at Michigan State, and Tony Golmont, who played at North Carolina State. Thirteen players off that 1960 team got scholarships to major colleges. We'd have been a damn good team even without Joe."

Namath, who never did well in the classroom, spent most of his spare time hanging out rather than studying. His favorite spot was the Blue Room, a pool hall behind a lunch counter on Seventh Avenue. A seedy, dilapidated place with fourteen tables and a clock made of pool balls, the Blue Room is the kind of place where teen-agers can smoke, affect Paul Newman poses, and bet a dollar or two on the eight ball. One college recruiter, who had come to Beaver Falls to visit Namath, reportedly saw Joe lying spread-eagled on the hood of a car in front of the Blue Room and left town without even talking to him.

"It hasn't changed much since Joe was here," says the proprietor as he punches time cards on a Saturday afternoon. "We used to have some posters of Joe on the wall, from that movie he did about a rebel or whatever, him in a cowboy suit. But you know how those things get all tore up if you don't put them on cardboard or something. A few years ago they shot a TV show here, about his childhood, I guess. But mostly folks don't ask too much about Joe anymore."

If the Blue Room has forgotten Joe, the rest of the town hasn't. Joe Tronzo, the harried sports editor of the *Beaver County News-Tribune,* claims that his paper is not going to help outside writers anymore because they have been so unfair to Joe's reputation. "I watched this kid grow up and I've seen all these people come in here since 1965," he says, his voice rising. "We give out pictures and work hard and get nothing in return. No thanks. Nothing. Writers just say all these slanted things about Joe. Why don't they write about a guy like Lance Rentzel, a guy who exposes himself, or that Steeler, Holmes, who took a shot at an FBI man?"

Joe, in fact, never was in serious trouble as a boy, though as Butch Ryan suggests, that may have been partly because he didn't get caught. "We used to do things like shoot out the lights over at Morrow Motors, but we knew the tunnels and scrapyards so well that there was no way the cops could catch us," he says. "I guess we were all borderline between being good guys and hoodlums."

Despite his lament about not having any money, Joe always spent his summers playing baseball rather than working. He had time to fool around with girls, although he was by no means a ladies' man. "He could have had a lot more girls than he did," says Butch Ryan. "But he was cool about them. It was sort of, if you're here, fine; if not, okay. You couldn't really tell who his lady was."

When Joe's parents were divorced, some people worried that Joe might be adversely affected. But if he felt any great inner turmoil, he kept it to himself. "Both of his parents were good to Joe after they split up," says Dom Casey. "His mother gave him money and his dad followed his teams. If the divorce had bothered Joe at all he couldn't have looked as good as he did. My God, he was a fabulous athlete in high school."

Though neither of Joe's parents like to talk about their divorce, John Namath hints at a certain bitterness over his loss of control of Joe's life. Larry Bruno, the Beaver Falls football coach, called John during Joe's senior year and told him that if Joe went to summer school he could greatly increase the number of colleges that would accept him. "I called up Joe and told him that if he'd go to summer school for half a day and play ball or whatever he wanted to do after that, I'd make sure he had enough money and I'd even let him use my car a couple of nights a week," says Mr. Namath. "He said okay. But then he called back two weeks before school was out and said his mom was going to buy him a car instead. I told him he wouldn't go to summer school. But he said he would. She bought him a car then—an old piece of junk it was, too—and he never went to summer school. Because his mother did that, he lost his chance to go to any college he wanted."

Joe doesn't get back to Beaver Falls much anymore, except for special occasions like Christmas, when he will stop by to give his family presents. He frequently gives them checks made out for something they may have mentioned they could use—a vacation or a home improvement. Sometimes, if Joe has time to kill when he is in town, he will go down to Seventh Avenue and look for a man named Sluggo, a feebleminded fellow who spends a lot of time helping the police direct traffic. "He'll see Sluggo and say, 'Come on, let's have a few drinks,'" says Mr. Namath. "Then, sure as not, Sluggo will see me later and say, 'Oh, Mr. Namath, I saw Joe yesterday, and guess what? He gave me twenty dollars for a Christmas present.'"

Money isn't the only thing Joe gives as gifts, nor is it always the most appreciated. Whenever someone asks John Namath what the best present Joe has ever given him is, he immediately reaches for his wallet and pulls out a picture. It is a snapshot of Joey, aged eight, his hair slicked to the side, smiling with the same deep dimples that now cause women to gasp and defensive linemen to snarl. "I got this on a card Joe made himself," says Mr. Namath. "It said, 'Daddy, will you please be my Valentine?' I wouldn't trade it for anything in the world."

ELEVEN

*I've found there are three things
everybody thinks they can do: star
in a movie, write a book, and coach
a pro football team.*

—CHARLEY WINNER

Each Monday after home games, a diehard group of Jets boosters known as the "First-and-Ten Club" holds a luncheon at the Americana Hotel in Manhattan where they fete and quiz one of the Jets' players. By some cruel twist of fate, right guard Garry Puetz was the featured speaker the day after Baltimore dismembered the Jets' offensive line and sacked Namath a record seven times, handing the Jets their third straight loss. Puetz, a basically lighthearted yet conscientious young man, had already begun his penance on Sunday by telling the press that he had no excuses, that Mike Barnes physically whipped him, that yes, indeed, he had "stunk up the field." As the First-and-Tenners asked such questions as, "Do you think the Jets will hold a team under forty points before the Dow hits two thousand?" Garry continued to punish himself. He admitted the Jets were awful, that he had personally played an "embarrassing" game, that despite the fact he knew what he was doing wrong, his feet seemed to be "encased in cement."

The press appreciated Puetz's gags and his candor, and they wrote headlines like Larry Fox's: "Jets' Line: No Punch, Lots of Punch Lines." Behind his apparently facile comments, however, lay the fact that Puetz was whipping himself for a specific reason.

"I guess I did it as a reaction to all the excuses being made around here," he says in the locker room on Tuesday. "The coaches are ignoring stuff, buying all these lines, as if maybe it'll all just go away. It's really sad. Hell, after guys make excuses for so long, they begin to believe they actually aren't making mistakes."

Winston Hill, the man who does not like praise, who admits that if he weren't playing football, he'd think about the sport as much as he thinks about soccer, also does not like criticism. After the Colts' game, in which he was beaten nearly as dramatically as Puetz, Winston refused to comment on his performance, saying he wanted "to see the films first." In the offensive line meeting later, Winston even had an excuse for being called offside. And after seeing the films he said that he had not been whipped by the defense but that it was "a matter of circumstance."

"You know, when a guy won't even admit that being offside is his fault, something strange is going on," says Puetz. "Winston just played terrible. I mean, he's not coming off the ball, he doesn't know the plays, he's not in shape—nobody's ever seen him work out. He's got that tremendous balance, but that's not enough when you're getting old. The point is that nobody is correcting anything. We're all screwing up but nothing is happening, nobody is leading us. Hell, we've been without a team leader so long we don't know what one is."

In Brother Herb's Tuesday Bible class, eight Jets sit attentively, sharing the Gospel. Only little Jazz Jackson finds the talk about "the gates of hell" and "the wages of sin" unenlightening. He tries to stifle several immense yawns; then, shaking his head, he walks off to the training room where he lies down on a taping table and falls asleep. Otherwise, the class is doing nicely during these weeks of tribulation, as players find the need for "the Man" growing with their sense of failure. The Jesus movement does well on the Jets even during the good times. ("I got one interception in three games already," said Roscoe Word earlier in the year. "It can't be all me doing that.") But it does best when used as a crutch or a shield. As Winston Hill says in his session-ending prayer: "With faith in Jesus we can suffer through the pain, knowing that all is temporary." Even a 3-11 season will end someday. All the players mumble, "Amen."

Ironically, Joe Namath himself has been cited as providing some of the impetus for the rapid growth of the religious movement in pro football. His drinking and carrying on have provoked many a gridiron evangelist, and as *Sports Illustrated* wrote in a series on religion in sports, "Joe Namath's love life keeps the entire movement in paroxysms of disgust." Even more ironic is the fact that no less a personage than Winston Hill calls Joe "probably one of the more religious people on the team, in the world."

Joe was raised a Catholic, was once an altar boy, and still wears a St. Christopher medal around his neck. He considers himself religious. "I must talk to God twenty times a day," he says in all seriousness. "Mostly thanking Him. I don't go by a crippled person without asking God to take care of me. If it's a nice day I thank Him. I say my prayers at night—two Our Fathers, two Hail Marys, and an Act of Contrition—and I'll say a few words for my family."

Still, even the hard-core believers on the team are eyed with a degree of suspicion by some of the players. "I think it's rare that they're sincere," says Garry Puetz. "You should see what some of those guys do after their meetings."

Mike Adamle sees the religious movement as yet another indication of the Jets' failure to come to grips with reality. "I don't want to get struck dead or anything, but, well, Christ and football make strange bedfellows," he says over the phone. "Before games the Jets say a long prayer and then they follow it up with a cheer. Have you ever heard it? It goes: 'New York Jets, badder than a Mother-fucker! Ooh! Goddamn! Get off your ass and

Jam!' It's absurd. Part of the problem is that football is a game of one-upmanship—use any kind of edge you can and don't forget God. It's like, if He doesn't exist, well, okay, no harm done—but if He does and He goes for that sort of thing, then great. But the other part is that the Jets are always looking for a gimmick. I remember this ex-junkie or something who had been with the Redskins helping them with God; one day the Jets just brought him in like a lucky charm. We won that week, so they brought him back for another week. Then there was the time that somebody got it in their head that what was really important for football players was not strength but flexibility. So they brought in these two freaks called the Stretchers to stretch everybody. I mean it's just not like it is with the old NFL teams where there is pride going way back, a sense of tradition. Bud Grant would never bring in some Stretchers. The Jets would do anything if they thought it would help, bring in a karate expert or a guy to paint helmets."

The bulletin board next to Joe's locker has started to reflect the mood of the Jets' 2-4 record. It is pocked with derogatory newspaper clippings, inspirational poems, and a notice from Greg Gantt explaining that he had to collect extra money from everyone for the Halloween party because "Roscoe Word would not pay!"

Near the bottom of the board is a cartoon showing a losing football coach asking his players: "What happened to all that teamwork you guys showed during the players' strike?" The joke is a bitter one for the Jets. They had no teamwork during the September strike, and in many ways their divisiveness then paved the way for their dismal performance now. "If you can't stand up for something you supposedly believe in," says Phil Wise, "it's gonna show in your character in a game."

Steve Tannen, who had been the prime mover behind the Jets' brief walkout that caused the cancellation of the last preseason game against New England, admits that things would be a lot better now if the players had only stuck together, pro or con. "I look around and I see that the guys who didn't want to strike aren't playing worth a shit," he says. "But then I see that the guys who did want to strike aren't playing worth a shit either."

One of the factors that seriously undermined team unity was Joe Namath. His standard refrain to reporters is, "My stand during the strike has never been made public and it's not going to be." But as any of the Jets' players will tell you, Joe did not want to strike. With his monstrous salary he, of course, stood to lose more than anyone else. But as David Knight says, "Joe wasn't against it just for selfish reasons. He got up and said, 'Guys, I don't think we'll get all these things we're asking for and we may get hurt in the process. We've got a game coming up we should be getting ready for.' I really think he just wanted to play ball."

The players voted to strike despite Joe's opposition, but without his support they were easily divided by management. "We just melted," says Knight, who voted against the strike simply because he didn't want to lose any paychecks.

"The team folded because they didn't want to fight," says Phil Wise. "They were looking for any excuse they could to get out of it. It's like that fight Caster and that safety had the other day where they were kicking and throwing punches from way back here. If you really want to tangle, man, you lock up, you gotta tear those guys apart. We got a lot of guys who'll say they want to fight, but it's all mouth."

The problems, of course, are not confined solely to the players. Charley Winner needs a big win, perhaps a streak of them, to keep a firm hand on his job. Several of the writers go in to talk with President Phil Iselin about Charley's stability and come back clucking and shaking their heads. "He says Charley has his confidence and he absolutely won't fire him," says Paul Zimmerman, lighting a cigar. "That's bad. If he'd given him three games to turn things around, he'd have a better chance."

For his part, Joe Namath seems to be rolling well with the punches. Before a cold Thursday practice he walks into the locker room and plunks down on his stool. His eyes are half-closed and his hair disheveled.

"Oh my fuckin' head," he says, grinning. "I went home last night at eight and slept till eleven, then I went out. See, that's the way to do it. If you just go out at nine, you can't last."

As I sit by my locker dutifully preparing to go out and pretend I am Buffalo's J. D. Hill and Bob Chandler, both of whom I once covered back in college, I am reminded of Bobby Layne. A profound hell-raiser in his days as the Detroit Lions' helmsman, Layne was the last quarterback not to wear a face mask and one of the last to insist he could party all night and not be damaged by it. "I sleep fast," was his motto.

"Oh, my head," says Joe. "This morning I took three Bufferin and had a beer and it still hurts." He is cheerful and pleased with himself, like a dog returning from treeing every cat on the block.

After he is dressed he looks around for something extra to keep him warm. Suddenly his heavy-lidded eyes brighten. "Oh, yeh, Joey," he says. "Hey, Joey, that's right!" He reaches into the depths of his locker and pulls forth a green knit dickey. "Oh, yeh, Joey. Wear your dickey." He pulls on the garment, tucks it in and trots merrily out the door.

After practice Charley Winner walks through the complex looking sorry for himself. His hair is perfectly in place and his face is tan but his eyes are sad, as if searching for a lost friend. I walk over to him and for a while we talk about injuries. "You take a young kid like David Knight—now, I'm not saying anything against him—but the doctor said he should be ready by the fourth game, and he still isn't ready," Charley says. "I remember a running back we had at Baltimore. He was thirty-nine years old, he tore his knee up, and they said he was through for good. He had surgery and one month later he was playing."

The coach stops and then changes the subject. "You know, people just don't understand what a coach goes through during the week. I work every day and every night and never get to see my wife. Sometimes on Fridays I'll try to take her somewhere, but usually I can't even do that. A game often comes down to three plays or less, and if you happen to be successful on them—say, you kick a field goal at an early point in the game and that turns out to be the difference—people say, well, they came ready to play, they prepared harder. But the thing they don't realize is that you work just as hard if you lose." He turns away for a moment, looking confused, almost dumbfounded by the ironies of the game. "It's getting so hard just to send your kids to school," he says with a sigh. "I've got a daughter at the University of Missouri and all she talks about is how awful the food is there. She says they call it 'mystery meat' because nobody knows what it is."

Jazz Jackson, the pint-sized reserve running back whose locker is one stool from mine, is in good spirits despite the touches of gloom around him. In the last game he put himself in for one offensive play before the coaches realized what had happened and quickly sent in a regular. Like Lou Piccone, Jazz's expectations may outweigh his talents, but he's always trying. Not long ago I told him that he probably had the best name in the history of pro football. Today he struts to his locker saying, "Jazz Jackson, the greatest name in the history of pro football." Seeing Charley Winner at the other end of the room, he sits down and directs a song he has just composed toward the coach. The melody is from the old Ruby and the Romantics tune, "Our Day Will Come," and Jazz sings it just loud enough not to be heard:

> *My day will come*
> *And I'll have everything.*
> *My day will come,*
> *Then I will do my thing.*
> *They say that I am too small to run,*
> *To block someone,*
> *My day will come.*

The press release before the Sunday game with Buffalo is accurate and to the point. "The Jets are faced with a do or die situation," it reads. "If they possess any championship fiber, it will have to be displayed this afternoon." O. J. Simpson and his powerhouse line, the "Electric Company," have the Jets worried, but the entire defense is keyed to stop the ground game. On O.J.'s first run from scrimmage, Barzilauskas nails him in the backfield for a two-yard loss and the stands erupt with cheers. Joe Ferguson, the Bill's quarterback, begins throwing instead and finds the airways a bit easier to work. He quickly moves the Bills down the field, capping the drive with an 11-yard TD pass to Jim Braxton for a 7-0 lead. The Jets come back with two field goals and then a third one to take the lead 9-7 in the second quarter. On the ensuing kickoff Buffalo fumbles, the Jets recover at the 28, and Namath uses just 11 seconds before passing to Boozer for a touchdown, making it 16-7 Jets at the half.

Joe fires a 31-yard scoring pass to Eddie Bell to open the third quarter, and the Shea Stadium crowd sits numb with disbelief. Abruptly the Jets own a 23-7 lead, and the fans start chattering about a runaway. For once luck and the bounce of the ball seem to be on New York's side. Twice the Bills have scoring passes called back—once for holding and once because Ferguson steps over the line of scrimmage before throwing. Even the Jets' defense and the previously sievelike offensive line play nearly errorless games.

Then late in the third quarter Buffalo scores a quick field goal and touchdown to close the gap to 23-17. With less than six minutes to go in the game the Jets find themselves with the ball at Buffalo's 19, third and one. Riggins gains only a foot, making it fourth and less than a yard, and Charley Winner calls time out. Pat Leahy, who has already kicked consecutive field goals of 42, 41, and 31 yards, warms up expectantly on the sidelines. Three points would put the game out of reach, but the entire stadium is rocking with the chant, "Go for it! Go for it!" Charley Winner and Namath confer on the sidelines, and then Joe goes back in with a play. The fans cheer but soon fall silent with fear, as though they really hadn't wanted the coach to listen to them.

Their concern is justified as Riggins, who recently painted his fingernails green to go with his red toenails, is stopped for no gain in a huge pileup off left tackle.

Buffalo takes over, and four plays later Ferguson calls a little dump-pass play known as "54 to the Juice." O.J., who has been bottled for most of the day, takes the pass between Richard Woods and John Ebersole, puts a dipsy-doo on Delles Howell, and streaks 64 yards to paydirt. The Jets get the ball back for one last chance, but it's obvious they've lost their heart. Buffalo wins, 24–23.

On Monday the Jets' players and the press are still talking about Charley's decision to go for a first down rather than kicking a relatively safe field goal. "Can You Believe That Call!" screams the headline in the *New York Post,* and at least a few of the players feel equally amazed. "It was one of the stupidest plays I've ever seen," says Darrell Austin. But some of the players simply shake their heads and admit that the point is not that they went for the first down but that they couldn't get it. "I tell you what," says Phil Wise. "If you can't make that much, you ain't much of a ball club."

At the Tuesday press conference Charley Winner stands grim and vulnerable. He weakly defends his decision and then states how there is something wrong with a society that harasses the family of a losing football coach, which has recently happened to Mike McCormack of the Philadelphia Eagles. He adds that the abuse he has received in New York is a frightening thing. "I guess I should have realized the intensity of things here, but I didn't. Thank God I don't have a listed phone number."

"Do you plan to change the lineup, shake it up at all?" asks a reporter.

"What do you suggest?" says Charley, his eyes burning.

The only sound is of several writers, myself included, munching on the free sandwiches laid out before us.

TWELVE

*Journalism is popular, but it is popular
mainly as fiction. Life is one
world, and life seen in the
newspapers another.*

—G. K. CHESTERTON

Through the years, Joe Namath's relationship with the press has been as tempestuous as any domestic war between embattled spouses, the major difference being that in Joe's case there are a dozen or more spouses. In New York, ten newspapers cover the Jets on a more or less daily basis during the season. Several of these papers often have more than one writer working, one to do the play-by-play, one to do Joe. Add to this the many local radio and TV stations and magazines, plus the national networks and publications that are based in New York and find the Jets easy copy, and one gets an idea of the bizarre clutter of newsmen milling around the team. Several times during the season I would actually count more writers than players in the Jets' locker room after games.

A good portion of this gaggle comes along free of charge on road trips, filling the front section of the team plane with their cigars, typewriters, and demands for more free food. At the foreign park there is always the keyed-up local news contingent waiting with eager smiles and rehearsed questions, and to these people Namath generally turns his most gracious side. "He's cautious with us, but he'll give interviews to the visiting press like gangbusters," says Ike Kuhns of the *Newark Star-Ledger*. The reason for this is that the foreigners ask less probing questions, plus the fact that, in general, Joe simply does not like the New York press. The problem for Joe is the basic one for any celebrity who is grilled and quoted endlessly. Daily he is expected to pick his own brain, repeat platitudes, form opinions, state the truth, and be satisfied with the many versions of his words that appear in print. Before the sportswriters come roaring around the corner to get their postgame stories, Joe visibly flinches. And one should never believe the concept that someone as independent as a football player is unaffected by what is written about him. Randy Beverly, considered the weak link in the Jets' pre–Super Bowl secondary, approached Ike Kuhns before the 1969 game, misery in his eyes. "Do they really think I'm that bad?" he asked, meaning the writers. "Am I really that bad?" He stared at Ike Kuhns. "I must be that bad," he said, answering himself, walking away in despair. Happily, he turned out to be not that bad. In the game he intercepted two passes, a new Super Bowl record. Sportswriters, if anyone still needs to be told, are not always right.

The New York press, everyone admits, is a special breed. "They're vicious," says middle linebacker Jamie Rivers, who spent seven years in St. Louis. "They'll put you through the third degree." Charley Winner calls the whole media atmosphere "amazingly negative." "Back when we were two-and-two, I found out an editor had sent his reporter to the Jets with the instructions, 'Find something wrong. There's got to be something wrong.' " Even retired Weeb Ewbank, who came out to the Jets' complex one day to chat with some of his old players, began ripping the press. He finished his spiel by calling Howard Cosell "a dumb sonofabitch," Murray Chass a "nasty bastard," and Red Smith a man with a "bolshevik attitude."

The competition, the fear of being scooped, the pressure from the sheer weight of numbers—all tend to make the New York news gatherers prone to hyperbole, both good and bad. "Every time a New York player makes three tackles, some writer nominates him for the Hall of Fame," says David Knight. Even Namath grudgingly admits the press has helped him, at least financially. "Initially, skill got me to a certain level, but then celebrity status took over. The money I get is out of proportion with anybody else in football—more than double anybody—so it has to come down to situations, to publicity, to the news media." But Joe is quick to add, that doesn't excuse all the "out-and-out lies and bullshit" that have been printed about him. In reality, most of the "lies" Joe complains about are merely truths he hasn't wanted to appear in print.

"I went through a period when I wouldn't speak to any of the news media about anything," he says. "Pete Rozelle came over and said, 'Joe, if you don't talk to them I'm going to have to fine you.' I said, 'Let me understand this: if I don't talk to a newspaperman you're gonna fine me?' He said, 'It's in your contract that you have to communicate with the press.' 'Well,' I said, 'I'm not going to.' And when Pete was leaving the house—we get along well—he said, 'Come on, Joe, talk to 'em.' And I said, 'No. They're turds.' And they were, writing lies about me being involved with certain people and other things. I just don't like the man who has so little pride in his job that he'll write something just to be writing it, not knowing whether it's factual, not even giving a damn."

The catalyst for Joe's antipathy came about during the Bachelors III incident during the summer of 1969. Prior to that, his attitude toward the press had been one of flippancy, but abruptly he found himself in the midst of a serious investigation for which a wave of the hand or a few wisecracks were no match. His tears of frustration were proof that he honestly could not understand the extent to which he was being interrogated.

The incident also seemed to polarize the press, dividing them into groups who felt Joe was justified or not justified in his claims—loosely, "friends" or "enemies."

Some writers skidded 180 degrees in their opinions of Joe once the affair ended. As late as June of 1969, Dick Young had written articles praising Namath for his loyalty and sensitivity and talent. "He is the type of guy who thinks about other people, and worries about other people and pays the bills for other people," Young wrote on June 7, the day after Namath had announced his retirement. Then Young abruptly made an about-face and began ripping Namath with a ferocity verging on vendetta. He coined his sneering "Joey Baby" moniker and started calling the quarterback everything from a phony to a has-been. In a 1970 column under the heading "Joey Baby Fools Everybody but Himself," Young claimed that Namath's poise was a front. "The cool cat actually is uptight. It was all a sham, a put-on, this bravado, this cavalier, bon vivant, let-the-world-go-whistle pose. He has the most common sickness of all. He has a fear of failure, a fear of criticism. He is so scared stiff of it that he tosses his cookies the morning before the game." In a 1973 column headed sarcastically, "Where Has Joey's Fastball Gone?" Young claimed Namath's arm was finished and then admitted he disliked Joe rather intensely. "I cannot respect the man's philosophies, nor admire his unquenchable thirst for yes-men, for flattery," he wrote. Part of the reason for the distaste is the fact that Joe stopped talking to Young shortly after the Bachelors III incident. But Young, a man whose barbs fly in all directions, claims he can handle the silent treatment. "He isn't talking to me. It's all right, I'll survive. Sometimes my wife isn't talking to me and I number those among my fondest days."

Namath's current hesitance with the press often takes the form of rudeness. Once in the locker room I watched as he spurned a radio man who had begun a brief interview and then apparently asked a question Joe didn't like. "What did I say?" pleaded the man. "Joe, I'm sorry, can't we start over?" Joe walked away, and a look of terror covered the interviewer's face. "I have to get something," he begged, following. "Please, Joe. Any question you want to answer. Please . . ."

"Don't you understand? I'm not talking to you!" Joe bellowed, leaving the room.

"One of the problems is that Namath lumps everyone together as 'The Press,' " says Ike Kuhns. "But he doesn't read 'The Press'; he reads one or two newspapers and makes his decisions from there."

There are even those writers who claim that if Joe likes you, you must not be doing your job. According to Dick Young, a sportswriter makes his decision early in life as to whether he will be a real "newspaperman," and provoke his subjects' ire, or become "a hero worshipper, a house man, a sycophant, a dispenser of pap."

Paul Zimmerman, who shares with Young the distinction of not having communicated with Namath since 1969, feels that, as a breed, reporters perhaps should *not* be liked. "Face it. We probably are not very good people. There probably *is* something wrong with us for doing this. I mean we're fringers, we're not participants. We're not the real people."

Nevertheless, it is through the eyes and ultimately the personalities of the New York press that Joe Namath is presented to the world. And a multihued crowd it is. There is Jerry Eskenazi of the *Times,* a calm, detached man with a lightly cynical sense of humor. Once in the press box he began quietly pleading for one of the Jets to do poorly. "He's such a jerk. Please, God, don't make me have to talk to him." Eskenazi approves of Namath, calling him a "great quarterback who plays under maybe the worst conditions in the game." There is Larry Fox of the *Daily News,* a portly, bespectacled man with the look of a smiling economics professor and the pen of an assassin. There is Bob Dixon of the *Morristown* (N.J.) *Daily Record,* a long-haired, bearded youngster who enjoys covering Namath. "The thing I like about Joe is that if he's going to talk, he'll talk to anybody. He doesn't care who you are. Some stars only talk to the biggies." And there is Zimmerman of the *Post,* an ex-semipro offensive tackle whose inner feelings about Namath probably were best described in his own book, *A Thinking Man's Guide to Football.* In it he related the basic differences between linemen and quarterbacks: "One is slim and the other is fat. One gets the girl and the other one doesn't. And if the quarterbacks don't like the pounding they have to take, then the hell with them."

It is probably foolish to do so, seeing as how a man's humor changes from day to day (not to mention his subject's), but it seems possible to list the major New York writers simply by their attitudes toward Namath. These were my impressions during the 1975 season; if nothing else, they show that Joe elicits a variety of responses:

Anderson, *N.Y. Times*	pro
Dixon, *Morristown Daily Record*	pro
Eskenazi, *N.Y. Times*	pro
Fox, *Daily News*	con
Janoff, *L.I. Press*	neutral
Kerlan, *Bergen* (N.J.) *Record*	neutral
Kuhns, *Newark Star-Ledger*	neutral
Pepe, *Daily News*	neutral
Schaap, *Sport* magazine	pro
Usher, *Newsday*	pro
Young, *Daily News*	con
Zimmerman, *N.Y. Post*	con

One of Namath's major flaws in dealing with the press, at least in the past, has been a sort of childlike naiveté that keeps him from seeing the relationship between what he does and what is then written about him. He seems amazed that his curfew violations, walk-outs, and other exploits start the writers salivating. Of course, there is no way he could prepare himself for the pseudo-psychoanalytic pieces that occasionally spring up. *Life* magazine ran a classic in 1969 which stated, among other things, that "Joe's form chart suggests that he reacted last week out of ego, resentment of authority, an almost neurotic need to make others conform to his wishes and, very probably, that same delight in anarchy which motivates the more typical 'revolutionists' of his age."

One day in the locker room I asked Joe if he ever thought it was funny how his words came back to haunt him. "Yeh," he said, thinking it over. "I remember one time a few years back we played Houston and they beat us, I think it was about twenty-four to nothing. The press came in and asked me what the story was. 'Well,' I said, just kidding around, 'too much booze and too many broads.' Hey, you know what the damn headlines were? 'Booze and Broads Down the Jets!' "

Murray Janoff covers the Jets for the *Long Island Press,* a paper with a circulation of nearly 400,000, distributed mainly in Suffolk and Nassau Counties. At 61, Murray is the veteran of the sportswriters, the only one to have been with the Jets every season since they started out as the New York Titans in 1960. His demeanor is that of a silver-haired grandfather, kindly, glasses hanging from a chain around his neck; and when he talks to the players he talks quietly, paternally. He doesn't dig too hard, and he appears to have no enemies on the team. But then his paper is one of the least read by the players. As of January, 1976, it was the only one to still cost a dime.

"I've been on the beat for fifteen years now, and you might say I've seen several eras," he states. "The Titans of the old AFL were one—an unbelievable three years. You couldn't even call them an organization; they were a weak spoke in a weak wheel. I remember after a practice in San Diego before a road game, the buses that had dropped the players off didn't return because they hadn't been paid. The players got mad but there was nothing they could do. They just started hitchhiking back to the motel wearing their dirty uniforms. In 1963 the courts awarded the team to a syndicate headed by Sonny Werblin, and the Titans became the Jets. Werblin was a great showman and he believed that you could build anything if you got a star, that you could treat football just like theater. So he got Joe and gave him that famous contract. Something funny about that time was that no one ever announced that Joe's contract was for four hundred thousand dollars. It was just a rumor that nobody ever denied. Another thing people may not know is that the St. Louis Cardinals were bidding for Joe in the NFL, but they stopped around three hundred seventy-five thousand.

"That winter Werblin introduced Joe for the first time in New York with great style and flourish. Then a couple of days later I went out to Shea Stadium on a hunch. I walked into the dressing room and, sure enough, there was Joe. A friend from Beaver Falls was with him, but other than that the place was empty. Joe didn't know me from a hole in the ground, but I started talking to him and he very nicely answered my questions. What he was doing was running up and down the ramps, already starting his training program, even though it was cold and rainy and he'd had knee surgery not long before. He was very determined, and I immediately sensed that deep inside this guy was an intense pride, a pride that might get him in hassles someday. Here was somebody who *knew* he had to make himself ready to fulfill an obligation. I mean that really got me, the pride.

"My first impressions of him were very good, and I truthfully have to say that I can't recall ever having any problems speaking with him. Having covered the Jets for so long, I find that an aura of understanding develops between the athletes and me, a feeling of trust. I remember one time I ran into Joe just by accident, while I was vacationing in Puerto Rico, but if you run into a guy like Joe, you're still a newspaperman. He gave me a good story about playing out his contract, and I sent it back and it was very nice. I have a good, professional rapport with Joe—maybe it's him, maybe it's me, maybe it's just the situation, an oddity. One thing I firmly believe, though, is that when I ask certain questions I must give explanations, even without being asked to. Maybe Joe respects that. To me it's basic journalism.

"In their own minds I think all the reporters feel they have been fair to Joe. Even Dick Young—I've never known him to say something he didn't think was right. But see, Werblin's idea was to make Joe a star, somebody that everyone would write about with different feelings. And that's what has happened. Personally, I think Joe has grown up, he's more sedate now, not as boyish, not as bubbly. But the writers didn't create him—he created himself. He has made it extremely easy for us because you don't *overlook* the kind of things a Joe Namath does. Since the beginning there has always been this urgency surrounding Joe, like there was with Babe Ruth. I remember preseason games when the headlines would read 'Joe Namath versus So-and-So,' Joe against the other team. And I think that's how sports are always going to be; it's the nature of the beast to have one focal point.

"And one other thing, this has been a hell of a lot of fun. There's always been more than football, always something happening—the Signing, the Super Bowl, Bachelors III, the Decline. You never know what's going to greet you, what you're going to fall over when you get to the camp. I'll keep covering this team till I'm ninety."

Dick Schaap is the editor of *Sport* magazine and a sportscaster and newscaster for WNBC–TV. An intelligent, witty, harassed man, and a former senior editor of *Newsweek*, Schaap admits that sports coverage is not the most important thing in the world and therefore must be handled with several grains of salt. Though he does not cover Joe on a day-to-day basis, he remains important to the scene because he is the only newsman Joe actually seems to like. This is due largely to the fact that Schaap appreciates Joe's worth as a commodity and harbors no desire to change Namath's style. In fact, the two men are remarkably compatible. One feels that if Joe could write, he'd do so in Schaap's catchy, lightly sarcastic way, and if Schaap were a quarterback, he'd try for a lot of 80-yard touchdowns and blondes. In the book he collaborated on with Namath in 1969, *I Can't Wait Until Tomorrow . . . 'Cause I Get Better Looking Every Day,* Schaap pretty much defined the shallow, carefree image of Namath that has persisted relatively unchanged to this day.

"The book was definitely a fair reflection of Joe at that time," says Schaap. "It was 1969, the year of the Super Bowl, and Joe almost never said anything serious or had a serious thought. He was a master of the put-on and the put-down. He never looked forward and he never looked back—he was very much of the moment, and he didn't remember things. The celebrity business had been going on for four years, and that's when it hit its peak, everything was fun.

"Still, the book was very difficult to do. I took more time to get material from him than I ever have with anyone else. He didn't particularly like to talk about himself, or even talk, and he was the least reflective person I'd ever worked with. As it turned out, not all of the words are Joe's, but certainly the mood and tone are his. Some things were actually wilder than I could put in the book. Joe Namath Day in Beaver Falls was one of the funniest things in my life. Joe brought back these two broads as gifts for his hometown buddies. One was a hooker but the other was just a dedicated amateur. It was hysterical.

"At the time Joe's philosophy was, 'I should be able to do anything I want as long as it doesn't hurt anyone else.' His explanation for doing something like wearing white shoes would be simply, 'I felt like it.' He never probed any deeper than that. Now, I think he feels a little more strongly about making other people feel good, not just not hurting them. He's superficial, I guess, but superficial has a negative connotation—I think 'surface' is a better word. What you see is what you get; there's very little phoniness there.

"Intelligence-wise, I don't think there's any question that Joe is not book-smart. He seems to react more through other people—I mean, like when he announced he was going to retire, he seemed more upset about how Bear Bryant was going to react than about his future. I remember the night he announced it we went out to dinner at Trader Vic's. He ate everything on his plate except for some rice, and I said, 'You better eat that and get used to it because that may be all you're going to get from now on.' He said, 'Okay, fine, if that's all I'm gonna eat, I don't care. It's not gonna bother me.'

"Intelligence really has nothing to do with being good copy, however, or even being a good conversationalist. Heavy intellectuals can be very boring. I've spent time with Norman Podhoretz and he can bore the hell out of you, and there's no doubt his IQ is probably as vast as any forty-three athletes in the world. After a while you find that just being smart doesn't mean a thing."

Ike Kuhns of the *Newark Star-Ledger* is a portly, forty-year-old sportswriter who says he's been a sports "fan" all his life. He went to Syracuse University when Jimmy Brown was an All-American running back; and one of his biggest undergraduate thrills was getting a free trip from his parents to watch Brown perform in the Orange Bowl. Ike had originally hoped to get into sports broadcasting but upon graduation found no jobs available. The reason: his voice was too high. He joined the *Star-Ledger* instead and in 1967 was sent up to Peekskill Military Academy to cover the Jets for the first time.

"What first shocked me was how free and easy the whole Jets' camp was," Kuhns says. "I'd played high school ball and it was all very gung-ho, and I'd read about Vince Lombardi and his nutcracker drills, and then I saw Weeb and this group and I could not believe they were getting ready for a football game. Everybody was smiling and taking it easy. I still have a vivid picture of that first day with Joe. I'll never forget it because all the writers got together to interview him in a corner of the field. He had long hair for the first time, and while we asked him questions he just sat on the grass picking buttercups and sniffing them. The whole time, just picking buttercups one by one and putting them up to his nose.

"By then Joe was already getting reluctant to talk to the press—he'd already had stuff appear about his swinging and missing curfews, and then the very next week he was apparently involved in a fight in a bar with the sports editor from *Time*. After the third preseason game, I asked him some questions by myself for the first time and he looked at me and said, 'Who the hell are you? Who do you work for?' And I'd already introduced myself to him several times. I was really turned off, so I went back to interviewing him in groups. The thing is, he felt and still feels the press gives him a bum rap. But he perpetrates his own myths, like he did in that book with Schaap. I remember him bitching about some *Daily News* photos of him where he was holding a glass in his hand. They said it was a drink, but Joe said it was just to spit tobacco in. In that book all he talked about was what a swinger he was. So how the hell is anybody supposed to know?

"I will admit that some of his claims are valid, like when he says he's been misquoted. I've been at press conferences and then read things later that I know he didn't say, where his answer to a question was changed. I remember one time when he wasn't giving interviews to newspapers, but he would for radio or TV, figuring that if what he said was taped it couldn't be changed. I listened in while he was taped for twenty minutes by Ed Ingles of WINS, and then I heard the tape on radio and they only used thirty seconds of it. It was a part where he said his knee was bothering him a little. Ed Ingles asked why, and Joe said, jokingly, that it was from dancing. It didn't come out as a joke. It came out: 'Joe Namath hurt his leg dancing.'

"But I also remember a time when Joe did a TV interview, and he told the guy that he was going to retire because he was sick of football. Other stations picked this up and ran it, too. But Joe had been putting the guy on, it was a gag, only nobody knew it. I'm not sure if the announcer got fired, but it sure didn't help his position any. I've found there are times when Joe says things tongue-in-cheek and you have to just sit there and wait and wait, to see what happens, to find out whether he means what he said or not. Joe won't answer a question he thinks is stupid, either, and that can be a problem because sometimes he doesn't understand that the writer may just want the obvious answer. Once when Joe was hurt, Al Woodall was starting and had just played a terrible game at Shea. I asked Al if the performance had hurt him, if he had lost any confidence because of it. Before he could answer, Namath turned around and said, 'What the fuck kind of question is that? What a stupid goddamn thing to ask!' And, of course, that turned the whole interview off. I knew what Al would have said but I just wanted it in his own words.

"It's good and it's bad covering Namath. Down in Miami before the Super Bowl some of the press were calling Joe this big-mouthed sonofabitch and saying why doesn't he just shut up. I said, Jesus, what do you want? More of that bland, gee-whiz, we-all-put-our-pants-on-one-leg-at-a-time garbage? But then little things can start to get to you—like the extra security, like this one time after a game when a truck sneaked Joe out of the stadium and dropped him off on an island in the middle of an expressway and the bus had to go get him. Or the time in St. Louis when a mob was pounding on the bus and we tried to leave and somebody's hand was reaching in Joe's window and they just pulled the whole damn thing out. We drove to the airport without a window. He's news but he's also pressure. My job would be a lot easier if he had gone somewhere else."

George Usher, a quiet, black-haired, worried man in nondescript clothes, covers the Jets for *Newsday,* the largest paper on Long Island. George seldom smiles, looking usually as somber as an undertaker. Once in the press box at Shea, Jerry Eskenazi asked him why he looked so serious. "It's my game face," said George, without a smile. Indeed, there are times when George seems to take his work a little too seriously, when he is bothered by things the other writers seem to accept. One day a few of the writers were talking about the players' religious convictions.

"I can't believe those guys can go in and pray and then come right out and get drunk and hustle girls and everything," said George. "It's so incredibly hypocritical."

"I'm surprised at you, George," said Paul Zimmerman.

"But really, how can they *do* what they do?"

George started his Jets beat in the summer of 1966, Namath's sophomore season.

"When I first went to Peekskill the place was in pretty bad shape," he says. "The showers didn't work, the food was bad, there was no air-conditioning. All the guys did was bitch. But they were a tight group and I think it was all the bitching that really pulled them together. This year at Hofstra with the beautiful conditions nobody's bitching, everybody's happy, and I think that's part of the problem.

"I remember the first time I saw Joe. I was awed because of his reputation, but somehow I expected him to be bigger; I just imagined him to be real big. Then I remember him talking about all the celebrities he'd met, like it was an everyday occurrence, and I started wondering if he was throwing names around to impress people. Overall, though, I thought he was a regular guy who was pretty close to everybody on the team. But he always gave me the impression of someone who was tormented by his publicity. He seemed to be trying to decide how to react, how to handle it all, like he was not quite in control yet. One day he showed me a press clipping he carried with him, a story in which a guy said something about how Joe deserved to have his knees torn up. 'How could somebody write this?' Joe asked. He was really very hurt by it.

"In 1968 when Sonny Werblin left the Jets, Joe seemed to get more serious, and the team came together more because of it. That same year he got voted captain and it really moved him. I can't understand why he wasn't voted captain this year, unless it's because there are more black guys now and they voted for Winston Hill because he's one of their leaders. Or maybe the young players just don't think too highly of Joe. Maybe it was just an oversight. I think it's a mistake, anyway, and I think it's hurt Joe.

"As far as I'm concerned, I could say I don't like Joe's

life-style, but then it doesn't really affect me one bit. He's moody, but he has a right to be. And his snuff and spitting, well, that's his business. Actually, there are very few things about him I don't like. Last spring I did a series about him while he was working out in Alabama, and it was like seeing a different person. He was in his natural setting. He lifted weights and worked very hard, but he was also amazingly relaxed. When I got down there he greeted me like an old friend and started telling me stories about how he used to daydream in high school all the time, and how he got the only hit off Sam McDowell in a baseball game, things like that. Hoot Owl was there, and one day we went over to his house in this little town that was just a shade above Tobacco Road. His house was all broken down, with doors falling off their frames and wood rotting and things all caved in, but Joe was completely at home. He had a drink and sat there happy as can be, holding Hoot Owl's baby.

"One day when Joe was working out in Tuscaloosa I got to catch his passes for the first time ever. When I first offered to do it, he said no, he wanted to throw to a regular receiver. But then I think he felt he'd hurt my feelings, because he came back and said, 'Okay, George, I'll throw it to you.' I'm an old end but it was amazing to catch those balls. My hands were sore for days.

"At night we went in to his restaurant in town, and a lot of times Joe greeted people at the door. He didn't do it to be showy but because he felt it was wrong not to. I remember there were three old ladies standing around outside with a camera, and Joe went up to them and asked if they'd like him to take their picture. He knew full well they'd want him in there, but he didn't want to come on like that. They said, 'Oh, Joe! Oh, Joe! You get in it!' And so he did, putting his arms around the ladies, and then they talked for a long time.

"The next night Jimmy Walsh, Joe's lawyer, called about some business with the WFL, and Joe immediately changed. He became upset, the balance had been broken. This girl came in the restaurant and sat next to him at the bar. She was bombed and Joe sort of moved away from her. She wasn't ugly but she kept calling him 'big shot' and 'big man' and moving whenever he did. He moved some more and she moved, and then he cursed under his breath and muttered, 'I don't need this!' and left the building. She drove him out of his own place. And I'm sure she probably hates him and is bad-mouthing him to this day."

If there is one major reason why the atmosphere surrounding the Jets and the press is so incredibly high-strung, it is surely because of Paul Zimmerman, the *New York Post* representative. A frenetic, driven man whose wife is a successful pediatrician, Zimmerman covers football as though many lives depended on it. A keeper of mind-boggling minutiae, Zimmerman times pregame national anthems ("The longest was 2:27 by the New Christy Minstrels") and charts every play on his own personalized graphs. "He keeps notes on notes and files on files," says one of the sportswriters. "I don't believe Paul has ever believed a press release," adds Jerry Eskenazi.

A $21,000-a-year avowed Socialist who readily admits that he "couldn't do what the players are doing, but with a little training they could do what I'm doing," Paul played college football at Stanford and Columbia and later won All-Service honors in the Army. At Columbia he also earned money as a human guinea pig for LSD research. He still has vivid recollections of those experiments—of time standing still, of nurses' faces disintegrating, of running through the winter streets of Manhattan without a jacket, sweltering with claustrophobia. These days he barrels through the crowds en route to the locker room, virtually trampling anyone in his way. His writing is incisive, biting, and filled with editorialisms; a wine-lover, he once had the *Post*'s wine column, but lost it because of his harsh criticism. Despite his abrasiveness, his facts are almost always correct, and he is not above making endless calls to check one minor point.

The other writers have mixed opinions about Zimmerman. "Sometimes Paul reminds me of my four-year-old grandchild," says Murray Janoff. George Usher admits that at times he thinks Zimmerman is "actually crazy." He is not, but he does have a formidable problem in that he must cover the Jets without being able to talk to their star. "I told Paul years ago, 'I don't want to stay mad at you, so you and I just won't talk,'" states Namath. The freeze-out has forced Zimmerman to periodically go to other reporters and ask them to ask his questions. Though still as aggressive as ever, Zimmerman seems to be carrying a certain weariness with him of late. "I don't have many friends left," he told me one day at practice. "Nobody wants to talk to me. It didn't used to be like that."

The old days, he implies, were a lot of fun. "In 'sixty-six, 'sixty-seven, and 'sixty-eight, my first three years, Joe was still pretty happy-go-lucky, and there was this tremendous divergence on the team between guys who disliked him intensely and guys who liked him. It made it interesting because the club was basically split. When they won the Super Bowl it was still split. That's why when people now say Joe splits the team apart and guys resent him and that's why they're losing, it's a cheap shot because all that was there when they were champions. Gerry Philbin and Matt Snell didn't like him at all, but they still played their asses off for him.

"One thing I've noticed through the years is that Joe is a very strong factor for black-white relations. I've seen him get on a bus or go into the dining room and deliberately—too many times for it to be an accident—go over to where the black guys are and plunk himself down in the middle. Pretty soon another white guy will come over, and before long it's an integrated group. I think he does it consciously because he realizes he's got to stay cool with everybody. He wants to do what's best for himself, which in turn means what is best for the team. I mean, Joe is all for himself—he wants the team to do well, but *he* doesn't make the big sacrifices. In 'sixty-seven, for instance, he partied all night with

Sonny Werblin and then blew the Denver game, knocking the Jets out of the race.

"I've never seen Joe actually drunk for a game, but I've seen him practice drunk. In Charlotte, there was a famous practice before an exhibition game in 'sixty-seven when he got plastered at a boosters' club party and then came out and was taking snaps backwards and throwing hook-shot passes behind his back and laughing and carrying on. The guy in Charlotte wrote a very funny piece about it. Weeb, I don't know if he even cared. He was afraid of Joe. All coaches are afraid of Joe. They can't control him. He's bigger than any coach.

"I don't know what it is about Namath—he drinks too much, he screws around. Who's the movie actor like that? Errol Flynn? Maybe Joe is the Errol Flynn of football. He appeals to something universal. I mean, my mother, for God's sake, *she's* hung up on him. She's mad at him because he won't talk to me, but still she hangs on everything he does. Has the media done it? How could we, we're slaves to our readership. Do you think I *like* to write about Namath all the time? But if I don't and the other papers do, I'll have a phone call waking me up at seven in the morning saying what the fuck's wrong with you! I hate it. I'd like to write about guys like Lou Piccone, that's where it's at. Namath is show business.

"It's very tough for me. I thought Namath was a pretty good guy until 'sixty-nine—but it's hard to say you like somebody when you know they hate you. It started with the Bachelors III thing when I was out at camp getting players' reactions and two cityside reporters were covering Namath in town, doing cheapshot gossip stuff. The paper insisted on combining our bylines and Joe quit talking to me shortly after that. I left a note in his locker saying let's talk about this, but he never responded. That was over six years ago and we haven't talked since.

"All I know about the actual Bachelors III investigation is what I've heard from other people. At the beginning I heard that there was all this police stuff involved, that the cops had a stakeout on some guys who were hanging around there, gamblers and people like that. I'm pretty sure Pete Rozelle, the NFL commissioner, had been notified that the cops were getting ready to move in on Bachelors III and Joe. Rozelle is very image conscious about the league and its players, so he called Namath in and told him to get out of the place. Some people construed it as Rozelle trying to run people's lives; others said he was just protecting his product.

"What kind of a place was Bachelors III? Well, I was in there once and I saw a bank of something like a dozen telephones downstairs. Now how many telephones do you usually see in a restaurant? One, maybe two? What does a place need twelve telephones for unless they're doing some kind of business? I'm not saying for sure I went down there and saw guys booking bets or pushers operating or anything like that, but I think Rozelle did Joe a real favor by telling him to get out of Bachelors III, to forget it. Then all of a sudden Rozelle comes out as the fascist, this guy who's telling people how to run their lives. George Sauer tearfully announces he's quitting. Pete Lammons says, 'Oh, God, they can't do this to us.' What bullshit. Rozelle simply protected his product, football, the NFL—just like they do in big business. Some people told me some things about the incident that made a lot of sense, but I never printed the stuff or used it. I never did anything with it.

"As a quarterback I believe Joe is flawed. He has a good arm but his physical liabilities affect his perform-ance—he can't get out of trouble. And another thing: he gives up on games. There comes a time when I see him say, 'Aw, fuck it,' and he just flings the ball out there. The quality quarterbacks are always thinking how can I beat you, how can I set you up, always working. Okay, Namath hasn't played on a winning team for six years. I don't know if that's his fault, but he hasn't. He's so used to losing I can see a point where he'll see a guy covered and he'll throw there anyway, saying shit, either we get a TD or we get off the field. Maybe if they'd had a good defense since the Super Bowl, history would evaluate him as the greatest ever. Who knows. Instead, every time he gets the ball he's got to put six points on the board because sure as hell the defense is gonna give it up, and it's affected his outlook. What's funny is that in the Super Bowl year we were all writing, 'What's Wrong with Namath? He's Not Throwing TDs!' Well, what had happened was that he knew he had a good defense and he had become the most meticulous, conservative quarterback I'd ever seen. He stayed out of the way and he didn't screw things up.

"He used to be able to move around, too, take sideways steps and even roll out. When Ben Davidson broke his cheekbone in 'sixty-seven, Joe had rolled way out there to the right. That was the year also when players started hitting him high. I remember in the Denver game Dave Costa speared Joe in the chest, and even though Joe threw a touchdown pass on the next play, he was in bad shape, gasping for air, with a big bruise. Costa was so upset he came into the dressing room after the game to apologize. I interviewed him and asked him why he was so concerned, and he said, 'Well, shit, he's the man who put our league across, he's the reason we're all making good money.'

"Two years ago I thought the Jets should have gotten rid of Namath, traded him for some defense and a new QB. At the time I wrote that it was like a guy on relief with a valuable diamond in his mattress—should he keep it or should he buy groceries with it? But the brass here think that if they traded Namath they couldn't face up to their fans. They should go sit in the stands. My wife does and she says you should hear what the people say, to a man they're screaming at Namath. But the owners here are bottom-line guys, jerks. Phil Iselin sits in his director's booth and has drinks with a couple of his garment center buddies and thinks he's running a football team. If the club got rid of Namath, made a dynamic trade, got a good defense, played competitive football, I know the fans would be happier. They're disgusted with this overbalanced, strange, megalomaniacal, off-balance, moody, introspective, weirdo-flake, fuck-up team.

"What will Joe do when he's through with football? I think he'll be a show-biz guy, a Dean Martin type character, somebody who plays in all the celebrity golf tournaments. He can't sing and he doesn't have a super agent, so he'll probably just be a personality, a host. I hate to admit it, but I think his name will carry him on and on. . . .

"You know, I haven't been having a great time covering the Jets. A lot of people think I'm a bastard. In this job you've got to keep telling yourself that the best reporters are the biggest pains, that nobody has ever liked guys whose basic job is snooping and prying. But we're needed. And I like to do it. Sometimes I enjoy being a bastard. I remember once we played a touch football game before the Jets' game at Shea Stadium—the newspaper writers against the magazine writers—and a guy on the magazine team intercepted a pass and I slugged him. Everybody starting booing. Then the captain of our team took me out of the game, and everybody really started booing. I talked to my wife after the game—she'd been in the stands—and I said what a thrilling thing it was to have thousands of people booing me. It was spectacular! Booing is great, it's sensational. Anybody can get cheers, Miss America gets cheers. But for fringers, booing is great.

"I'll tell you the truth, as far as this Namath thing goes, I don't know what to say, I've been removed from him for so long. I see him now as an embittered reporter who has been forced to go to war. And I don't take Namath on in print because of one reason: I absolutely can't win. He's bigger than any of us."

THIRTEEN

*When the world has once begun to
use us ill, it afterwards continues
the same treatment with less scruple
or ceremony, as men do to a whore.*
—JONATHAN SWIFT

As the Jets prepare for their second game against Baltimore, they give the distinct impression of a team on the run. "The call" against Buffalo has not been forgotten, nor has the fact that the Jets are slipping in every category. Cornerbacks Roscoe Word and Rich Sowells, in particular, have become frighteningly vulnerable, and their ineptitude is seen as part of the general malaise and mounting confusion. "Man, when the other team comes up to the line and it all looks like Chinese checkers to you, how can you play right?" asks safety Delles Howell.

More than a few of the players are bothered by the lack of effort that seems to be coming from certain quarters. "I remember other seasons when guys were just putting in time," says Richard Caster. "And there are some guys who just want to finish up now. I've already been a part of the worst team record ever, and I don't want that to happen again. I have to live here year round and hear how terrible we are. And poor Joe, the other day I heard a TV announcer saying he ought to retire, that he looked sad out there. But I'll tell you, Joe still tries harder than anyone. He must feel like he's pissing straight up."

Godwin Turk, the young and promising outside linebacker, has recently threatened to quit football entirely because of all the sandbaggers on the Jets. His alternative—working in a funeral parlor—is something he looks forward to with bizarre relish. "I got interested in it when I was a little kid in Houston," he says. "There was a funeral home right behind the church, and when everybody went to church I went over there. I hated church. At first the man would see me coming all the time and he wouldn't say nothing, but then one time I was messing with one of the bodies and he hollered at me. He asked me what I was doing, and I said I liked being around there. I'd been dreaming about the business; I'd even had a dream where I was getting embalmed. So he gave me a job. I started going to wakes, seeing all sorts of things, like women with Bibles in their caskets, their glasses on their faces like they was gonna read their way into heaven. I was about twelve, but I was never scared. It was something I was meant to do. I'd be in the back with four or five bodies, cleaning 'em up, moving 'em around. Ain't no problem, they ain't going nowhere. I've already been to embalming school and had my two years apprenticeship, and I want to open my own place this off-season. I'm serious about quitting football. I want peace of mind. Embalming and football don't relate—I'm dealing with the dead, and football, it's with the live."

On Monday, Paul Zimmerman wrote that the Jets were taking the entire skid a little too lightly, that their rowdiness on the way home from defeats was embarrassing. As his main source he quoted Dave Herman, for ten years an offensive guard with the Jets and now a radio announcer.

"I remember plane flights back when we lost by a point," said Herman. "Guys like Paul Rochester and Jim Turner and Carl McAdams, you couldn't talk to 'em. If you'd look at 'em the wrong way they'd kill you. I remember twelve-hour plane flights from the Coast in the early days . . . twelve hours wasn't enough time for them to unwind enough to even smile."

As a veteran of the Super Bowl team, Herman knew, as did the others who played then, that something was basically different about that team. And it was not simply a matter of talent. "Right now we've definitely got more talent than we had on the Super Bowl team," says Randy Rasmussen. "No doubt about it. But the difference comes from potential and output. In 'sixty-eight we had a funny team; we couldn't beat you physically—the linebackers couldn't stay with the backs out of the backfield, the defensive backs couldn't stay with fast receivers, the lines weren't big or strong—but damn, we'd find some way to beat you." Don Maynard, the veteran wide receiver who was cut from the Jets in 1973, recalls that the team was "loose" but sure of itself. "It was a very mature group; even a guy like Rasmussen, a rookie, was very mature in his thinking. We didn't have pep talks before every game; nobody had to wind us up to do battle."

Along with the overall team shrewdness was a decided intensity, a gutsy quality that allowed relatively small or untalented players like Pete Lammons, John Elliott, Johnny Sample, or Gerry Philbin to consistently play over their heads. In a classic statement to that effect the undersized Philbin told a reporter, "If I could put my desire in Verlon Biggs's body, people would have to pay me to let them live."

Namath recalls, more than anything else, the intelligence with which the team played. "They said we didn't have talent. Okay. But mentally we never missed a block or a pattern. Goddamn, those last six games including the Super Bowl were close to perfection mentally."

Whatever the qualities were that brought the Jets to the top back then, it is interesting that they accumulated so quickly and dissipated so rapidly. One could almost say the injection of Joe Namath in 1965 led to a magic one-shot transformance, like the addition of yeast to unleavened bread, or a princess's kiss to a frog. That there was no staying power whatever simply makes the catalysis that much more provoking. With or without Namath, the Jets have been losers—before he came they were 29-39-2 and since his arrival they have been 71-79-4. Indeed, in sixteen years of existence they have managed only three winning seasons—the season before, including, and immediately after the Super Bowl. A graph such as the one on page 165 can perhaps best show this strange history.

On Friday, with New York City sinking deeper in its accumulated financial woes, there is a good deal of discussion in the media about what will happen if the city defaults. Before practice, I decide to ask a few of the players what default, if it occurs, will mean to them.

After thinking deeply about the question, Winston Hill starts in on a long, involved lecture about free things, parks, social conditions, and revolving tax brackets. After a few minutes I tell him that he's given a good answer.

"What do you mean, good?" he asks, his brow wrinkling. "Does there have to be judgment? I'm not trying to make a *good* answer . . ."

Richard Wood, the rookie linebacker from USC, says he's worried everyone will flee New York for California. "They'll go from default to the fault," he says. "Then the whole place is gonna fall in the ocean. Not just maybe, either. I got shook twice by earthquakes back at school. One time I almost got thrown out of bed."

Garry Puetz speaks for most of the players, however, with his rather selfish concern. "If it affects the price of an off-season shot of bourbon in Valparaiso, Indiana," he says. "I'm demanding two billion from Ford to bail the city out."

While the team is out practicing I stroll up to the reception area to see if there is any gossip to be learned from the secretaries. Tim Davey, the short, plump assistant trainer, is there hunched over one of the desks, signing a stack of eight-by-ten glossy photos of Namath.

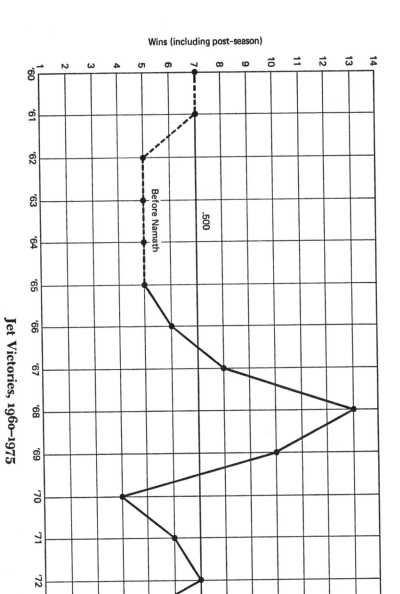

Jet Victories, 1960–1975

Wins (including post–season)

.500

Before Namath

I look over his shoulder as he writes, "Good Luck and Best Wishes—Joe Namath."

"Doesn't he do a lovely job?" smiles Elsie Cohen, the head secretary.

I look again and, from what I can tell, Tim Davey's script is a dead ringer for Joe's. I ask him if he's had a lot of practice, and he turns to me with a what-do-*you*-think look. The pictures, it turns out, are to be sent to a school or a Boy Scout troop or something along that line. Joe gets a lot of such blanket requests.

In fact, a great deal of Joe's time in public is consumed with autograph signing, something about which he is remarkably good-humored. Even in the locker room he continually signs pictures for teammates, their wives, their friends. He even signs a number of photos for the coaches. One day after Joe had been writing for quite a while, Roscoe Word approached with a program he wanted him to sign. "No," said Joe, backing off with exaggerated steps. "No more."

"Come on, Joe," said Roscoe. "This is for a kid in the hospital."

"Roscoe, you're always hounding me for autographs."

"Please, Joe. See, what the problem is, the kid's got disease."

Joe suppressed a grin.

"He's got disease?"

"Yeh, he's got disease."

"Well, why didn't you say so. Gimme the pen."

Through the years Joe's signings have varied. For a while he drew peace symbols after his name, and during another period he drew smiling faces. For quite a while he signed "Joe Willie Namath" but stopped doing that in the early '70s. One thing he has always done is try to make his notes personalized, following the person's name with a message. Business Manager John Free remembers one time when he had a picture for Joe to sign. It was for an eight-year-old boy who was dying of leukemia, and John had no idea what a suitable inscription might be. He gave the picture to Joe, who thought for a few seconds and then wrote: "To Billy—

Wherever you go, may you go in peace—Your friend, Joe Namath."

On Thursday it is cold and raining, but after bundling up I join the team for practice. Charley Winner had asked me where I'd been lately; and after thinking about it I realized it was all the losing going on that was making me less excited about running patterns.

Today I help Joe loosen up, catching his twenty-yard passes and lobbing them back. Periodically I break into a deep smile simply because catching a pass from Namath is such a luxurious thing, like biting into a good steak or slamming the door of a Rolls-Royce—precise, well-crafted, and exceedingly pleasurable to experience, it is something I feel I could do endlessly. After a while, though, I move over by Joe to catch the return passes from Barkum and Knight. Joe's left wrist is so sore from the pounding he took in last week's loss to Miami that he can no longer catch the ball and must have it handed to him. After that game, in which he was sacked three times and battered several more times, headlines on sports pages asked, "How much more pain can Namath take?"

Before the game, however, Joe had been in a light-hearted mood. If he had any worries, they were about the team rather than himself. In a midweek interview with Dick Schaap for ABC-TV, Joe had deadpanned all his lines until Schaap asked if the Jets were confident. "Oh, yeh, we're very confident," said Joe. "I mean they only beat us by forty-three points the last time."

All week long the entire team had been rather odd. While standing in the hallway at the dorm I had watched Roscoe Word grinning out at me from between the closing elevator doors, playing with the blade of a knife. All night long Delles Howell played his stereo so loud I could hear it through three walls. Then one day the motif seemed to be shoes. Jazz Jackson came out for practice wearing one white shoe and one black shoe. "See, the black one's for cuttin' and the white one's for glidin'," he said. Then he shrugged. "Too many blows on the head, I guess." After practice Greg Gantt went into the shower nude except for a pair of cleats. "All you need is a mask and you could star on Forty-second Street," one of the players hollered at Gantt as he tromped off to the sauna.

But the height of the absurdity came in the team meeting held at the Miami Beach hotel the night before the game. A good number of the players had been drinking beforehand, and they sat restlessly as Charley Winner spoke.

"I don't like us taking a back seat to any team," he said. "I'm tired of taking a back seat to Shula, and I know Joe's tired of taking a back seat to Griese . . ."

Joe stood up, angry. "I'm not taking a back seat to anyone!" he cried.

Immediately after that, John Riggins got up and began telling the team how Kansas, his alma mater, had upset Oklahoma that day. He held a cigar in his hand, waving it as he spoke, and before long a few of the players started giggling.

"This is not funny!" Charley yelled.

Riggins continued his speech and then finished by yelling, "We can beat the hell out of 'em! Isn't that right!"

The room was silent. Riggins tried again.

"Isn't that RIGHT!"

This time everybody cheered and whistled and pounded on the tables. Riggins put the cigar in his mouth, smiled, and sat down. After that the team split into offensive and defensive meetings, and Garry Puetz, who felt the situation demanded a show of enthusiasm, picked up a glass, bit it in half, and ate it.

On the way out of the meeting room, several of the players could barely control their laughter. "I don't think the guys were too fired up tonight," said Darrell Austin. "Mostly they were just pretty drunk."

The Saturday before the Baltimore game, Charley Winner is in relatively good spirits, feeling that this may well be the week the Jets' fortunes change. "Anything can happen," he says. "I remember back in about

1954 when I was with the Colts and we played the Redskins. The fog was so thick you could barely see. I was on the phones at the fifty-yard-line, and we put another coach on the phones at the goal line. We were down six with about a minute to go and we fumbled away the ball. The coach at the goal line threw down his head phone in disgust and said, 'I'm sick of this! I'm quitting!' He walked off and he never came back. And the funny thing is, we got the ball back a few seconds later. We threw a pass, and for some reason the safety tried to intercept instead of batting it down, the ball bounced off his hands, and the tight end caught it and ran for a touchdown. We won, but the coach was gone and he didn't even know it. Funny game."

While everybody else was getting on the bus, Charley then called me into one of the meeting rooms. He was very earnest. "I know we can win if we just follow this checklist," he said. He very solemnly raised a screen in front of the blackboard to reveal the notes he had chalked out for his players. The list looked rather simple and clichéd to me, but I listened attentively as he read through it.

Check Points to Beat Colts

1. Protect the QB—time to pass
2. Block for runs—don't get fancy (last week we tried to finesse)
3. Control the ball—no turnovers
4. Contain #7—Jones
5. Don't Give Up the Big Play
6. Control #26—Mitchell—know where he is
7. Force turnovers
8. Think positive—think win
9. BE PHYSICAL
10. Second half

On the bus, David Knight sits near Wayne Mulligan, and the two begin eyeing each other suspiciously. Mulligan is wearing a dark three-piece suit, and Knight, sporting a three-day growth of beard, wears his faded blue jeans, maroon shirt, and Earth Shoes. As usual the two soon fall into a debate.

"So you think Gus Hall shouldn't be allowed on the ticket because he's a Communist?" asks Knight.

"That's right."

"Thank you, Senator Mulligan."

"Thank you, voice of the left."

"Thank you, voice of my father."

"Now I got him mad. He's gonna get his bomb kit and blow up the bus."

"Look at you, Wayne. I bet you even have shoe trees."

"Knight looks like something out of *Rolling Stone.* That's a compliment to him—'Do I really?' "

"Wayne's idea of coexistence is to drop the bomb on them first."

"You want to get on your knees and be friends."

"I'll put dirt on the bombs and grow flowers on them."

"Go read *Ramparts* and *National Lampoon.* "

"What about *Time?* That's Commie-slanted isn't it?"

"Here," says Mulligan, pointing at Knight and addressing the front half of the bus, "is a perfect example of freedom without responsibility."

At the Baltimore Hilton a suite has been reserved for the Jets' officials and coaches and the press to have a small party. The main treat is to be steamed Chesapeake crabs, and everyone sits around drinking and watching TV, waiting for the food to arrive. An hour goes by with no sign of delivery, and a few of the guests begin to leave. Paul Zimmerman sits on a stool by the bar with two cups of wine, sniffing and snorting and sloshing, but for the most part things are oppressively dull. After two hours, all of the Jets' brass have left, as have most of the writers. When the crates of crustaceans finally arrive three hours late, the only people left in the room are Charley Winner, Larry Fox, backfield coach Jim Spavital, the two Jets' public relations men, Frank Ramos and Jim Trecker, and me.

There are enough crabs for dozens of eaters, and Charley Winner's eyes grow large. A man with an astonishing appetite, he sets to with knife and wooden mallet, boring through one crab after another like a hamster shelling seeds. No one else knows how to eat the animals, so Charley must give constant demonstrations. "Here, this is called the 'key.' Pull it out like this . . . now tear this back and yank this thing off and cut here . . . that's right, Jim . . . now scrape out that black stuff, that's fat, and dig in right back here . . . and here . . ." All the while he's talking, Charley continues his onslaught, a man possessed. He plows through six, ten, a dozen, eighteen, two dozen crabs without a sign of fatigue, stopping only to guzzle beer or check his watch.

There is a reason for his mania. During World War II, Charley was shot down over Germany and sent to a prison camp where he was interrogated and starved for two weeks. After that there was still very little food; Charley spent a lot of time wandering the grounds eating dandelion greens. Combined with an underfed childhood in New Jersey, the experience made him vow that if he survived he would never slight himself for food again. Even so, tonight's performance is a rare one. Charley continues to eat after everyone is done, and then an hour or two later stops at the hotel restaurant for ribs and chicken. A short while after that, he calls assistant coach Ken Shipp into the restaurant to help with a platter of oysters.

If there is meaning to the feast, it may be that Charley has felt the weight of forces beyond his control, that he is indulging in the last pleasures of a condemned man. Certainly the Jets' spectacle on Sunday is enough of an atrocity to warrant such actions. The defense gives up 502 yards, Namath is sacked five times, another punt is blocked, and the Jets are utterly humiliated, 52–19.

The players themselves seem to be motivated by a massive death wish. Darrell Austin knocks himself unconscious while crashing through a wedge. Bob Prout gets knocked cold on a punt. Rich Lewis and Ed Taylor manage to collide while missing a tackle and knock each other out. But the crowning act comes in the third quarter after Baltimore scores its 37th point and the Jets' defensive unit walks to the sideline. Ed Galigher, the 6-foot-4, 253-pound right tackle whom Mike Adamle has described as "just a good old California beach boy," abruptly goes berserk with frustration and rage and attacks reserve linebacker Steve Reese, punching him repeatedly in the face. It takes two of the largest Jet players, Richard Neal and Carl Barzilauskas, to calm Galigher down. By the time they do, the writers, most of whom have watched the fight in silent disbelief, are bending to their typewriters, tapping out that now, finally, the Jets have lost all semblance of respectability.

After the game Jerry Davis, a defensive back who had joined the team only five days before, moving into the room next to mine at Tower F, stands shocked and silent. "I mean, I can't believe it," he says finally. "I'm from the WFL and all, but this is like a dream. Are these really the New York Jets?"

FOURTEEN

*There is this loose projectile flying
through space and it's destined to
fall unless you intersect with it.
There is an incredible pleasure
involved when you and the object
meet perfectly. That, I think, is the
thrill of catching a pass.*
—DAVID KNIGHT

*They aren't even playing the same
game we are. It's like they're out
there having their own little picnic.*
—RANDY RASMUSSEN, ABOUT THE JETS'
RECEIVERS

"Well, Eddie Bell is a speedster, mostly an outside
threat, the out-and-ups and the goes. And then in tough
situations Joe would rather go to Barkum, because he's
bigger and he can get his body in front; he can come in
and play tight end on most plays. For shorter stuff Joe
likes to go to me because I'm even bigger and more
durable than those other guys. Now David Knight, he
probably has the best hands of any receiver I've seen in
the league, and he's got great moves. But he doesn't have
a lot of muscle; even Eddie's better put together than he
is. David's taken a lot of whacks where they've had to
help him up or carry him off. But he's got those flypaper
hands."

173

That is the way Richard Caster describes the Jets' receiver corps, one of the more diverse groups on any pro team. Until the total collapse of the Jets at midseason, when every element of the team became suspect, the receivers were considered by many to be the best unit in the game. They still are one of the most colorful. Jerome Barkum, the split end, is a lighthearted four-year veteran with a striking resemblance to Muhammad Ali, a characteristic he exploits in frequent locker room battles with Steve Reese, a Joe Frazier look-alike. On one thigh Jerome has a "J" and on the other a "B" tattooed in blue ink, homemade markings done as a boy back in Gulfport, Mississippi. He is friendly and easygoing, and never far from his stereo or portable tape deck. "Jerome says the music relaxes him," says Caster. "Sometimes I think it relaxes him too much." At 6 feet 4 inches, 212 pounds, Barkum presents Namath with a large target, and his strength enables him to outwrestle opponents for the ball, something he did in the 1974 Buffalo game when he literally tore the winning touchdown pass away from safety Donnie Walker. Always smiling on the field, Jerome enjoys talking to opponents and handing them the ball after he has beaten them. He says that playing with Joe is "a thrill, something I can look back on forever."

Flanker Eddie Bell, though much like Barkum in spirit, is vastly different in the flesh. At 5 feet 9 inches, 160 pounds, he is close to, if not *the* smallest man in professional football. He has excellent speed, however ("Otherwise I'd probably be dead"), and better-than-average hands. As a senior at Idaho State in 1970 he set three national small-college records, including an amazing one-season total of 96 catches for 1,522 yards and 20 touchdowns. He astounded his hometown buddies in Waco, Texas, by getting drafted into the pros. "They see me now and they say, 'Damn, Eddie, if you made it, I *know* I could have.' They're right, too. But they never did anything except stand on corners." The flashiest dresser on the Jets, with several stunning hat, cape, and suit ensembles, Eddie has had to work hard to maintain respect throughout the league. "In my first game as a rookie we played Buffalo, and I was lined up opposite Butch Byrd, their 215-pound All-Pro cornerback," he says. "I put my head down, and when I took off he knocked the absolute shit out of me. While I was lying there he smiled and said, 'Welcome to the NFL.' "

The differences between tight end Richard Caster and Eddie Bell begin with their jersey numbers, 88 and 7, and continue from there. Eight inches taller and seventy pounds heavier, Caster is one of the most imposing figures ever at a receiving spot. A two-time Pro Bowl selection who began his career as a split end, Caster is considered the fastest man on the team and the possessor of more natural tools than anyone except possibly Namath. With a career average of nearly 20 yards per catch, he has done as much as any receiver to hasten the growth of zone defenses. "Normal coverages just weren't designed for a tight end like Caster," says Kerry Reardon of the Chiefs. "No strong safety can stay with him man for man."

Caster's description of himself as being a primary target only for short passes is somewhat incorrect. One of Namath's favorite tactics is to throw a 20-yard pass to Caster and then let him run 50 yards with the ball. In 1972 when the Colts tried to cover him man-to-man, Caster caught 6 passes for 204 yards and 3 touchdowns, two of the scores coming on bombs of 79 and 80 yards. In 1974 he snagged an 89-yarder against Miami, the longest pass in the Jets' history. This season he reset the record against the Colts with a 91-yard slant off a safety blitz. "Sometimes you get lucky," he says. "But on that one we weren't lucky because Joe and I knew exactly what they were doing. It's performance and execution in that case."

Caster also has an intelligence nearly the equal of his physical prowess. He has found, however, that a high IQ is not necessarily an advantage in his profession. "Richard is an insecure, nervous young man," says Paul Zimmerman, and indeed there was a time when it seemed Caster's mind might stand between him and stardom.

His first few years he constantly dropped easy passes, and the Shea Stadium boos rang out. "I'd drop a ball because I was careless," he says. "And then I'd worry about the next one and about the fans getting on me. I'd be so tight, the ball would hit my fingers and they wouldn't even react." With time he recovered his confidence and says now, "I'm programmed. I'm like a computer." He still struggles for an evenness of flow, however—something he works at by practicing yoga and figuring out runs on his bass guitar. Occasionally I'd hear him thumping away at the dorm, and I'd walk over and watch his huge fingers climbing the bass frets. "I've always wanted to be a bass player," he'd say. "You see them onstage and they're the coldest bitches up there."

Blessed with a photographic memory, Richard has never had any trouble remembering the Jets' elaborate "tree of learning" pass routes. "I just write the plays down on paper, depending on circumstances, and after I look at them I can remember which ones I wrote first, second, third, however they went." What he calls his "tendency to look at things as problems to solve" has also enabled him to make valuable in-game suggestions. For instance, this year in the Kansas City game he called the winning play. "I told Joe in the huddle and he snapped his fingers and said, 'Right!' It was a play-action pass off what we call our crossing Jet patterns, the one-thirty-three Jet. After the game, Coach Shipp told Joe he was glad he called it, and Joe said, 'I didn't. Caster did.' That was nice of him."

The biggest anomaly among the receivers, and, for that matter, the entire Jets team, is long-haired, undernourished, self-contained David Knight. Although supposedly recovered from his preseason knee surgery, David has barely played at all this year, the coaches evidently feeling he isn't ready mentally. Dave has given them little reason to believe otherwise, limping for half the season and never once stopping into the coach's office to discuss his condition. "That's not the way I am," he says with a shrug. Instead he sits through meetings daydreaming about 1974 when he finished eighth in the AFC in receptions with 40 catches and 4 touchdowns and made some of the most acrobatic grabs since Raymond Berry. "I close my eyes while they're showing films, and I can see the ball coming at me in slow motion. It's as big as a beach ball, coming right in, and the instant I catch it the crowd just goes bozo." Catching passes is David's prime motivation in life. "I'll tell you this," he says. "I'd trade forty catches again for about five years of sex."

The only white receiver of the group, David is not fast or large (6 feet 1 1/2 inches, as low as 170 pounds), and with his hair and teen-idol face, he more closely resembles a wayward rock star than an athlete. In fact, he considers his craft to be a similar type performance, and allusions to the music scene constantly fill his dialogue. Upon meeting Namath as a rookie in 1973, Dave told newsmen it was just like seeing Mick Jagger for the first time; and after thinking for a while, he will state that the only thing that might approximate catching footballs is being Jimmy Page, the lead guitar player for Led Zeppelin. "I make no bones about it," he says. "I love people cheering for me. I only wish I could play without a helmet so my hair would flow in the wind."

Dave did not play organized football until his junior year in high school, limiting his involvement to after-school contests with his brothers in front of their Alexandria, Virginia, home. "My brothers were rough guys," he says now. "One of them undercut another on pavement and broke both his elbows. They used to call me 'Watermelon Head' and hold me down and shoot me with BB guns." In the pickup games, Dave always played receiver, finding that chasing after a pass was something he was meant to do. "I just found it so inviting to try to catch anything," he says. "I would literally dive over the top of a car for a pass. I remember the first time I caught a ball I caught it exactly like I do now, with my hands out, fingers around the nose, following it with my eyes. If you'll excuse me, I knew right off the bat I was good."

Dave's preoccupation with his art has led him into a

certain vain, effete posture. When the Jets put him back for punt returns his rookie year, he fair-caught everything, regardless of the coverage. On kickoff returns he downed everything in the end zone. Once when he was a freshman at William and Mary he was forced to play a half at offensive guard because of team injuries. He blocked no one. "On the snap I rolled into a ball and dropped to the ground," he states. Oddly enough, David was once a head hunter. As a defensive back his junior year in high school, he remembers that "if there was a pileup and a guy's head was sticking up, I'd come through there—and boom!—shave it right off." As a senior wide receiver, however, he began getting instructions from his coach to the effect that he was special, that receivers didn't demean themselves like common football players, by blocking or hitting or getting dirty. "I didn't like it at first," he says. "But after a while I'd watch Fred Biletnikoff on TV, and I'd say to myself, 'That sucker doesn't block at all.' So eventually in games I'd just trot off to the side if I wasn't on a pass route."

"I was a wide receiver for a while," says Richard Caster, who understands the metamorphosis. "And I could feel myself starting to fall into certain patterns that go with the position. You know you're isolated and people are watching you, so you develop a personalized jog, you dress up with wrist bands and spatted-down shoes, you try to become almost pretty."

David Knight has become aloof enough even to enjoy the catcalls from dissenting crowds. "They throw things at me and call me a hippie faggot and I love it," he says. His basic insouciance led him to ask for a $50,000 bonus his rookie year, despite the fact he was an eleventh-round draft choice. "They sent the letter back saying an imposter named David Knight wrote it," he recalls. He now makes $40,000 a year, sleeps on a bare mattress, owns virtually no worldly goods, and claims he'd be happy making nothing at all if the Jets would give him free room and board. "There's not a whole lot I care about," he says. "If somebody would take care of me and let me catch passes I'd be content."

All the Jets' receivers admit that catching a Namath pass is a pleasurable thing. "When I first got here I couldn't believe Joe's anticipation," says Eddie Bell. "He could drill it to you or lay it in like he'd walked down and handed you the thing." David Knight calls it the "easiest" ball he's ever had to catch. "Some guys throw too early or too late, but with Joe you can turn your head and focus and get comfortable. The ball settles in but it doesn't float. You can't really describe it." Richard Caster points out that Joe is very protective of his receivers: "A quarterback has your fate in his hands. Some guys will lead their receivers right into a bunch of broken ribs or a concussion. Joe never does that." Indeed, not once the whole season would I see a receiver run into a clothesline or a waiting forearm while trying for a Namath pass.

Oddly enough, one of the things Caster likes about Joe is the fact that he can't scramble. "There's always just one place to look for the ball," Caster says. "It makes it easy to pick up the ball's true trajectory so you can figure how to handle it best. Sometimes I can't even see Joe at all, he's completely buried in the pocket. But it doesn't matter, because I can just look to an area. I know he's still there."

When blinded by a rush, Namath will sometimes simply throw to an area, counting on his memory for accuracy. And other times he will communicate a new variation of a pattern in midplay. "Last year against Buffalo I was running a corner route, but since they were in a zone the cornerback just stayed back there," says Caster. "There was no place else to go, so I just kept on, figuring Joe would hang the ball up and I'd try to outjump the guy. But what he did was he threw it to my left even though I was facing right. It was a desperate situation but he knew I'd be able to read what he was doing. It looked like a real bad pass, an out thrown way behind me. But we got a touchdown, and now all the teams are doing it."

Despite their appreciation of Joe's skills, none of the receivers are too awestruck to be unaware of his flaws.

"If Joe would only use all his receivers, we'd have the best attack in football," says Eddie Bell. The fact that Namath throws only sporadically to his backs is one of the reasons his completion average is generally low (five years below 50 percent) and his interceptions so high (an average of 22 for each of his 8 complete seasons). "I remember a game or two where Joe really went to Riggins with short stuff," says David Knight. "The next game those linebackers were all over the backs, and it just opened everything up for the wide receivers. This year Joe just seems to toss a token one over there every so often, and then it's bombs away."

Ken Shipp sees Joe's problem as being physical as well as mental. "The name of the game now-a-damn-times is short stuff," he frowns. "It's something I've tried to teach him ever since I've been here. But you're talking about a guy who was brought up when they were playing man-to-man and you could always hit so many long ones. And I'll tell you what, Joe doesn't throw short very well. In the St. Louis game last week we had Caster wide open on a third and three early in the game and Joe overthrew him. It was a good call but he just missed the pass. Throwing short ain't as easy as you might think."

According to the receivers, Joe's famed quick release is not overly effective because of the pass routes the team uses. "It's actually negated by our patterns, which are six yards longer than anyone elses," says Knight. "I don't know why, I think Joe said he likes the longer patterns because he likes the time to read, plus he says, 'I can throw it that far easily, so why get ten when you can get twenty.'" In a way, however, the long patterns —the post-flags, the out and ups, the QPs, the streaks, the flies, the goes—are as much the receivers' favorites as they are Joe's. "We can't win with Joe," says Knight. "I think it's impossible. But see, I don't care. It's just a game and I'm more than willing to play on the same team with Joe because I can have a good time with him. He'll throw deep to you even if you've only got a half-step on the defender. And I love that."

Eddie Bell knows the thrill of the deep ones, his favorite being a last-minute 83-yard reception that beat the Colts in 1972, after which he went "totally bananas." But in chatting with defensive backs, Bell has found they like Joe to go long, too. "They tell me Joe's long ones are easy to intercept. I guess that makes sense. If a ball's easy to catch, it should be easy to pick off."

Aside from Joe's normal tendencies, the receivers have noticed special changes this last season. "Is there a difference in the way he throws now?" says Eddie Bell. "I'd rather not answer that. . . . Yeh, there is. What do the other guys say?" For the most part they say things like David Knight, who readily admits Joe's arm is slowly fading. "When I was a rookie he threw an out perfect ninety-five percent of the time. Now I'd say it's down to about seventy-five percent. I guess when you're thirty-two things just start to happen."

Of course, not all of the passing problems are of Joe's doing. Qualified as they are, none of the Jets' receivers has true deep-threat speed à la Mel Gray, Cliff Branch, or Isaac Curtis. "What Joe could really use is a true burner," says Coach Sam Rutigliano. "Somebody who just scares the hell out of defenders."

With the Jets' sophisticated "read on the run" patterns, a heavy burden is placed on Jet receivers to be accurate as well as agile. They must analyze zones correctly, make proper decisions, and reach proper depths, or else coordination becomes mere guesswork. This year, in particular, Joe has been plagued by a rash of undisciplined, incorrect, or just sloppy patterns. "I told Joe after one game, 'Hey, man, this is a conspiracy,' " says J. J. Jones. "I was joking but I might have been telling the truth. It's almost like those guys are screwing up on purpose."

Eddie Bell, in particular, is notorious for his less than precise routes. But David Knight sees the problem as still being partially Namath's. "What happens a lot of times is you go down to your proper depth and turn and Joe's already been sacked. So you want to cut things off and get into your pattern quick. Eddie sometimes cuts off five whole yards on a pattern, which really messes up the timing. But after you've gone ten yards you always think, man, it's been a long time."

Don Maynard, the Jets' split end from 1960 to 1973, recalls that his group of receivers, which included Pete Lammons, George Sauer, and Bake Turner, were a very disciplined crowd with a great rapport with Namath. An eccentric penny pincher from Texas, Maynard put the same type of effort into his pass receiving as he did into his money-saving routines. During training camp Don saved such things as toilet paper and light bulbs, and for a long time he drove an ancient turquoise Ford coupe known as the "El Paso Flame Thrower," a 160,000-mile heap he had converted to burn butane rather than gasoline. While practicing catching footballs, Maynard worked constantly with one eye closed ("It maybe makes you grasp a little harder"), and though right-handed he usually returned the ball with his left ("Heck, I already could throw with the right one").

Such diligence paid off as Maynard became the first player in the history of the game to go over 10,000 yards in receptions. He caught Namath's first professional touchdown and feels that the relationship he and the other receivers developed with Joe was the real secret to their success. "I don't believe there has ever been a team to have its three receivers plus its quarterback make the All-Star team like we did in 1969," he says. "Everybody got along with Joe. He was just a plain old guy. We used to go out for chili or something and shoot the breeze. I remember right before the Super Bowl with the millions of people watching on TV, old Weeb said, 'I don't know who to introduce, the offense or the defense.' And Joe said, 'Well, just introduce the seniors, Coach.' I tell you, the place cracked up.

"Some guys used to razz Joe a little—Wahoo McDaniel especially. Finally, it got so bad a few of us said, 'Well, bull corn, Wahoo, why'nt you shut up and leave people 'lone.' All the receivers liked Joe. George was a little different, but Bake and Pete and I were all Texas types, never any problems. When we were playing, Joe only had to take care of Joe, because we knew what we were doing. I mean if he told me to run a post at seven yards, he knew I'd run it come heck or high water. We had timing. I remember one game when the defense blitzed and Joe threw quick because of the rush. I turned to the left, and just when I did the ball hit me and sorta stuck between my left elbow and my chest, and I was tackled all at the same time. That was good timing. Now, well, I wouldn't want to say this, but some of those guys have got Joe so hesitant it's a shame. Some of those guys you could flush down the commode."

If Namath and his current receivers aren't the best of friends, they still get along quite well on the field. "This is the closest I've ever seen a team—grade school, high school, or college," says Jerome Barkum. "I think Joe brings about unity. I mean, he's a cat it's hard to tell he's a millionaire." Richard Caster feels Joe has opened up in recent years. "He's more personal now. When I came here in 'seventy, it was like I'd see Joe in practice and then I'd never see him again. Things were mostly formal. Then starting last season it seemed guys would give parties, and Joe would be the first one there. Sometimes in the huddle now, if we're ever way ahead, Joe may say, 'Where you going after the game?' And I'll say, 'I'm going out to dinner,' or something. Then he may say, 'There's a chick behind the bench, she keeps calling you. Why don't you check her out?' Maybe he's trying to atone for things he did in the past."

Namath's coolest relationship is with David Knight, part of which may stem from Knight's ambivalence toward him. Though they hardly ever speak, Knight claims he's never lost an argument with Joe. One such incident occurred last season in the Houston game when Joe audibled to an out pattern because of man coverage. On the play the receiver has the option of turning upfield if he sees the cornerback coming hard. Knight did this, while Joe threw the out. The ball was intercepted and run back for a touchdown. On the sidelines Joe got mad at Knight but Dave said, "No, Joe, it's your fault." In the films Dave turned out to be correct, if not entirely reasonable.

"I don't know if Joe likes me or not," Knight says. "But sometimes he does strange things. I remember a game in Atlanta when I came in for Barkum because he bruised his knee. I could tell it was only for one play because Bark had walked off the field by himself. Joe must have known, too. He called a thirty-five-wham where I have to come in and play tight end. Joe was laughing when he called it. He knew the play was going over me, and he knew I had to go one-on-one with Claude Humphrey, their All-Pro defensive end. It was absurd. It was like I didn't even hit Humphrey; he just made a sandwich out of me and Boozer about five yards deep in the backfield."

Nevertheless, a completed pass carries with it the ability to transcend petty irritations, something David recognizes in his relationship with Joe. "After a big completion the two of you feel really close," he says. "I remember last year I caught a long touchdown over Zeke Moore's head, and when I looked up the first thing I saw was Joe running down to shake my hand. He said, 'You really make me smell like a rose,' and I just said, 'Man, you put it right there.' It's an incredible feeling, but it's over almost immediately. Still, you'll play a lot of football trying to feel it again. To have it last forever would be heaven."

FIFTEEN

He was a hell of a guy. He went farther out of his way to correct things than anyone, but he just couldn't find the answers.

—JOE NAMATH

On the Wednesday before the St. Louis game I walk over to the training complex, scarcely noticing the unusual number of cars in the parking lot. Inside the building I can't help noticing the throngs of people milling about—men with writing tablets, men with TV cameras, men in business suits. I walk over to Connie Nicholas, one of the secretaries, and ask what is going on.

"Didn't you hear?" she says. "They fired Charley."

Although it shouldn't have, for some reason the news shocked me. Perhaps I believed Phil Iselin's statement that Charley Winner had the confidence of the directors; maybe I was beginning to believe that a six-game losing streak and a 2-7 record were pretty standard fare for the Jets. Certainly I knew things weren't in the best of shape. The New York press, in a rather bad moment of excess, had tried to label the Galigher-Reese incident a racially motivated flare-up. It wasn't, but the air had to be cleared via needless interviews, and some of the tension lingered. "Ed's excitable like that," said Richard Neal. "I remember one time he went after Tannen the same way, but we got to him first. What's funny is that I've never seen a year like this. Until now there haven't been any fights. Turk and some other black guy got into it in training camp, but that's it."

Yesterday, Bob Prout, the reserve safetyman who lived down the hall from me, had been released. In the Colts game he'd blown a blocking assignment, allowing Gantt's punt to be blocked. Bob was a nice person, although rather high-strung, as defensive backs tend to be. I'd bring my guitar over to his room and we'd try to play together, but it was impossible because he strummed with such frenzy. "I can't play slow," he told me. "I just go faster and faster. Some Beatles songs I play in fifteen or twenty seconds." He was gone, and Jamie Rivers and Phil Wise had been put on injured reserve, and there had been those chants coming from the stands at Shea: "Good-bye, Char-ley, we hate to see you go." There had been, after all, sufficient warning.

The mimeographed press release that is being circulated quotes Phil Iselin as saying, "I had truly hoped that we could turn it around like we did last year. That's why I made my earlier statement that we would not change coaches in the middle of the season, if at all, but the turnaround is not there. The continued public speculation was damaging to everybody, including Charley. Therefore, we decided to make the change now."

The new interim head coach will be Ken Shipp, the offensive coordinator and receiver coach. His job, Al Ward makes it very clear, will last only until the end of the season, regardless of the team's performance. He has been chosen to fill in simply because "he'd been handling half the team" and because "he has a good rapport with Joe Namath."

As the reporting hubbub continues, Shipp, a forty-six-year-old down-home boy from Old Hickory, Tennessee, wanders the halls, his pipe in hand, looking anything but ecstatic. "When they told me what was happening, I had no emotion at all," he says. "Here's a man I've worked with five years, gone. I've always looked forward to being a head coach, but now it happens and I feel nothing."

The players are of mixed opinions, although most seem to have accepted the firing as easily as they have accepted everything else this season.

"Maybe my thing—maybe we needed something bizarre to shake things up," says Ed Galigher. "With Prout gone and now Charley, maybe it'll throw some fear into guys. Fear has been missing. The season doesn't mean shit now, anyway."

Jazz Jackson is trying to let the situation just slide by, to keep his world simple and clean and absurd. "Look at me," he says walking into the locker room with both biceps flexed, wearing nothing but a jock. "I come to camp weighing two forty-five and now I'm down to one seventy-three. I blame this, ladies and gentlemen, on a serious lack of soul food here on Long Island."

For his part, Namath, who has never been through an abrupt coaching change before, is a bit more pensive. "For the first time I've had to ask myself why a coach was fired," he says. "Okay, it came down to the fact that we couldn't win and Charley, being head coach, got the blame. That's just the way it is. But I know that I am in part responsible for not doing my job right. We looked for answers, we'd sit down and talk, but we couldn't find 'em. We had meetings where Charley brought up him personally taking over the defense. But he said he wouldn't because what we were doing was sound, there was nothing to change. And he was right.

"I started to say this sounds corny, but it's not corny— I remember down at Alabama when Coach Bryant was getting interviewed by the Northern press and they kept asking him about his defense. How can you stop running games, stop kickoff returns, hold punt returns to negative yardage, this and that—what kind of defense do you teach? they asked. He said, well, it's not the defense, it's the people playing it. And that's where it's at."

I knock on Charley's closed door and he says to come in. He has a box on his desk and he is filling it with his things—books, papers, a football with a handle on it ("You can't fumble this one," he'd laughed), pens, pencils, a racketball racket.

"I got a call from George Allen," he says. "And he told me the most important thing is to keep active. Play something, he said. Stay active."

Charley's hair is neatly combed and his eyes are still a bright, pale blue, nearly as light as Namath's, but they are red-rimmed and hurt. He whacks the racket on the palm of his hand and takes a few steps back and forth, the equivalent of pacing in this small room.

"I just felt we were on the verge of doing something," he says as though talking to himself. "Of turning it around. Maybe they didn't want me to turn it around, I don't know. . . . It's a cruel business. . . ." He shakes his head and moves behind his desk. As a coach, Charley had never seemed to be in complete control. Even I, as a semiparticipant, could feel the lack of inspiration coming from his on-field speeches. He had seemed like the kind of coach a player could cheat on, if he were so inclined.

"You know, you have a guy like Joe on your team and people say you should be able to win it all. But you look at his record over the years and—I don't know. . . . Well, maybe with somebody like J.J. in there, a young guy making mistakes, maybe they wouldn't have expected as much. . . ."

Charley's voice had cracked slightly during his last comments, and I have the feeling he would like to be left alone. I prepare to leave, thanking him for his kindness and suddenly being overwhelmed with the odd realization that he is now more an outsider than I am.

"I'll tell you, Joe has such a big heart, though," Charley adds. "It's a strange world . . ."

I am not sure what else to say—losing a coaching job is not the same as catching a disease or having your house burn down. "He's been fired before," linebacker coach Buddy Ryan had said, explaining the situation. "We all have. When you decide to become a coach you don't look for a permanent home." It is probably best that Charley has been relieved, for the Jets pose a dilemma he is obviously not capable of handling. But then, one wonders, who would be capable?

Charley and I shake hands and I leave. Earlier, in the locker room, Jamie Rivers had probably summed the problem up best. "Charley's such a nice guy," he said. "And that may not be the best thing to be."

SIXTEEN

Joe can't do everything forever.
Hell, even God died once.

—MATT SNELL

On the plane ride to Boston for the December 7 Patriots game, Namath sat quietly scanning a *New York Post,* concentrating mostly on the sports. "Man, look at this," he said to Winston Hill. "They got Buffalo down as two-and-a-half-point favorites over the Dolphins. I can't believe it!" The Dolphins and Coach Don Shula are probably Namath's favorite team.

"Yeh, but they're missing their first two quarterbacks," said Godwin Turk, pointing out what had most influenced the bookmakers. In recent weeks both Bob Griese and Earl Morrall had been injured, and unknown Don Strock was set to start.

"So what?" said Joe. "The kid's been there two years. The game is a matter of the offense and the defense. All he's gotta do is stand in there and just not fuck things up."

Joe had not been downgrading Strock or the Bills but simply making a point which he periodically felt obliged to do. Other quarterbacks had made similar noises. As James Harris of the powerful Los Angeles Rams put it, "The most important thing a quarterback can do is be on a good team." Even 1975 NFL Most Valuable Player Fran Tarkenton constantly diminished the helmsman's role. In a postscript to Dick Schaap's book

Quarterbacks Have All the Fun, he wrote that "the quarterback isn't all-important, that he can't by himself make the differences between victory and defeat, that if he were so important, Joe Namath would never lose a game." Because of the complexities of the game, Tarkenton explained, one-man rule is a thing of the past, and future quarterbacks will "be even less important." Most pro football analysts agree. In the 1974 Super Bowl, Bob Griese "led" the Dolphins to a 24–7 rout of Tarkenton's Vikings by handing the ball off 50 times and stepping aside. In 1968 Namath went six games down the stretch without throwing a touchdown pass, content to let the Jets' juggernaut, which included the league's best defense, roll of its own momentum.

But no matter how unimportant quarterbacks' roles are or become, they will always remain the focal point —the day seems highly unlikely when fans will start to blame wins or losses on the performance of guards. A quarterback for the Jets, furthermore, will always be a highly visible position; the precedent has been set. As retired running back Matt Snell said, Joe can't play forever (his contract covers 1976, and Joe says he doesn't think he'll play beyond that), and whoever steps in had best be ready for comparison—as a thrower, a play-caller, and a personality.

The two heirs apparent through the 1975 season are substitutes Al Woodall and J. J. Jones. Woodall, twenty-nine, is the veteran of the two, having been drafted just a few weeks after the Jets won the Super Bowl in 1969. At 6 feet 5 inches, 194 pounds, he has the size for a pro quarterback, and the football savvy, but his game development has been stunted by the seven seasons spent playing in Joe's shadow, waiting for routs or a Namath injury. The inconsistencies in his playing time might have finished a less even-tempered competitor: in 1970 he threw 188 passes; in 1972, none; in 1973, 201; in in 1975, none again, spending the entire season on the injured reserve list with a separated shoulder. But Al is an easygoing type, a classic "nice guy" who smiles a lot and laughs and accepts his fate much as it is handed to him.

Whenever we talked, he would listen intently to my part of the conversation, nodding frequently and saying, "That's an interesting point" and "Yes, I agree," and "I think you're right there, I really do." Al enjoys drinking and partying but not in the more cosmopolitan climes, not in the style that made Joe Namath famous. A good time for him is an evening spent at Bill's, drinking beer with Riggins and the boys, swapping stories. His standard attire includes blue jeans and a Massey-Ferguson tractor hat, and his voice still carries touches of drawl from his hometown of Erwin, North Carolina.

"When I was at Duke I was definitely not a star," Al says. "I led the conference one year in passing, but I never thought about playing pro ball; it was just something very far away. I think the main reason I even started playing quarterback as a kid was because the way I'm built and with my speed I couldn't have played anywhere else. Quarterback is kind of funny—it's hard to say why a kid starts right out there. Having a good arm doesn't have much to do with it. I really think a lot of guys might say they want to play quarterback, but when you get right down to it, they don't. They don't want to come off the field with a clean jersey; they want to get down in the pits.

"At Duke I was red-shirted my sophomore year, and then after my fourth year I purposely held back on one course so I could play a fifth year. Then during the summer a big thing came out about coeds writing papers for athletes, and because of that I got kicked out of school. I played semipro ball that fall for the Richmond Road Runners in the Atlantic Coast League—and brother, was that an experience. Outside of three or four guys sent down by the New Orleans Saints, the rest of the team was way beyond any hope of playing NFL ball. They were real dirty players, too. We had about ten guys under twenty-five years old, and I considered them fairly sane, but the older ones were maniacs. They'd bite your leg, incredible things. They were just these has-beens who'd say, 'Hell, I still got it,' then they'd go in and tear up a bar and come out for the team.

"When the Jets drafted me I knew I'd be the third quarterback behind Joe and Babe Parilli, but that was fine with me. It was better than Richmond. Everybody told me how fantastic it was to be playing behind one of the greatest quarterbacks ever, and I'd always agree and say, 'Hey, yeh.' If somebody asked me, that's what I'd say. But now, looking back, I see that that was totally wrong. If you're playing behind the greatest, what do people expect when you get on the field? Another Joe Namath, right? But I couldn't do the things he did. I could score points but I did it in a different way. It was a handicap for me, something I didn't realize at the time. I just let everybody create my opinions for me. I'm more or·less easygoing, a relatively happy guy. If a building falls down and I don't get hurt, then I'll be okay. I don't have a lot of emotion. And that's hurt me because I personally think the cockier you are, the better you'll be as a quarterback. I wish I were cockier but I'm not. I wish I had a bigger ego. The whole time I was here it was like I was saying, 'Gee, I'm sure lucky to be with the Jets,' instead of saying, 'Shit, get me out of here.'

"Joe was always real nice to me, though. Right from the start he came up and said hello and was very friendly. But looking back, was he worried about me beating him out, did he have any reason *not* to be nice? Still, he impressed me. I thought he was going to be very snobbish and conceited. You know, I've always felt that players like Joe and O. J. Simpson are few and far between, but that if some wheeler-dealer got a hold of a good football player he could make a star pretty much like them, create one. Take a kid like Steve Bartkowski, a big, good-looking guy—I'm sure if they'd wanted to they could have made a celebrity out of him. Of course, he'd have to want it, too. And as it turns out I'm not sure he has the color for it. Maybe it takes being a little bit shallower than the average person to be a star. But I think in the long run the shallow person might be the smartest, because I think a lot of these people who want to come across as introspective and deep are playing a big game. It's like they're trying to create something rather than just being themselves. If you can be yourself by going out and getting drunk and screwing around all the time, then I say more power to you. It's more natural to live it up.

"When I first came to camp, Joe was supposedly retired over the Bachelors III thing, but everybody told me he'd be back. He did come back, and I ended up playing about three minutes the entire year. I hardly did anything in practice either. In fact, during that season I gained forty-five pounds. I came in at one ninety and finished at two thirty-five. All I did was eat and drink beer. But I didn't feel that bad about not playing because Joe was at his peak then, and he really, really impressed me. His reactions and the way he read defenses and his motion were the things that impressed me most. And the timing he had with receivers. When he and George Sauer got working, they were so precise that on a twelve-yard out Sauer's footprints would be in the same spot and Joe's pass would be within a two-foot circle every time.

"Playing backup behind Joe has probably made me more known than I would have been backing up someone else. People can say, well, if it weren't for Namath he'd be a starter. I think I'm rationalizing the hell out of this, but if I had to look for some good, I would say that. Also, being an unemotional person, in a way I sort of couldn't give a shit. I've been making money and playing some and I've been happy. So what's important, where are your priorities? We all want to be number one, but to be realistic, I've been leading a pretty good life, so why should I complain? I remember my third year when I wasn't doing anything, I went to Weeb and told him I was a little bummed out. He said, 'I'm not going to tell you what to do, but look at the players who have forced teams to trade them so they could play—a lot of them aren't around anymore. Why don't you just let things happen?'

"The way it is now, I think the whole Jets' system is going to change. It's got to. This has been like the rise

and fall of the Roman Empire. The Jets built themselves up, won a Super Bowl, and now if we are not the
worst, we are close to the worst team in the league. I
don't know why exactly; I think Weeb stayed a few years
too long, and then he brought in his son-in-law, and
that's a very hard situation. And I liked Charley—I
thought he was a hell of a guy, but I also thought they
had to get him out of here. But the biggest thing, I think,
is that the organization has relied too much on Joe. I
believe the owners didn't care as much about winning
as making money, that far and above everything it was
Joe Namath *and* the New York Jets. And I could see it
rub off on players; I'd see young guys come in and maybe
they'd see Riggins have a bad game and they'd say he
played bad, but then they'd see Joe play a bad game and
the next night they'd see him in a movie or something,
and it's like, 'Hey, there's our man!' He's such a celebrity
that things get completely out of context. You can't
really describe it. You have to live it to understand it. As
far as my plans, well, I don't really want to talk about my
future. Basically, if I keep on playing ball, that's fine.
But if I don't, that's fine, too.''

J. J. Jones, unlike Woodall, is filled with a great deal
of youthful ambition. He is twenty-three years old, 6 feet
1 inch, 185 pounds, and where Woodall has had to wait
and wait, J.J. may get his shot soon if, indeed, Namath
retires after the 1976 season. As a black he is pushing his
luck trying for a starting quarterback job in the NFL.
But the precedent has been established—Marlin Briscoe
at Denver, James Harris with the Rams, Joe Gilliam
with Pittsburgh—and J.J. points out there were two
black pro quarterbacks as far back as 1918 and 1926. "I
don't know their names," he says. "But I think you could
check it out." He was pushing the odds from the very
beginning, having played his football at tiny Fisk College, getting overlooked in the draft, and finally surfac-
ing amid the chaos of the Jets' 1974 free-agent tryouts.
His most impressive quality was a howitzerlike arm.
"J.J. even throws fly patterns on a line," says David
Knight.

J.J. sat out the 1974 season with a very minor back injury, primarily so he could study films and learn the basics about pro defenses. This year he played sporadically, and unimpressively, finishing last among all NFL quarterbacks in statistics. He completed just 16 out of 57 passes for 181 yards, 1 touchdown, and 5 interceptions. At times he seemed to be visibly overwhelmed by his surroundings. Randy Rasmussen recalls that in the San Diego game, J.J. checked off a play at the line without even knowing he had done it. In the St. Louis game he was so flustered by a safety blitz that he forgot to hand the ball off. "They knew he was a rookie and they just destroyed his mind," says Ken Shipp. But J.J. has a willingness to learn, and combined with a natural humility, it makes him exceedingly coachable. His favorite teacher is Joe Namath. Frequently when the reporters mob Joe after a game, J.J. will be unable even to reach his locker. "I don't mind," he says, standing off to the side, a towel around his waist. "It's the least I can do for the man."

J.J. is married and deeply religious; he is one of the sincere members of Brother Herb's Bible class. He also is a rarity among Jets quarterbacks in that he can scramble, run for his life if necessary. In the business they say he possesses "young legs."

"I first started playing football in about fourth grade, out in the street," he says. "This was in Memphis, in a city neighborhood, and you had to be agile because, if you fell, it's a lot worse than Astro-Turf and you had to watch out for cars because they're a lot worse than linebackers. I played my first organized ball in junior high, but I almost didn't play at all because I'd already joined the band. I was going to play the tuba and I had my uniform and everything, and my mother said no football. I appealed to my father, who'd played a little pro baseball in the old Negro League, and he overruled the verdict. Back then I was short and awkward and hardly a great athlete. When the coach said everybody who wants to play a position line up behind that position, I watched everybody scramble around. I wanted to play defensive back or halfback, but it was outrageous, there were at least twelve guys in every line. But there was only one kid in the quarterback line, and I knew he was a chump, so I became a quarterback. At the time there weren't too many blacks playing football so everybody wanted to imitate Jim Brown and Lenny Moore. I couldn't think of any black quarterbacks, so my dream became that maybe someday I could be the first.

"In seventh grade I couldn't really throw the ball, just heave it up in the air and hope somebody'd run under it. Most of the plays weren't passes anyway, but things like quarterback keep the ball right, quarterback keep the ball left. But I don't think that old stigma is true—that blacks don't have the arm to be good quarterbacks. I don't think it's in the black man's physique; I think it's a stigma from society. With a quarterback, you're talking about the head of something, the top, and when it's denied in society, it's natural it will be denied somewhere else. Now I think it's gotten to the point where if your talents are needed and you can win, you'll play, no matter what color you are. One thing that happened in junior high was that we only won one game, and I almost became too paranoid to play the position. I was ridiculed and I realized then that a quarterback has an awful lot of chances to be ridiculed—a fumble, an interception, a bad call, anything that hurts the team.

"I came on better in high school. My arm developed, I got taller and more agile, and we started to beat teams sixty-three to nothing, things like that. The school was in a neighborhood that had just changed racially, so we were an all-black team with all-white coaches. I think the fact that I had a white coach may have been why I got so many scholarship offers. But another thing was that the head coach called me into his office one day and said, 'John, you don't want to think about going to this school, Fisk. It's not a very good school.' It was a small, all-black college, and I was perturbed because he was telling me it wasn't any good when he hadn't said anything about any other college. That was part of the reason I went there. And also I suppose it was a shelter, a way to develop myself. Maybe if I'd gone to a big white school they might have said forget it, and that would have been the end of my quarterback career.

"When I came to the Jets I knew that I wasn't going to step in and fill Broadway Joe's shoes, but nobody tried to destroy my confidence, either. John Schmitt was the center then, and he'd been with the team for years and years. He worked with me and he never said anything that made me feel that he thought I was incompetent. Then Joe started working with me, and the first thing he told me was that on dropbacks I was watching where my feet were going instead of looking downfield. Then in a preseason game against the Giants, I was looking to the left and I saw Caster break open on the right, and I threw way over his head for an interception. After the game Joe told me that he'd never been able to throw a decent pass unless his shoulders were squared up with the line. He didn't say any more, just that he couldn't do it. Well, if Joe couldn't, I knew I couldn't. So I never tried it again.

"From then on I tried to pattern myself after Joe. I read his book, *A Matter of Style,* and I took things directly from there. It isn't baloney either; Joe is actually telling his secrets for success. His upper motion has revolutionized football. See, most quarterbacks cock the ball, rear back and then throw; but the way Joe does it, the ball is carried at shoulder height, and when you throw you just twist your trunk and the ball is gone. It's unique because it eliminates two entire steps. I did get in a little trouble at one point during training camp because all my balls were nosing down, and I finally realized it was because I was imitating Joe too much. I can't do everything like he does, I just don't have the strength.

"I can throw the ball hard, though. Eddie Bell is always telling me I throw *too* hard. Sometimes I guess I do. In eleventh grade I got my lip split, and this receiver on our team, Andre Johnson, was laughing and calling me 'Big Lip.' Then in practice one day he ran an out, and when he turned the sun was right in his eyes. I'd thrown the ball with perfect timing and it hit his face mask, shattered the plastic and busted his lip. All I could do was laugh. Another time I stuck a ball right on a guy's chest, and he came back and lifted up his jersey and showed me where his heart was just pounding, his whole chest moving. I thought he was dying.

"But just because I can throw pretty well doesn't mean I'm going to pick up all of Joe's tendencies. In high school and college I had most of my success setting things up and then throwing short—you know, throw a three-yard pass and let the guy run for five yards. Joe says that isn't his bag. Since I'm a young guy, Coach Shipp is going to make sure I do what he wants, take what is there. I know Joe has had some trouble this year, but I certainly won't criticize him because I've sure done some stupid things, and nobody can say why. And then Joe has been getting hurt by things that aren't his fault: he'll catch a team in a blitz, drop back to throw, and somebody will miss a block and he'll go down. One time a receiver ran a go pattern on the twenty-yard line and he was supposed to do a down and in. The middle was wide open, but Joe had to throw out of the end zone; it looked real bad but it was the receiver's mistake, not Joe's. As far as Joe retiring, well, that's a decision each man has to make for himself. It was sad the way Johnny Unitas ended, because he had done so much and then he waited till they had to put him out of the game.

"It's sad when anybody plays longer than they should. Last year I sat in the stands at Shea and I heard them singing 'Goodbye, Charley,' and I heard them saying, 'Joe, go put your panty hose on!' There are people there who haven't missed a game since the Jets became the Jets, and when you're messing up they can really get down on you. But I think they've accepted me. I hear little words of encouragement, you know, like 'Go, J.J.' I see myself here in New York. The Jets have spent two years grooming me. I hope they don't give up now."

A major stumbling block suddenly appeared for J.J., and to some extent for Al Woodall, when the Jets used their number-one draft pick of 1976 to select quarterback Richard Todd of Alabama. A handsome, 6-foot-1, 206-pounder, Todd had worked out with Joe several times down in Tuscaloosa and admitted openly that Joe had been his idol since age nine. The comparisons between the two began immediately, including a picture in *People* magazine of them working out bare-chested, the headlines calling Richard "A Blond Version of Broadway Joe." A powerful young man with good knees, Richard Todd was a former high school discus champion who liked to run, having thrown only for a modest 661 yards and 7 touchdowns his senior year at Alabama. He admitted to liking beer and girls but called comparisons between him and Joe "silly."

When Joe was first introduced to the press, it was at a wild cocktail party at Toots Shor's saloon in Manhattan. Richard Todd met the press as just one of sixty-three players attending an orientation weekend at Weeb Ewbank Hall. He smiled a lot, verifying early society page reports that labeled him "amiable."

"Joe is the best player who ever played the game at the quarterback position," said Richard. "Nobody is going to take his place on and off the field. I'd be a fool to try."

Someone asked him if he had any nicknames.

"Just plain Richard," he said.

Then one of the writers asked if he'd had any acting lessons.

"Any what?"

"Any acting lessons."

"Oh, acting lessons. No," replied the young man. "I thought you said 'acne,' but that's all cleared up."

Throughout Jets-land one could almost hear the sighs of relief. For the many who felt one Broadway Joe was enough for a lifetime there lay a treasure of elegance in the words of Just Plain Richard.

SEVENTEEN

But there is an intensity and
a danger in football—as in life
generally—which keep us alive and
awake. It is a test of our awareness
and ability. Like so much of life, it
presents us with the choice of
responding either with fear or with
action and clarity.
—JOHN BRODIE, EX-QUARTERBACK
FOR THE SAN FRANCISCO 49ERS

Richard Neal, a 6-foot-3-inch, 260-pound black from Shreveport, Louisiana, is the Jets' right defensive end and Joe's best friend on the team. Neal has one of the most astounding physiques on the squad, with muscle overlapping muscle, and if it weren't for an easy smile and a generally relaxed attitude, his presence would be rather terrifying. He joined the Jets in 1974, and this year was elected their player representative after Winston Hill resigned the post. It wasn't a job Richard really wanted—"Do you realize that last year twenty-one player reps were traded?"—but it was one he accepted dutifully. Verbal and perceptive, Richard is the player writers go to first to determine team attitudes. After the Galigher-Reese fight his word on the racial implications was considered gospel.

One day he and I were sitting in the training complex discussing the motivations of pro football players. We talked about the prolonged adolescence and the insecurity and the rewards and about the type of behavior best suited to the game. Richard stated that after seven years in the pros he had begun to notice distinctive patterns associated with each position. It wasn't a new theory—psychologists have already determined that environment and genetics are as important to the making of a football player as they are to the making of a scientist or a poet, and that a player does best when his position fits his personality. But Richard claimed it was more a matter of culturization than of innate suitability.

"Look," he said, gesturing with his massive arms, "players *become* their positions. It's like what somebody said about the President—the office makes the man. Hell, these guys have been programmed for half their lives. You take offensive linemen—they have to learn plays and assignments—they're rules obeyers. Defensive linemen are rules breakers. Look out there in the parking lot, in the no-parking zone. I'll bet, I know, that four out of five cars there belong to defensive players. I'm a rule breaker—I *look* for no-parking zones. If there's an offensive player's car in there, it'll be a first-year guy, somebody who hasn't settled down yet.

"This stuff carries over to players' homes," he went on, "even to their lockers. I mean, I can look at a locker and tell you what position a guy plays. I gotta go now, but one of these days we'll take a tour and I'll show you what I mean."

At the end of the week he had some free time and we took the tour, beginning at the far end where the offensive linemen's lockers were clustered. As a group the cubicles were nondescript and orderly. "Look at this," said Richard, stopping in front of Robert Woods's locker. "A jersey actually on a hanger."

We walked farther along. "Look at Ebersole. Now he's a businessman. You know how he shoots right out of here. He's fast, efficient. See, his shoes are placed perfectly, his Skoal is neatly stacked." After that came Reese, the loud, effusive reserve linebacker. "Chaos," said Richard. We stopped at David Knight's locker and observed the mess of letters and tape and new white shoes. "He's not like most offensive players. He's a wide receiver," said Richard. "Also, he's injured."

"Now look at Piccone," he pointed. "A little guy who's trying to get bigger and stronger. What's he got in his locker? Cookies." We continued past Carl Garrett's locker, which was surprisingly neat for a man generally considered a discipline problem, past mine (virtually empty, hence unreadable), and stopped at Namath's.

"Joe Namath," said Richard Neal, sizing up the scene. "He's the quarterback, the leader, and he has to know the plays and know where everything is. He's ordered but he's wild, too. Quarterbacks have to take chances." In Namath's cubicle were a pair of sunglasses, some Skoal snuff, a toothbrush and toothpaste, several small boxes, a bag containing something the size of a flashlight, shoes, letters both opened and unopened, an empty paper cup, a pencil, two red practice jerseys and a green warmup jacket, on hooks. There was a sort of neat confusion to the arrangement; one imagined Joe could find anything with a reach, an order known to him.

Richard Neal first began observing Joe when Richard was a starting defensive end for the New Orleans Saints. "I remember when we played the Jets, I put Joe out with a tackle," he says, chuckling. "Shit yes. But we always hit him high because we knew he was money for all of us. We got to him four times, and on the last one they had to take him out. He was lying there on the ground screaming, holding his helmet. The trainers came running out and they immediately started checking his knees. Joe yelled, 'My ass, you dummies!' We'd destroyed his ass."

After Neal was traded to the Jets it wasn't long before he and Joe became friends, cementing their relationship with a common bond—drinking. "I guess Joe took to me because I'm one of the few dudes who can keep up with him," says Neal, who can and will consume prodigious amounts of alcohol. The Jets as a group are a heavy-imbibing team, being issued 360 cans of Miller's on the return flights from all away games. But they are not supposed to drink on the way to games, and they are not allowed hard liquor. For Joe this can be a little stringent. "He gets immature, like a kid, when he's been drinking," says Howard Goldberg, the Eastern flight coordinator who comes along on road trips. "On one flight I asked him to sign a ball for this friend of mine. He'd already had a few beers and he said, 'Okay, but get me a bottle of vodka.' I said, 'You know I can't do that.' He said, 'Well, then I'm not signing your ball.'"

With Richard Neal, Joe has found a way to circumvent the rules. On most flights Neal carries a shoulder bag containing, among other things, a bottle of liquor. The two players sit next to each other and secretively pour themselves cocktails, keeping an eye out for coaches and nosy airlines personnel. On the December 12 flight to San Diego, Richard and Joe managed to sip their way through a quart of vodka, after which Joe put on his sunglasses to conceal eyelids made of lead.

Though the two players are close, Richard admits that their friendship is more one of expediency than depth. "When we talk, we talk about football," he says. "Joe doesn't talk about his personal problems with anybody. I guess the main thing we have in common is having fun and drinking. Right now Joe's favorite drink is vodka on the rocks with a twist. It used to be Black Russians, and before that I think it was Scotch. Remember 'Johnny Walker Red and the women blonde'?

"Something that happened before I got here, I think it was 'seventy-one or 'seventy-two, was that the guys on the team got together and said, 'Joe, if you're so good when you drink, how good would you be if you didn't drink?' Joe said all right, and he didn't drink anything all week, I think it was before the New England game. On Sunday he went out and threw six interceptions, and when he came back in after the game he told everybody to go fuck themselves."

Richard points out that Joe drinks for pleasure, that if he didn't enjoy it he could take it or leave it. "To my way of thinking there are three points to problem drinking," he states. "Number one is you can't afford it; number two is you drink and hurt people; number three is you drink and hurt yourself. I don't believe Joe has any of those faults." But he also admits that the point of their drinking is usually drunkenness, and that both of them, he feels, are "lonely people."

"Joe's in that big house all by himself, with an ego that needs to be built up just like any athlete's. I think at times he's lonely despite all the crowds. I guess what I'm trying to convey is that emotionally he's like the rest of us, even though I don't think many of us could switch places with him. It takes a very strong man to live in that type of environment without breaking out or going crazy."

There are shelters Joe has erected, Richard adds, and one of the biggest is the avoidance of complications. "His life is awkward," he says. "You don't really want to get too deep with him, and he definitely doesn't want to get too deep with you." Close friendships, including those with women, have necessarily been avoided. "But I'll tell you this," adds Richard. "Joe doesn't feel he's through playing around yet, but when he does and he gets married, he'll fulfill that damn contract to the word. He'll be a one-woman man. He believes in institutions."

Richard feels that "as long as there are telephones," he and Joe will remain in touch, regardless of trades or possible retirements. Already Joe has asked him to come to Fort Lauderdale during the off-season for a week of fishing and relaxing. When Joe is criticized, Richard defends him. "You know, right now a lot of people are tired of the way Joe is because we're losing. If we were winning, his style would be number one again just like before. Kids would be imitating him and wearing number twelve. People will accept anything when you're winning. But when you're losing, everything you do is wrong. If you drink, it's wrong. If you stay out late, it's wrong. If you go to bed at eight o'clock, it's wrong. But see, Joe doesn't believe all the criticism and that's because he knows what is his fault and what isn't. If he believed what is said about him, he'd be destroyed. He has too much confidence for that."

As the season has progressed and I have seen Joe in action and watched him at ease and listened to him and to what others have said about him, I have found that everything about him seems to come together as a whole, to be interconnected and interrelated. Rather than being a mystery, his character makes a great deal of sense. Everything he does seems to stem from a basic desire for excellence, for the test, for pleasure, but most of all from an intrinsic, almost childlike understanding of the meaning of competition. If that means limiting one's deep relationships, as Richard Neal points out, then Joe has done it. If it means being shallow, then Joe has been it. If it means feeling above certain rules, then Joe has gone his own way. "Joe says, 'Put the burden on me. I will dare to be great,' " says Phil Wise. Joe has, according to his teammates, never choked. Even the people in Beaver Falls can never remember him clutching. There is an ingenuousness to such a record that can't be manufactured. Several times I have asked him questions that he answered poorly and, in fact, seemed hardly to understand. Only after reflecting did I realize that questions such as "Weren't you afraid of failure?" have only a limited meaning to a man like him.

It has become fashionable recently to compare sports with the teachings of various Eastern philosophies. A glut of books and articles have related the similarities between an athlete's mind—his concentration and reliance on experience rather than thought—and that of a meditator or a Zen master. "Every great athlete has learned to concentrate whether he can talk about it or not," says Timothy Gallwey, the author of *The Inner Game of Tennis.* "He's learned how to block out irrelevant things about the past and the future to a large extent; he's learned how to be fully present in the here and now." John Brodie, the ex-quarterback for the San Francisco 49ers, who speaks of a mystical "clarity" that entranced him in some games, states that concentration is something we probably have from birth but that we lose "as we grow up."

Namath, clearly, has not grown up in the sense that he has ever allowed self-doubt to disturb his concentration. "I don't let anything interfere with my job as quarterback," he says matter-of-factly. Not girlfriends, not hate mail, not bad knees, not glory. Thus, in crucial situations Namath sees only challenge, not pressure. Nor is his eagerness a product of positive thinking. "It's *not* positive thinking," says Timothy Gallwey. "Positive thinking is trying to replace a negative belief with a positive one. Positive thinking always originates with self-doubt. There's really no need for any *belief* at all."

Dick Schaap, who once cohosted a TV interview show with Namath, claims Joe "never, ever" got uptight. "It wouldn't have mattered if we'd had the President or the King on, Joe wouldn't have sweated. I was jealous of him. But all he had was just a reasonable amount of self-confidence and a sense of perspective. After all, it was just another human being up there with us."

Joe himself says that challenges are meant to be pleasurable. "If a man is convinced that he knows what he's going to do, boy, he can have a heck of a time," he states. "Maybe you don't know exactly what's going to happen, but you can be confident you'll be able to confront it and do the right thing when it arises. As a team, Miami best reminds me of that, just the way they work.

"I think it's something you can develop; I know I did. Hell, I used to get such a bad stomach, get that pain in there—did you ever when you were young have a girlfriend and break up or have a fight and get an actual pain? Well, I used to. I remember one time I had some change for my mother from the store, and I went into the pool room and I lost the damn thing. She was waiting on the money and I lost it. I was so sick leaving that pool room I wanted to die. And all the way home I had that awful feeling inside, suffering. That stuck with me, remembering the damn thing. It might be one of the reasons I never got married or seriously involved with a girl."

Joe claims that a few years ago he felt slightly tense during a game and decided to put an end to the feeling. Oddly enough, that game was the Baltimore contest in 1972 when he threw for six touchdowns and 496 yards, statistically his best performance ever. "I didn't feel good before, during, or after the game," he says. "It wasn't worth it. It went against one of my basic philosophies: don't do anything to cause worry and mess up the nervous system."

Since that time he has not gone into a game uncomfortable. Two years ago he picked up transcendental meditation from Bob Oates, Jr., his collaborator on *A Matter of Style,* and he feels it has made him even less tense. "Winston took the course, too, and he thought it had something to do with religion, but it's just in the mind, just relaxing. There's no concentration at all. Just close your eyes and your mantra will come into your head. Finally it will be the only sound and eventually it will disappear, and you'll wake up and twenty minutes will be gone. It's so restful. Sometimes when I meditate I can feel an arm jump, and that will be a stress I won't get. People say they can notice when others start meditating, but I don't think they can notice it in me. It makes you more mellow, but I've been pretty mellow for a while, anyway."

While Joe has been talking, he has been sitting on his stool in front of his locker, absentmindedly toweling his hair. He stops now, wads up the towel, and throws it at the laundry basket, watching it curve off to the right and land on the floor. The locker room is deserted; practice has been over for more than an hour. Gradually his brow furrows and an uncommon look of introspection covers his face. He seems excited.

"You know," he says. "Being able to eliminate worry is one of the—Goddamn—it's one of the greatest parts of life. Not worrying about what you said to this guy or if he's gonna say it to somebody else. Not lying or cheating or stealing. Not having *anything* to worry about. I told you one thing that helped me was making money, and then I guess getting a job and a general direction. But now, I am without stress. I mean, I am *without* stress. And you know what's funny? Randi, my girl friend, says I'm nervous. I don't know how she can say that. I'm fidgety, I like to move, but I don't feel that bad feeling in my system. That knot.

"Sometimes, though, it does come back. Like at Kansas City before the second game this year." He shakes his head with the memory. "We were in the hotel and I was with my father and stepmother trying to get through the lobby into the bar so we could have a drink. This fellow ran up to me with his camera and stuck it right in my face, and I pushed it out of my way and started going, and then he said something. I turned around real quick and I grabbed him and I said, 'How would you like it if somebody stuck a camera in your face? Do you like looking at flash bulbs?' He sort of mumbled and then he left. Well, I felt so goddamn bad for doing that that I sat my parents down, ordered drinks, and went out and looked for the guy. I felt like shit. I looked all around but I couldn't find him. And I felt that feeling then." Joe lofts another towel at the basket. This also misses.

"But I'll tell you, if you don't learn to be at peace, especially in a job that's in the public eye, you just can't stay in it."

EIGHTEEN

*If men live decently it is because
discipline saves their very lives for
them.*

—SOPHOCLES

November has passed. December is here, and the
skies over Long Island have grown gray and harsh. The
footballs are cold and no longer pleasant to catch. As I
retrieve field goals for kicker Pat Leahy, he complains
that it feels like he's smacking his instep into blocks of
ice. The practice fields, once so green and soft, are now
hard and disheveled, with a color fading its way to
brown. The wind whistles and the kids in the school
buses on Hempstead Turnpike no longer lower their
windows to chant their shrill greeting, "Hi, Joe! Hi, Joe!
Hi, Joe!"

"It seems like this season will never end," says General Manager Al Ward, and indeed a sense of eternity
does linger with each practice, each repeated pattern.
Nobody seems to care about the Jets anymore—the few
people who come to practices have obviously stopped by
only to look at Namath. A feeling of anonymity pervades
the squad. Several of the players have started growing
beards. David Knight has begun one out of boredom and
a sense of decadence. "I wish I could grow something
else," he says. "Something really gross. Some long nose
hairs or a huge patch of zits on the side of my face."

Still, the season goes on in its prescribed fashion, following the schedule written out several years before. As the Jets prepare for their game with San Diego, their moment of exposure on *ABC Monday Night Football,* it is hard to imagine a contest of less import. The Chargers are one of only three NFL teams with a worse record than the Jets; combined the two teams have a total of 4 wins and 21 losses. The only element of interest is to be Joe Namath himself. Ironically, Charger officials have already said they are expecting their largest crowd of the year.

To be fair, the Jets are coming off a one-game winning streak, their first victory in nine games. It was a modest win, no doubt about that, a 30–28 squeaker over New England with the gun mercifully sounding before the Patriots could score again. But it was a win, Ken Shipp's first as a head coach.

Since he has taken over, Shipp has been making an effort to settle things down and instill some order in the household. He has demanded that everyone wear pads to practice, and he has brought in each player for an individual conference, telling them among other things that if they don't put out "they're gone." But the Jets are creatures of habit now and scare tactics barely register, or if they do they cause mostly confusion. On the ride to New England, Shipp had puffed on his pipe, looking confused himself. "I think we can win," he said. "But hell, I don't know. We've had some good practices, but practices really don't have anything to do with games. I think a team psychologist might be a good idea. I really do."

The first two games he coached were indications that nothing had changed. The St. Louis Cardinals destroyed the Jets, 37–6, with wide receiver Mel Gray scoring twice —once on a 74-yard bomb in which he beat the Jets' defenders much worse than he beat me four years earlier as a college senior, and then again on a 20-yard pass in which he appeared to look around to see why nobody was covering him. One of the reasons was that Delles Howell, the free safety whose zone he had entered, was standing alone in the middle of the field with a broken arm. Delles spent several days in the hospital after that, returning to the dorm early one morning with a crash. He had been out drinking and was bringing back some company; and finding the main door locked, he kicked it in.

The following game with Pittsburgh was a very dull affair, highlighted only by Namath's four interceptions and the team introductions. Apparently fearful of the boos that would greet either the offensive or defensive units, someone in the organization decided the Jets should salute their second-stringers. Out came the stream of unknowns—Hoey, Fields, Browne, J. Davis, S. Davis—to a smattering of applause, while the rest of the team sneaked toward the bench. Donny Walker, a journeyman safety acquired only a few days before, apparently found his first appearance in a Jet uniform spiritually uplifting. As his name was announced he jogged across the field with his right arm held high, first finger waving toward the heavens in the traditional "We are number one!" salute. Fortunately most fans missed, or failed to comprehend, the gesture. The Jets' brass didn't, however. Within ten days Donny Walker was back on the road.

On the Tuesday off after the Pittsburgh game Joe came limping into the training complex to get some treatment for his bruised body. "I need to get the blood flowing to various parts," he said, heading off to the heated swimming pool. Newspapers were now routinely speculating on Joe's future—whether he would last the season and, if he survived, whether he would play again next year. "Is This Joe's Last Fling?" read the headline to an AP story that quoted Joe as saying he'd be doing "some heavy thinking" before next year.

After his swim he felt much better, and as he dressed he mentioned that it was the cold that was truly bothering him. "It never gets like this down in Alabama," he said. He then began talking about the South and about his college days and, as he often does, about Bear Bryant. "My sophomore year before the Orange Bowl against Oklahoma I remember it was about as cold as it gets in Alabama. Bear was watching films and all of a sudden he yelled, 'Run that back!' They ran the film back and forth a couple times. 'Why, those are colored boys!' he said. 'I thought they were wearing stockings.' "

Joe chuckled with the memory. "You know, Bear is a big man," he added. "About six feet four and he's got those cold, gray eyes. He can be witty as hell, like at the crap tables in Las Vegas when he's yelling and cursing, but he can sure be tough, too." Joe told several stories about Bear's toughness and then finished with the one that had most impressed him.

"I was a freshman and I was running the option play and a guy had me by the legs. I pitched the ball back and missed the halfback, and the ball was just rolling around. Bear came running over and yelled, 'You idiot, you turd!' I went back to the huddle like this, shaking my head and sorta going, 'Yeh, yeh.' Well, Bear ran up to me and grabbed me by my face mask and lifted me off the ground. I swear to God. He had his fist back behind his head and he said, 'Boy, when I talk to you, you look me in the eyes.' From then on I was all 'Yessir, yessir,' and if he was fifty yards away I'd come running."

On the Wednesday after the New England game, Carl Garrett, who remained behind in Boston, still has not arrived for practice. Rumor has it that his grandmother has died. "That'll be his nineteenth," says Sam Rutigliano.

Late in the afternoon, Garrett finally comes in, blaming his tardiness on the fogged-in Boston airport. Immediately he is surrounded by reporters. As they grill him, his face turns to an ugly scowl. "I wasn't here for practice," he snaps. "So what'd I do except be late?"

"We've got to ask you questions," says Paul Zimmerman. "Otherwise you'd accuse us of not getting your side of the story."

"Why you accusin' me?" Garrett asks. "Why do you think I'm so different? Would you ask somebody else all this?"

"Nobody else has been late."

"Fuck it. You guys gonna print what you want anyway. I know you guys."

Ken Shipp has announced that Garrett will be fined, plus he is being benched for the Monday night game in San Diego.

As a continuation of the shakeup, Al Ward has recently hired Babe Parilli and Ralph Baker, both ex-Jets, to begin viewing all available film of this year's team. They are to evaluate each player according to skill and effort so that Al can begin paring away the dead weight. Neither Babe nor Ralph is talking about their findings, but they are obviously making progress. One day when I looked into their darkened room I saw Buffalo run a twenty-yard draw play over and over. "Look at that, Ralph," said Babe Parilli, indicating middle linebacker Jamie Rivers, who was blocked completely out of the play. "That just isn't right."

Despite the new measures, the Jets are keeping their cool off the field, remaining, as ever, loose and festive. If anything, the party tempo has picked up. There has been a Halloween party at Twigg's, a Thanksgiving bash at Shea Stadium, a veterans' party at Mother's, assorted birthday parties at homes, and dozens of smaller affairs at various local bars and discotheques. On the Friday before the St. Louis game, the Jets held a kangaroo court at Bill's Meadowbrook with virtually every player in attendance. The beers came fast and furiously, and Magistrate Mark Lomas had to pound his gavel repeatedly to bring order and present the cases. The official paper had been drawn up several days before:

Kangaroo Kourt Docket

Nov. 21, 1975

1. Treasury report—E. Galigher
2. *Jets defense* vs. *E. Bell*
   Slander & defamation of character, Phil "F. Lee Bailey" Wise—prosecuting attorney

214

3. *Jets* vs. *G. Turk*
   Threat of desertion; mutinous behavior
4. Jeff Snedeker
   Continuance of validity of "Asper-rub" charges
5. *Galaxy* vs. *Steve Reese*
   Failure to answer charges:
   a. 1974 locker room dues (and probably 1975)
   b. Invasion of privacy—Colonel Darrell Austin (Six-Million-Dollar Man)
6. *Steve Reese* vs. *E. Galigher*
   Assault & battery
7. John Riggins
   Sanity hearing to determine competency to stand trial for a second treason charge, D.A.—Big Guy Puetz

The cases were tried and the defendants routinely hooted down. Eddie Bell was fined ten dollars and warned against granting interviews to "that tabloid *New York Times.*" Godwin Turk wept and threw himself "on the mercy of the court" but was found guilty, as was Steve Reese. When Ed Galigher stood up to be tried for slugging Reese in the Baltimore game, Roscoe Word came marching out of the back room wearing a white sheet with eye holes cut in it. He announced himself a member of the Ku Klux Klan and said he would defend Galigher. Galigher immediately pleaded guilty and was fined twenty-five dollars.

The main event came as John Riggins was tried for treason, the basis of which stemmed from his sham pregame speech in Miami and certain vague comments construed to be in defense of Charley Winner. To be found guilty, however, he had to be proven sane. Lou Piccone, his defense attorney, assured the group that John was not, "that even brain-damaged people can occasionally act normal." Riggins made the most effective plea himself by leaping up and speaking in his own behalf. "I don't want to be known as sane and logical while I'm bumming around this league next year!" he cried, jumping up and down and pulling on his green suspenders. A precedent of sorts was set as the overwhelmed gathering found him incompetent to stand trial. Riggins let out a mighty cheer, lit a cigar, slapped Piccone's back, and donated twenty dollars to the court "out of the goodness of my heart."

Later in the week, I sat down with Darrell Austin, one of Riggins's best friends, and asked him a little bit about the fullback. Both Darrell and John grew up in small towns—Darrell in Union, South Carolina, and John in Centralia, Kansas—and both had been the biggest boys in town.

"Is Riggins crazy?" I asked.

"Definitely. But he's a good kind of crazy. The kind of guy you'd like your son to be, have your daughter bring home."

"Why is he crazy?"

"Might be hereditary. Playing pro ball might have something to do with it. Farm boy makes good, that can be hard on you."

"Did you know any crazy people in Union?"

"Lord, the town was full of 'em. I remember some guys I knew had a poker game one night. One of the guys passed out, so the others carried him up to his bed. Then when the game was going again, they got in a big fight and beat one of the players to death. They put him in bed with the first guy. In court the judge asked the guy who'd passed out when he first realized his buddy was dead. He said, 'When I woke up I hit him and said, "Wake up, Sam," but he didn't move. "Get up, Sam," I yelled. Nothing. So I turned his head around and, sure enough, he was colder than a well-digger's ass.' The courtroom broke up."

"What does Riggins do that is crazy?"

"He's got those costumes. He dances like Alice Cooper. He's got that motorcycle. But he hasn't really done anything crazy like this guy I know named A. J. Maggot."

"What do people think about Riggins?"

"That he's the greatest fullback in the league right now. Believe me, he's only crazy off the field."

"Are there a lot of crazy guys in football?"

"Oh, yeh. Most of 'em on my college team at South Carolina. I started to mention A. J. Maggot. He missed a turn in New Orleans once and ended up in Texas. He was so drunk they put him in a hospital. Then he bought a quart of whiskey and drove back. His real name was Bob Perry; A. J. Maggot was just his other self. One time he told us that he was through with A.J., that he was going to settle down and be normal for a while. We were coming home from a football players' party on a bus, and Bob had on a nice suit and was sitting next to his beautiful date. He had a Styrofoam cooler beside him and we were drinking a few beers and Bob was acting real calm. Then all of a sudden he just stood up and picked up the cooler and held it in the air. Then he smashed the whole thing on his date's head and yelled, 'A. J. Maggot is back!'

"We had another guy named Matt Wall, who used to walk around in the rafters at night. He had dreams about being in a whale and having to eat his way through dead babies. Another guy was a professional thief. He had lock-picking tools and a blowtorch and used to rob country clubs during the week. This linebacker named Guillotine Brown sometimes would shoot his own room up with a rifle. Another guy worked high steel and liked to pretend that he was falling off buildings just to scare people down below. We had another guy named Blind Hog, about six-three, two-eighty, and one time he reached down for something and fell through four or five rows of people in the stands. He was a mountain boy and there was a billboard on his land, and every so often he'd get a twenty-dollar check as rent. Then he'd buy some beer and pass out in the sun and have second-degree burns on one side."

"Does it help being crazy to play football?"

"Hell yes. You'll be crazy at the end, if you aren't when you come in. Just think what it must be like to have your ass run over by some huge fullback with green fingernails."

On Friday the Jets leave for their four-day road trip to San Diego. As usual the plane is filled with a number of freeloaders—friends of the owners, children, obscure pressmen. And as usual the players are in high spirits. Card games immediately start up, tape decks come out, and the back of the plane takes on the appearance of a casino.

Several of the players discuss the fact that they will be on national TV Monday, and they try to think of ways the exposure can be exploited. "Football, especially on this team, is nothing but theater," explains David Knight. "There are so many things to be done, things that years from now people will be saying, 'Why didn't they do that back then?' " What he would like to do, he adds, is get a David Bowie haircut, dye his hair white, and then touch up his face with glitter and lipstick.

Before he was traded to the Bears, Mike Adamle had been planning a back flip off Garry Puetz's shoulders after his next touchdown. Puetz now says he is considering wearing earrings for the game. But the players all realize that the cameras will be focused primarily on Namath, that what they do is largely irrelevant. In one TV game, Puetz decided he should be seen, so he stayed as close to Joe as possible, at certain times even feigning dialogue with the side of Joe's head. "Monday night," he says, "I'm gonna be Joe's shadow."

The few days before the game pass rather uneventfully. On one bus ride Ken Shipp severely scolds running-back Bob Gresham for using profanity in the presence of women, a move that startles most of the players. "That's the first sign of discipline in two years," says a stunned J. J. Jones. And while visiting Tijuana, Ken Bernich has $120 lifted from his wallet by a bar girl. But the routine, aside from the sunny weather, is much as it would be in New York.

On Monday afternoon I spot Namath and Ken Shipp talking in the courtyard of the motel. Joe is wearing blue jeans, a khaki jacket, and sunglasses, and Shipp is wearing a leisure suit and chewing on his ever-present pipe. Having brought along a camera for this trip, I walk over and ask if they'd mind my taking a picture. Neither of them says anything, apparently being lost in thought, so I snap a shot and move on.

That night at the stadium before the teams have taken the field, PR man Frank Ramos comes running through the press box throwing out mimeographed sheets like a hyped-up paper boy. As each writer gets the sheet his eyes open wide. I get mine and read it: "NAMATH WILL NOT START VS. CHARGERS." Because Joe missed the Sunday night curfew, states the release, he will be fined and benched, and J. J. Jones will start at quarterback. "Neither Shipp nor Namath will be available for comment until after the game." The benching is the first time such a thing has happened to Joe since 1963 when Bear Bryant suspended him from the Alabama team for drinking.

Al Ward hurries down to field level where he informs TV commentators Howard Cosell, Alex Karras, and Frank Gifford of the sudden development. Alex Karras snorts through his nose. "Curfew?" he says in a high voice. "He missed curfew? Holy shit. The guy's got gray pubic hairs and he has to be in at ten o'clock."

Cosell rises to the occasion, quickly composing an impromptu bulletin. When the red light comes on he addresses the audience with full-blown hyperbole. "Joe Willie Namath, the highest-paid, most flam-boyant quarterback ever . . . healthy and happy for once, but suddenly . . . inter-cep-ted . . ."

As the word trickles out to the fans, thousands of whom have come only to see Joe play, a dark murmuring spreads through the stands. "Joe's infraction is serious. Really," says Al Ward. "There are only fourteen nights a year like this."

President Phil Iselin stands alone near the fifty-yard line, a thoughtful look on his face. Unlike Sonny Werblin, who set the precedent for Joe's pampered, "special" treatment by interfering with Weeb Ewbank's control, Phil Iselin has backed up his coach's decision. "Shipp slept on it. We stand behind him," he says. "We can't treat Garrett one way and Joe another."

When the official announcement is made over the public address system, boos echo through the stadium like thunder. The suspension, however, turns out to be less than permanent. In fact, all it has done is set up a dramatic entrance for Joe midway in the second quarter, an entrance heralded by cheers and rippling banners reading "JOE, WILL YOU MARRY ME?" and "JOE, WE'D LIKE TO GET IN YOUR PANTY HOSE." The move causes a number of writers to speculate on the purpose of "benching" someone for twenty minutes. Isn't it possible, they ask, that Shipp merely wants to be known as the coach who tamed Namath as he, Shipp, searches for his next year's job?

Despite the fanfare, Namath adds little to the game except his physical presence. He throws a touchdown, an interception, and fails to take the team in from the one-yard line. The Jets lose, 24–16, for their tenth defeat of the season, tying the club record. In the locker room a reporter hands Joe a copy of the pregame announcement. He sits hunkered down on his stool, his head almost below the newsmen's knees, and when he finishes reading, he gives a short, resigned laugh. "I got caught up talking with some friends from Beaver Falls," he says. "I got in at eleven twenty-five. The coach had to do it. It's cut and dried. I blew it."

On the plane home that night Joe sits with his head against the window, sleeping comfortably. The entire plane is silent, with coaches, executives, press, and players all dozing as best they can. Only a handful of people are still awake. Richard Caster stares blankly at the seat in front of him. Lou Piccone talks nonstop to a drowsy stewardess. "I'm wired," he says. Randy Rasmussen paces the rear kitchen area. "I'm so intense," he says. "It's like I've gone through a five-day business week in three hours." John Riggins sits alone, eating peanuts, his body too beat up for sleep. The night sky slowly begins to lighten in the east, the stars fading in the purple. Somewhere over Illinois we pick up the first orange of sunrise, as we speed our way toward New York and Tuesday's headlines.

NINETEEN

*Don't you think if you were Joe
Namath's lawyer you could do
a good job for him?*

—PAUL ZIMMERMAN

One evening at Bill's a few of the players were sitting around when Joe Namath's image appeared on the overhead TV. Namath demonstrated how the Hamilton Beach Mini-Mac could broil one tiny hamburger in two minutes, his voice filled with sincerity. Joe Fields was the only player who paid any attention to the ad. He waved at the screen, said, "Hi, Joey," and turned back to his beer.

Namath's face is seen so often in various forms of the media that the Jets, as a whole, are immune to it. They have seen him promote Schick razors, Braniff airlines, Noxzema shaving cream, Olivetti typewriters, Ovaltine chocolate, La-Z-Boy chairs, Beauty Mist panty hose, Fieldcrest sheets, Arrow shirts, Fabergé cosmetics, Franklin Sporting Goods jerseys, and Hamilton Beach Mini-Macs and Butter-Up Poppers. In that last ad Joe comes up with perhaps his best Madison Avenue line. Seated behind a device that resembles a space-age gumball machine, he states: "There's only one thing I like better than football. My new Hamilton Beach Butter-Up Popper."

As a rookie, Joe Fields is more impressed by such pitches than some of the veterans; but certainly no one comes to the Jets believing that Namath is going to be *just* a quarterback, *just* a team member. They can learn soon enough by examining the official Jets' autographed footballs. Mechanically signed, the balls carry everyone's signature except for Namath's; even his name must be purchased and royalties paid.

Joe is literally more than a football player—in the business world he is known as Namanco, a corporation consisting of five people: lawyer Jimmy Walsh, Jimmy Griffin, Sam Iselin, Mike Martin, and Namath himself. The company is unique in the athletic management field in that it promotes just one athlete. It is also unique in its curiously interwoven, almost incestuous relationship with that athlete's employers, the New York Jets. Sam Iselin is President Phil Iselin's brother, and Mike Martin is the former Jets' assistant to the general manager and the son of the Jets' chairman of the board, Townsend B. Martin. On the day I visited the Manhattan offices of Namanco, Jet publicist Frank Ramos was already there on business, and shortly afterward ex-coach Charley Winner came in on what was apparently a search for employment.

The prime mover of Namanco is thirty-five-year-old bachelor attorney Jimmy Walsh, a chunky 5-foot-7-inch nonathlete with stiff red hair and the afterimage of Woody Woodpecker. In business dealings Namath maintains the low profile while Walsh, an ex–New Jerseyite who calls himself "Jimmy" because people "can relate to somebody named Jimmy," plays the heavy. Despite his name, Walsh is tough, adamant, blunt, and, according to various businessmen, virtually impossible to negotiate with. Some of his favorite expressions are "Do you understand what I'm saying?" and "I don't think you're listening to me." As to why he seldom budges from his predetermined prices, Walsh says, "If Dustin Hoffman asks for five hundred thousand dollars for a movie, that's exactly what he wants. If Joe Namath asks for five hundred thousand for something, that's exactly what he wants, too."

As a man of ideas, Walsh receives mixed reviews. "I

think Joe might have been able to get somebody with more impressive credentials than Jimmy," says Dick Schaap. "But I doubt if he could have found anyone who's more dedicated. Walsh is one hundred percent loyal to Joe." Cosmo Currie, Namath's hairdresser friend and drinking buddy, is less complimentary. "Joe has not gotten good management," he states. "Walsh just happened to be lucky and come along at the right time."

That he came along at the right time can scarcely be denied. Walsh started at the University of Alabama in 1959 and became friends with Ray Abruzzese, a defensive back who later played two years for the Jets. Through Abruzzese he met Namath in 1961. Though Joe was two years younger than Jimmy, they had a good deal in common, being northern Catholics at a southern, predominantly Baptist school. "We were very much like outcasts," Jimmy recalls. "One of our major social functions was going to church at the university chapel." Still, the young men's friendship was not an immediate success.

"My first meeting with Joe came one night when Ray and I went out to shoot pool, and Ray brought this kid with him," says Walsh. "The kid stood off to the side and kept saying things like, 'Let me play this guy.' I resented him and thought he was a cocky wise guy. Later I'd see Joe around school. He wore weird peak-billed berets and did things like carry a golf ball with him; when he'd turn a corner in the corridor, he'd throw it against the far wall, which was just a little bit dangerous with all the people coming and going.

"Then one morning near the end of Joe's freshman year I had the occasion to go to breakfast with him. We had a nice, genial conversation and I found out he was Hungarian, which my mother is also. We became friendly after that, not close friends, but I no longer perceived of him as being a wise guy. And even though he was a freshman, he was a very important person who knew all the athletes, and when you're from New Jersey and nobody knows who you are at all . . . well, in my mind he was a celebrity and it was nice to say hello."

The friendship was cemented at the start of Namath's junior year. As is the case in all Joe's close associations, each had to prove his loyalty to the other. Jimmy Walsh was returning for his first semester of law school, and after his car broke down in southern New Jersey he was forced to fly to Birmingham, sixty miles from Tuscaloosa. He arrived at two in the morning, and despite numerous calls to school none of his friends would pick him up. All of sudden Jimmy remembers hearing a loud scream. "There was this guy who I barely knew, Joe Namath," he recalls. "It was September, football had started, and he had jeopardized his entire scholarship just to come out and pick me up. I guess he'd heard from someone that I was stuck and didn't have a ride. I didn't realize he thought that much of me."

In November, Jimmy had a chance to return the favor. Joe's brother needed money badly, so Joe asked Jimmy for a loan. Jimmy withdrew $1,000 from his school savings account and gave it to Joe, who sent it to his brother. By January, Joe had repaid the debt. "I think he did it by selling the tickets some alumni got for him," says Walsh. "Joe never forgot what I had done for him. After that we were the best of friends."

When Joe was done with football his senior year and no longer obligated to live in a dorm, he moved into a house with Walsh and Abruzzese and two other men. "One of our roommates was a guy named Chris Vagotis," says Jimmy. "When they did this exposé on television on injuries in football, he was the high school coach who was beating kids up. Vagotis was a funny character. It was great. We had a lot of fun."

The roommates' favorite fun place was a redneck bar outside Tuscaloosa called the Jungle Club, a dive Walsh refers to as "the worst place in history" with a lot of "emotionally disturbed people" among its clientele. It was after a session at the Jungle Club that Joe had one of his most serious brushes with the law. While driving back to town with Hoot Owl Hicks in the doorless car they had bought together, Joe was stopped by a policeman who immediately recognized him. As Hoot Owl pitched beer cans out the door, the cop approached Joe, smiling. "The police didn't particularly like Joe down there for some reason," says Jimmy Walsh. "This guy came up and said, 'Oh, the Pennsylvania Kid.' He was really enjoying the fact that he had happened on the situation. Joe got a little annoyed at that. He'd had a few drinks and he said, 'Tell me something: Is it true that to become a Tuscaloosa cop you have to be able to flunk out of the state police first?' The cop jumped back and drew his gun. He called in about forty squad cars and they took the two of them in. Hoot Owl was really scared. He said, 'Joe, you're the star and they'll probably let you out right away, but they may leave me in here forever.' The funny thing is, an assistant coach came right down and bailed out Hoot Owl. But Joe he just left in jail."

Jimmy remembers that he and Namath were constantly doing favors for each other. One time Joe was invited to speak at a banquet in Fort Walton Beach, Florida, and he and Abruzzese went down for the weekend while Jimmy stayed home to study. "At five o'clock Sunday they walked into the house and said, 'Just to show you we didn't forget you, we brought you a present," Walsh recalls. "And then in came this beautiful girl. She stayed for about two weeks. She was terrific."

When Joe left to join the Jets he had a local attorney representing him, and it was not until just prior to the Super Bowl that Walsh became his official agent. "The way it happened was that we went back to his apartment after a football game and he told me that Milt Woodard, the commissioner of the AFL, had asked him to shave his Fu Manchu mustache which he had at the time. Joe casually said, 'Why don't you call around and see if you can get a mustache commercial?' I was only a quasi lawyer at the time, but I called a friend who was a publicist and he contacted Schick; and they had some money left over from their yearly budget and the deal was worked out."

The deal had Namath shaving the mustache in front of TV cameras for $10,000, or, as was later computed, roughly $10 per hair. From there the wave of money-making schemes began to roll in. "In 1969 Joe Namath was seen as something to be exploited," says Jimmy Walsh, who rapidly and easily adjusted to that concept. Joe, himself, was more than willing to be exploited; there seemed little, if anything, he would not do for money. As late as 1975, while Walsh negotiated with Fabergé for a multimillion-dollar contract to promote Brut cologne, Namath told him that if they got what they wanted, he'd even drink the stuff. "We're talking about a guy from western Pennsylvania, not some fucking kid from Park Avenue with a trust income," says Walsh in defense of Namanco's cash consciousness.

However, one thing Joe wouldn't do for money was star in a porno movie, for which he was reputedly offered one million dollars cash. After deliberation he also refused to become the first nude centerfold for *Cosmopolitan* magazine, telling Jimmy that he wasn't sure if he could face his mother afterward. He did agree to do the Beauty Mist panty hose commercial in which millions of men were first titillated, then shocked to find the smooth-shaven legs being slowly panned by the camera belonged not to a woman but to Joe Namath in drag. "I thought about that one for long time," says Joe. "Then I said, 'What am I, crazy?' This is a fun commercial and it should be looked at the same way. The people who don't like it, that's their hangup, and I'm sorry they feel that way."

As the numbers on the contracts got bigger, Jimmy Walsh became more demanding that Joe's macho, women-slaying, superstar image be presented properly. *Sport* magazine's art director, Al Braverman, planned a cover photo of Joe seated in a high-backed chair lecturing to a group of young boys, all wearing jerseys with number 12 on the back. "Joe's people said it made him look too old," recalls Braverman. " 'Maybe if they were girls,' they said. 'Why not just use a cover that says, "The King Is Back!" ' I asked them where in the hell he was supposed to have been."

Walsh kept asking for more and more money. Several seasons ago, ABC was after Namath to cohost its Monday night football show before offering the job to Fred Williamson and then Alex Karras. "They offered many millions of dollars," says Walsh proudly. "But not enough." Perhaps his biggest coup was negotiating the Fabergé contract, believed to be the most lucrative advertising deal ever for any celebrity, in or out of sports. The contract guarantees Namath a minimum of a quarter of a million dollars a year for eight years, with the company having the option of extending the terms for an additional twelve years. Such an extension would have Joe slapping on lotion or, perhaps, hair dye at the venerable age of fifty-two.

With his wealth, Namath has found there come certain drawbacks, most notably the stilted postures of the rich. "A lot of times now I have to take limousines," he says. "For tax reasons. And sometimes when I go through certain parts of the city I just have to crouch way down in my seat, it makes me feel so bad. I don't want those people to know who I am." As Jimmy Walsh sees it, such is Joe's education in stardom. "The fact is that the concept of Joe Namath is much, much more than the physical, living, breathing human being," he states. "He may be standing in front of me, but he is also a display in a department store in Pittsburgh and an ad for La-Z-Boy chairs in a magazine. The concept of Joe Namath transcends the person. At first it was awkward for him to understand that, but now he does."

And the concept continues to sell. Walsh estimates that Namanco currently turns down more than 80 percent of the offers it receives. What is it that advertisers find so appealing about Namath? George H. Hill, the vice president in charge of advertising for Arrow Shirts, the company that has begun a Joe Namath Signature series of upper-price-range shirts and jackets, feels, ironically enough, that Joe is "very typical of the average guy." "He's not conservative but he's not ultramodern or far-out, either," says Hill. "We picked him because we feel he nicely typifies the eighteen- to thirty-five-year-old age group. Also he has a ready-made image that we don't have to create."

Arrow, of course, was aware that not all males are in love with Joe Namath. "We realize a lot of people don't like Joe," says Hill. "But we also know we can't satisfy everyone. Then, too, we've found that if you have someone everybody likes, the product becomes much too bland. We had Fran Tarkenton once, and he'll get more attention than the average stock model, but he's nothing like Joe."

Jimmy Walsh is well aware of how Joe's controversial qualities enhance his market value. "Thank God for Dick Young," he frequently smiles. The fact is that whenever Joe is written about, pro or con, his fame increases. Al Woodall points out that Joe has always gotten "good" press in that regard, "controversial" as opposed to "negative." "If they said Joe was suspected of raping and killing a girl, now that's negative press," says Woodall. "Joe absolutely does not need a publicity firm," adds Jimmy Walsh. "Just like that thing last week in San Diego, Joe's benching. No PR man could have done that. It was worth millions."

An odd thing has been created at the tail end of Namath's career: the usual roles of performance and demand have been reversed. The more ads and off-field appearances Joe makes, the more valuable he becomes on field, the more football groupies appear, the more of a demand there is for him to be *seen* in uniform. Despite the fact the Jets have been a losing team for six years and Joe has not been overly effective, the club remains incredibly healthy at the turnstiles, a factor everyone from equipment boy to general manager attributes solely to Namath's presence. On the road the Jets always attract huge crowds—10,000 more fans than this year's O.J. Simpson–led Buffalo Bills attracted in Baltimore, 14,000 more than the average in Kansas City, 7,000 more than the average in Miami, 20,000 more than the preseason average in Washington, 20,000 more than the average in San Diego. "You take that San Diego game," says John Free, "the second to last game of the year for what you could almost call the championship of last place. You multiply 20,000 times $10 per ticket and come up with $200,000, maybe $150,000 after freebies. The Jets get 40 percent of that, or $60,000—as a direct result of Namath. And people wonder if he's worth his salary."

But for all his success, Joe has had one glaring, embarrassing, stupendous failure: movies.

Cosmo Currie went to the premiere of one Namath movie with Jimmy Walsh and afterward turned to Jimmy in shock. "How could you let him do this?" he asked. It was a valid question, the answer to which, of course, was money. Joe's first flick, a thing called *Norwood,* was so bad that Jimmy Walsh claims Joe probably wouldn't have done it, even for money, if Phil Iselin hadn't "demanded" he be in it. *"Norwood* had no story and no acting," says Walsh succinctly. "It was a poor version of a beach movie. Glen Campbell and Kim Darby were the stars; Glen Campbell never made another movie, and I think Kim Darby's career took a terrible decline afterward."

One shameful experience wasn't enough for Namath or Walsh; after *Norwood* they moved to *C.C. and Company* (billed as "the *Ben Hur* of motorcycle movies") and then to Joe's third and final effort, *The Last Rebel,* a 1971 spaghetti western costarring Jack Elam, Woody Strode, and Victoria George. The show recently appeared on daytime TV, and I was able to view it in its entirety, an effort of considerable will power, indeed. Almost surreal in its idiocy and lack of communication, *The Last Rebel* is designed to feature Joe, a never-say-die Confederate soldier, in various "natural" situations. There is Joe eating, Joe drinking, Joe lying in bed, Joe shooting people, Joe grinning at whores, Joe (shades of the Beaver Falls Blue Room) playing pool. Most of the characters speak only in grunts, and Joe's best line is a reasonably well muttered "Git." The rest of the time he says, "Put 'em down" and "Come on out" with the enthusiasm of a ventriloquist's dummy.

"The problem," explains Jimmy Walsh with deep

conviction, "is that Joe Namath's credibility as an actor is undermined by the fact that he is already known." In truth, Joe Namath's real problem is that he can't act—not even as well as Jimmy Brown or O. J. Simpson or even Dick Butkus. Joe, who is so good at presenting products for sale, seems to lack even the tiniest bit of insight into a character's emotions. Being so calm and one-dimensional himself, he seems unable to imagine how someone acts when they are very mad or near tears.

In his defense, he has had little practice. "Before *Norwood* I'd never been on a stage or acted in my life," he says. "I'd always wanted to be a cowboy or a soldier, and I loved movies, but it never entered my mind to be in a high school play or anything like that. Then one day after working in films I sat down and said, 'What am I doing? I'm trying to do something without ever having had any training.' There's nothing I've ever done without training."

Joe is not tainted with actor's ego, either. "When I first saw myself on screen, I *hated* it," he states. "I've never seen any of my movies in full. I didn't even like the rushes. I can't even watch myself on TV when I do a Sonny and Cher or Flip Wilson show. Sometimes I'll turn the set on for just a second; then I'll look and cringe and turn it right off. I just get so paranoid, so weird. It's funny because I like watching football films of myself. I don't like to see myself screw up, but I can usually rationalize what happened, and I appreciate the good plays. I guess acting's a whole different thing mentally."

Joe has turned down all movie offers since *The Last Rebel* and claims he'll be much more cautious the next time around. Though he has no specific roles in mind, he has started taking acting lessons at Hofstra. The problem of image is the major one if Namath is ever to achieve any respectability in films. Dick Schaap, who admits he watches a little bit of *The Last Rebel* every time it comes on TV, "until I break up laughing," feels that movie acting can't be all that hard. "You do what—fifteen-second takes? I should think that with proper training and a decent script, Joe could pull that off. But

I think he should do comedy, funny stuff. He has a good ability to make fun of himself and to be so cute. He is cute. He is cuter than he is a sex symbol, which is what he's promoted as. They put him on a motorcycle or make him a tough cowboy, but I don't think—knowing him— that he's a sex symbol. In the abstract, maybe. But in the locker room he sure as hell isn't a sex symbol; he's not in the top thirty-five."

It seems unlikely that such a change will occur, however. Joe talks fondly about roles in Harold Robbins books. Jimmy Walsh has always preferred Joe the stud to Joe the clown. "I thought it would have been great for Joe to do the *Cosmopolitan* centerfold," Walsh states. "It would have gotten attention and been tremendous for publicity." For the man pulling the levers behind the scenes, it is not so important what Joe Namath is as what he is made out to seem. "Eventually," says the attorney, his hungry eyes gazing into the distance, "Joe Namath the football player will not be as significant as the *idea* of him." When it comes, that idea will certainly be largely Jimmy Walsh's creation.

TWENTY

Football is not, after all, a summer game.

—ROBERT LIPSYTE

On the Wednesday before the final game of the season the players voted John Riggins the Jets' 1975 Most Valuable Player. According to several sources, Riggins won by a "healthy margin" over runners-up Rich Caster and Ed Galigher. In a brief question-and-answer period with the press, Riggins stated that on his own ballot he voted for Greg Gantt and Pat Leahy, claiming that the kickers are "sort of unappreciated." "He did it as a joke," said Gantt when confronted with the news. "He was just foolin'."

Riggins always seems to be half-joking, but on Wednesday there was also a note of sadness in his tone, a decided unhappiness over circumstances surrounding his career with the Jets. He seemed almost to regret his cornball antics. "The toenail polish?" he said. "No, it really didn't have anything to do with my toe being hurt. I don't know why I did it. The fingernail polish was just something to do, I guess. I'd rather not talk about it."

On Friday he talked about his hometown of Centralia, Kansas, and the reputation he earned there for his wackiness. "Every time in grade school when they'd send us to the board to do problems, I'd draw dirty pictures instead. Then the teacher would come by and erase them. The next day it was always, 'All right, everyone, go to the board. John, sit down.' My shop teacher, every time he left the class I had to go with him. He wouldn't leave me alone with the tools." What John was rebelling against in Centralia was partly his status as the local athletic *wunderkind.* "You'd have to understand what it's like coming out of a town where everybody knows everybody else and where you're more physically developed than all the other kids," he says. "I know I'm sounding smug, but I think even with something like this MVP those people may feel more jealousy than pride."

Like Piccone, Riggins is playing out his option this year, taking a 10 percent pay cut, down from $75,000 to $67,500, so he can peddle himself on the open market. His salary, which is approximately one seventh of Namath's, has been the major reason for his discontent with the Jets. This year he needs only 57 more yards to become the Jets' first 1,000-yard rusher. In 1972, his sophomore season, Riggins gained 944 yards on 207 carries despite missing two games. After that performance, coming on the tail of a rookie season in which he led the Jets in both rushing and receiving, John felt he had proved himself as a first-rate fullback worthy of top pay. Weeb Ewbank, so accommodating to Namath's demands, said not so. A lengthy and bitter 1973 walk-out ensued, and when Riggins returned it was with a Mohawk and strange clothes. He admits he played the 1973 and 1974 seasons "without a heart." Now after proving himself again, Riggins has hinted that he will be moving on.

(By the spring he would become more specific. "The Jets have deteriorated," he told a reporter in late May. "It's like being with an outfit expected to go bankrupt. If you got any smarts you ought to get out of the damn thing." Having fixed his price tag at $1.5 million for five years, payable at $100,000 a year until 1990, Riggins set out on the road to visit interested NFL clubs. The fresh air seemed to revitalize him: news photos showed him with hair neatly trimmed, horn-rims, and a three-piece business suit. "If you're asking for a million dollars, you've got to look like a million dollars," he said. "I want these people to know I'm a solid-citizen type, not the flake some people say I am."

The inner stress that has come from playing so long in Joe Namath's shadow showed in Riggins's handling of the Jets' contract reoffers. Though willing to negotiate with other teams, his only comment to the Jets was either to pay him exactly what Joe gets or bid him goodbye. "It wasn't feasible, and they knew it and I knew it," he said of his request on June 11, 1976, the day after he signed a five-year pact with the Washington Redskins. "The demand I put on them was my way of saying, 'It's been nice.' ")

Other Jets are also nearing the end of their relationship with the team. Veteran Emerson Boozer says he is "leaning toward retirement," making it clear that "they're not just going to use my body during training camp." Winston Hill, who has been methodically following a fifteen-year game plan, claims he'll probably be back in 1976. Still, he has made an uncustomary move, having just purchased a new Lincoln, "the first luxury car I've ever had." He rationalizes the extravagance by stating simply, "It's near the end."

For the others, if they are not traded or cut, next year will most likely mean business as usual. In February the Jets announced the signing of new coach Lou Holtz, a former college coach with a winning record and an abundance of confidence. Whether he could change things would have to be seen. As Mike Adamle had said, "Playing on the Jets might have permanently maimed some people as football players."

During the first few days of the final week, the biggest topic of conversation among the players is Ken Shipp's benching of Namath in San Diego. Shipp himself had tried to explain the action at the Wednesday press conference. He started lightly, saying he hadn't received any hate mail from Namath groupies yet, but soon he was bogged down by the apparent magnitude of his act. "I didn't sleep much the night before," he stated, his jaw thrust forward in defiance. "I felt it was too big a thing for me, so I talked to Phil Iselin and he said he'd go along with my decision. It would have been real easy to duck the thing. I'm not even gonna be the coach next year. But I couldn't have looked the squad in the face. Everybody knew—players knew, the owners were in the bar—how the hell you gonna look people in the face? You gonna have two standards? You gonna run a team like that?

"Just last week I told everybody to wear thigh pads to practice. Everybody did except Gantt. So I chased him in. Because we're *all gonna do things alike*. That's how it's going to be."

The big justification for Shipp's move, he claimed, was the fact that he had benched Garrett the week before for a rules violation. The parallel was not a perfect one, however; there were those who felt Garrett didn't deserve to start anyway. "It wasn't the same thing at all," said defensive back Jerry Davis. "What I've found is that Joe's not a prima donna, that he doesn't try to act any different than anybody else. He's a good guy. Shipp was just trying to make a name for himself."

What Shipp had actually been trying to do was maintain his dignity. "It hurt me that Joe would do that to me," Shipp said finally, his lip quivering. "Five hundred or a thousand dollars doesn't mean anything to him. I wanted to *punish* him."

"The coach took it personally," said Eddie Bell, another player who felt Joe shouldn't have been benched. "He may have thought he was punishing Joe, but he was really hurting the forty-three-man team. Especially since Joe was throwing better last week than ever." The complexities surrounding so simple a disciplinary move made its hoped-for effect impossible. "Nobody from inside this system can pull off something like that," summed up Steve Tannen.

On Thursday, Weeb Ewbank comes out to the complex. An old man now, short and rotund, with a nervous disorder called myasthenia gravis that requires him to tape his eyelids open with Band-Aids, Weeb hardly looks like the only coach to have won championships in both the AFL and the NFL (where he coached the Baltimore Colts). According to the secretaries, Weeb has little to do these days and he enjoys "just hanging around" the team.

A deceptively complex man, Ewbank gives the initial appearance of someone as innocent and befuddled as a pet rabbit. In one of his books Namath tells about a halftime speech Weeb made in 1967 while the Jets were losing to Boston. "All right, you *Colts,*" Weeb supposedly shouted, "now get out there and win this *baseball* game!"

But from most player accounts Weeb was craftier than he was naive, and his toughness during negotiations is legendary. "I'll tell you what," says Don Maynard with lingering resentment, "I was tight, but Weeb, oh brother, he was cheap."

Having been the coach during the years that the word "double standard" became part of the Jets' vocabulary, Weeb bears some of the responsibility for the present situation. In a strange way he denies now that there was ever any favoritism. "Sometimes Joe didn't like to get up in the morning," he says. "So I used to put dependable people like Jim Hudson or Ray Abruzzese as his roommates. Down at the Super Bowl, Joe was late for the picture-taking session and Hudson said, 'I quit trying to get him up. I left because I'm not getting fined.' So Joe just had his pictures taken the next day. There was never a double standard. Oh crap, no. He didn't want any favors. We just never told the press nothing about it. After he missed that session we just said, 'Appropriate measures taken,' and let it go at that."

If Weeb didn't mind Joe's habits, there is abundant evidence that the players sometimes got upset. When Joe walked out of training camp in 1967 because of alleged "personal problems" and then headed straight to the East Side bars, a number of Jets felt intense anger. "We didn't think he could pay a fine big enough to pay the debt he owed us," said veteran guard Sam DeLuca. "It wasn't a question of a fine anymore. It was a question of his moral obligation, as our leader, to make bed-check and to do what everyone else did."

Joe has never seemed to understand that "obligation." In a sense, it is both his genius and his flaw that he has not. "Joe was a very conscientious football player," insists Weeb Ewbank. "I thank the Man upstairs that I got to coach him."

On Friday, Christmas carols blare from the locker room stereo while *F Troop* reruns flash on the overhead color TV. A few weeks ago I had walked into the locker room late in the day and been somewhat startled by sounds of passion coming from the TV speakers. The equipment men and trainers were sitting on the benches staring raptly at the screen. I looked up and saw what appeared to be a close-up of open heart surgery. This scene faded into something resembling action shots of worm ranching, the camera finally panning back to reveal the distinct workings of human arms and hands and mouths.

Unless I was mistaken, I was seeing hard-core porno being broadcast over public television. I found out later that film man Jim Pons had brought in a videotape of *The Devil in Miss Jones* and plugged it into the hall's tape circuit.

Today's holiday music has apparently overly relaxed Jazz Jackson, for he lies curled on the floor in front of his locker, asleep. Someone has seen fit to cover him with several pages of newspaper. Al Woodall sits on his stool and studies Jazz's figure.

"Son," he asks, "what have you got to look forward to?"

Jazz rustles in his nest.

Carl Garrett frowns down at his fellow running back. "Man, why don't you go home at night?" he scowls. "That's what they always tell me."

After a few minutes Jazz stirs and gets up, his face lined by the carpeted floor. At the receptionist's desk Namath talks over the phone to a grade-school class that has called him as part of their Christmas treat. The youngsters are assembled in the school gym and are listening to Joe's voice over the intercom.

"I like the game," Joe says. "It's a challenge. . . . Yes, a lot of ups and downs, a chance to experience good feelings and bad feelings, things you can't feel other places. . . . I like New York. . . . Once you've played here you don't want to go somewhere else. . . . Uh-uh. . . . Listen, I have to go to a meeting now. . . . What? No, I don't think the coach would accept a note. Ha-ha. . . . Okay. . . . Merry Christmas."

Lately Joe has become less desirous of interviews than usual. I had asked him if he'd have time for a final tape session with me, and he had said no, that he was truly tired of answering questions. "I'm really beginning to feel like I've said it all before," he added.

The last time he said anything to me without being asked occurred several weeks back. When I first came to the Jets I had a beard, but I shaved it off after a few weeks because it had become a nuisance. One day at practice I stood behind Lou Piccone, simulating a soccer-style kicker, as Lou took practice placement snaps from Joe Fields. "I was standing next to Ken Shipp," Joe said afterward, "and all of a sudden he nudged me and said, 'Who's the new kicker?' I looked at him and said, 'Goddamn, Coach. The guy's only been here about three months.' You think football doesn't fuck your mind up?"

After practice the players stream into the locker room in high spirits. Several wrestling matches start up, with the main bout between undersized Lou Piccone and Darrell Austin. "Get the Bionic Man!" scream the observers as the two thrash up and down the room. After a while, Austin gets Piccone in a headlock, lifts him up and, holding him in midair, drops with a thud to the floor. Austin winces at the pain in his right knee, and the contest ends shortly afterward with Darrell limping to his locker.

On TV an ad for Gulden's mustard comes on, and Winston Hill's image abruptly fills the screen. He is wearing a Joe Namath T-shirt and standing beside several young boys. Though the sound cannot be heard above the locker room noise, Joe Fields lip-synchs the words:

"Kids are really eating a lot more hot dogs at Joe Namath's Camp this year. And it's not the hot dogs. It's the mustard . . ."

While the ad is still going on, Caster, Bell, Turk, and several others jump Steve Reese and hold him down, performing what is known as the "annual tape-up." As they tape Reese's legs together, Coach Shipp walks in and looks at the action. He smiles thinly and leaves. Namath watches the proceedings with his customary nonchalance and tacit approval.

Abruptly Reese reaches a free arm into his locker and pulls out a clawed garden tool which he swings wildly. His attackers flee. Reese, who has been screaming the whole time, starts yelling now that he'll kill anyone who gets near him. He is covered with sweat, his eyes are dilated, and his chest is pounding. Caster calls him a coward, and Reese hurls a string of epithets.

"I'll kick your ass," says Caster.

"You fuckin' asshole!" screams Reese. "You footstep-hearin' bitch!"

"Put that thing down and I'll kick your ass here and now."

"I'll always have it!" says Reese, swinging the tool. "And when I don't, I'll have something else!"

Trying to dispel the tension, Eddie Bell climbs on a table, nude, and holds his arms out like a crucifix. "Here, tape me," he says. "Make it easy on yourselves. Go ahead. Tape."

His suggestion goes unheeded. Caster and Reese continue to glare at each other. Where Reese's name plate is affixed to his locker, the name "Elmer Squatlow" has been taped on. Godwin Turk points at it.

"That's his real name," he snorts.

"You can call me anything you want," jabbers Reese. "But in two days you can call me long distance!"

After the season Steve Reese will be among the first of the Jets to be shipped away.

For the Dallas game on Sunday the weather is almost unbearably cold. The temperature hovers at 20 degrees while 25-mile-an-hour winds and 50-mile-an-hour gusts roar over and through Shea Stadium. The stands are more than half empty, the fans huddled in tight pockets to conserve heat. The field itself is frozen like a box of old spinach, with small jagged pinnacles rising where dirt clods have been kicked up and allowed to freeze.

In the locker room the players wrap their feet in Baggies and pull on extra pairs of thermal underwear. Darrell Austin sits on a bench with his right leg straight in front of him. He is not suiting up, having just learned from the doctor that the cartilage in his knee is torn and he will have to have surgery within the week. On Friday night at the "Last Tango in Point Lookout" Darrell had staggered painfully from bar to bar, playing the mandolin he had borrowed from film man Jim Pons, a onetime guitarist for the Turtles and Frank Zappa. When he was ten, Darrell had played in a rock band back in Union, South Carolina. The group was called "Uncle Henry and His Cousins," had ten members, and featured a sixty-year-old man as lead singer. With me accompanying on guitar, Darrell had hoped to recapture a little of the Uncle Henry's excitement, but his damaged leg had made the songfest a spiritless affair.

The only interesting part of the night came when a customer perhaps half Darrell's size began harassing him. Claiming he had lost money all year betting on the Jets, he proceeded to toss out insults in a loud voice. I had heard that little people often picked on big men, but I had never witnessed it. To his credit Darrell merely bulled his twenty-one-inch neck and looked the other way.

Before the game, Coach Shipp gives his last attempt at a team speech and then calls on Winston Hill for the invocation. The room is filled with the sound of grating chair legs as the Jets drop to their knees.

"There are three words I think we can think about today," Winston says in his best preacher's voice. "Those words are: All is well." He goes on to talk about pride and friendship and happy families and ends by saying, "Next year we'll know we're all doing well whether we're in football or not, because no matter how bad things get we're not quitters. We're not gonna bow to any situation we've been placed in. All is well."

The words achieve their maximum irony as the Jets run on to the field to choruses of boos. Aside from Riggins they have no one in the top five in the AFL in scoring, passing, receiving, rushing, intercepting, punting, tackling, punt returning, or kickoff returning. Namath is aware of the jeers directed specifically at him, having recently commented on some of the more obscene ones. He is aware that many people think he should quit, that they feel he is only dragging himself down. But he steadfastly maintains that he will honor his contract and play at least one more year. "Nobody plays this game for fun," he says. "You need money to justify yourself. But it won't be money that keeps me on and on. With Johnny Unitas, that was money. But that's not my situation. I don't *need* a good paycheck. If I play more than next year it will be because I legitimately in my heart and mind feel I can contribute to a winning cause, that I can improve."

Among other people, Joe's father feels he should get out. "I've told him since 1968 that he should quit before he's crippled. The day that he retires, that is when I will smile again," says John Namath. Another person who believes Joe should quit is Fran Tarkenton. "Fran thinks he's through," says Dick Schaap, who recently talked to the Minnesota quarterback to inform him he had been voted *Sport*'s Man of the Year. "Fran has always been a real big, big fan of Joe's. But just from watching films and playing against him he thinks Joe should stop playing. Fran said the only way Joe could survive was if he played for a team like the Rams or the Vikings where they're so good it doesn't make any difference who the quarterback is. I thought that was a funny line."

When the game begins, Joe plays poorly. Two of his passes are dropped, but the rest are badly thrown, and at the half he has thrown no completions. At the end of the third quarter Riggins, whose Joe Namath Model Arrow sports shirts are still untouched in his locker, finally gains his 1,000 yards. The game is stopped briefly and Riggins is given the ball.

In the unheated, wind-blown press box the writers, some of whose pens have stopped functioning, dance up and down in the cold. "Don't stop the game!" several of them cry. "No measurements! No time outs!" A drunk falls over two chairs, saying only that he's "with the Cowboys." A few of the writers begin singing their college fight songs, and Bob Kerlan of the *Bergen Record* starts babbling that "nothing means anything," that he has begun "hallucinating with cold."

In the fourth quarter Namath completes his first pass, a seven-yarder to Caster. Immediately afterward he is run over by Harvey Martin, a 6-foot-5-inch, 250-pound defensive end. Namath lies motionless for a frightening amount of time on the icy turf before finally being helped up and led out of the game. J. J. Jones comes in to finish up.

In the press box the report comes that Namath's injuries are not thought to be serious—bruised ribs and a twisted knee—but that he will not return to action. With his game statistics set at 1 completion in 8 attempts for 7 yards, the worst in his entire career, Namath has finished the 1975 season as the twenty-seventh best quarterback in the NFL. He leads the league in one department only—interceptions, of which he has 28.

After the game, which the Jets lose, 31–21, to cement their worst season ever, Winston Hill gives the final benediction. He finishes by saying that everyone will be fine in whatever they're doing, wherever they go, because "we know that we're not gonna stop. Nothing can stop us. Thank You for Riggins. Drive safely."

The last sentence bears the most meaning for the Jets, since many of the players have their cars parked outside, loaded and ready to leave town. After a few brief handshakes I run to my own car and begin my journey back to Chicago, a curious sense of relief filling me as I put miles between myself and Shea. In Pennsylvania I stop at a Howard Johnson's along Route 80. Looking into the dining room I see Carl Garrett and two companions seated at a far table. Carl and I had not exactly been close friends during the season, but now he motions me over to his table. "Have a seat," he says.

I can't help marveling that he could have played in the game and still have beaten me out of New York.

"I can drive when I have to," he says. "When I got traded from Boston to Dallas I drove straight through. Saw the sun go up and down twice."

While eating, I ask Carl what he thought about Riggins gaining his thousand yards.

"Man, he's some dude," he states. "Did you see him bowing to both sides of the stadium?" I had. After that Riggins had given a small military salute as a finale.

The meal arrives, and Garrett starts talking about this being redneck country and how he's a crazy nigger in the midst of it all. His female companion giggles and tells him to stop talking that way. As he sops up some gravy with a roll, I ask him what he was looking at when Namath got knocked down in the fourth quarter. He drops his roll on the plate.

"Man, I wanted to see what happened," he says. "Joe was sort of all scrunched up on the ice, and I didn't know if he was hurt bad or what. When I could finally see his face, you know what I saw he was doing? He was *laughing*. The sonofabitch was lying there on the ice *laughing*. So help me God."

Garrett picks up his roll and continues mopping his plate. "They think I'm something," he states, shaking his head. "But, man, that dude is ca-razy."

Sometimes, some seasons, it surely must help.

Acknowledgments

Many people deserve thanks for their assistance while I was writing this book. In particular, I want to thank newsmen Paul Zimmerman, Gerald Eskenazi, George Usher, Ike Kuhns, Murray Janoff, and Dick Schaap for their aid to a somewhat confused and naive out-of-towner. Jets PR men Frank Ramos and Jim Trecker granted me countless favors, and secretaries Connie Nicholas and Elsie Cohen helped by letting me use their telephones and giving me hot tips. I also want to thank Dr. James Nicholas for his erudite medical opinions, Al Ward for his kindness, Weeb Ewbank for his time, John Free for his patience, Jim Pons for his films and musical knowledge, Phil Iselin for his observations, and Bill Hampton for the best equipment in the bin.

Special credit should go to coaches Charley Winner, Ken Shipp, and Sam Rutigliano, to Mike Martin and Jimmy Walsh of Namanco, and to Dom Casey and Butch Ryan of Beaver Falls, Don Maynard of El Paso, Tom Bettis and Willie Lanier of Kansas City, and Cosmo Currie of the Upper East Side.

I need to thank Pat Ryan and Linda Westervelt for helping me wade through the files in the *Sports Illustrated* library and for providing moral support. Tad Parsons's research and tape transcriptions were masterful. Kerry and Peggy Reardon did more than they needed to; Mike Adamle assisted beyond the call of duty; and John Namath was as gracious a host as a man can be.

I am particularly grateful to Tom Wallace, season ticket holder and editor-in-chief of Holt, Rinehart and Winston, without whom this book would never have come to be, and to Keri Christenfeld, a production editor who throws spiraling commas like a pro. Also, Lois Wallace, who is the Vince Lombardi of literary agents.

Most of all, for allowing me into their fold and for being themselves, I must thank Joe Namath, Godwin Turk, Darrell Austin, Lou Piccone, Winston Hill, Richard Caster, David Knight, and all the other guys on the New York Jets football team.

About the Author

Rick Telander, twenty-seven, played quarterback on his high school football team but never felt comfortable there because his ends threw the ball harder than he did. At Northwestern University he switched to defensive back and made second-team All–Big Ten and was drafted by the Kansas City Chiefs. He is currently a Special Contributor to *Sports Illustrated* and has written one other book, *Heaven is a Playground,* a chronicle of street basketball in Brooklyn.